CONCORDIA UNIVERSITY

3 4211 00132 6399

WITHDRAWN

DR. BETTE J. KRENZKE

DATE DUE			
OCT 2 6 2004			
12-7-05			

DEMCO 38-297

hild

VOLUME 4

WITHDRAWN

W9-ABZ-522

DR. BETTE J. KRENZKE

The Young Child at Play

REVIEWS OF RESEARCH, VOLUME 4

Editors

GRETA FEIN
University of Maryland
MARY RIVKIN
University of Maryland

KLINCK MEMORIAL LIBRARY
Concordia University
River Forest, IL 60305-1499

A 1985–86 Comprehensive Membership Benefit

National Association for the Education of Young Children
Washington, D.C.

Cover photograph by David Greenberg

Copyright © 1986. All rights reserved.
National Association for the Education of Young Children
1834 Connecticut Avenue, N.W.
Washington, DC 20009-5786

Copyright © 1986 for "Children's Playgrounds: Research and Practice," pp. 195–211 is held by Joe L. Frost.

MASTERS OF THE UNIVERSE and associated characters are trademarks owned by Mattel, Inc. and used with permission.

Library of Congress Catalog Card Number: 67-24993

ISBN Catalog Number: 0-935989-02-1

NAEYC #320

Printed in the United States of America.

Table of Contents

List of Contributors

Greta G. Fein
Department of Curriculum and Instruction
University of Maryland
College Park, MD 20742

Joe L. Frost
Department of Curriculum and Instruction
University of Texas
Austin, TX 78712

Nina Howe
Department of Psychology
University of Waterloo
Waterloo, Ontario
Canada N21 3G1

Nancy R. King
Department of Education, Policy Planning, and Administration
University of Maryland
College Park, MD 20742

Marsha Liss
Department of Psychology
California State University
San Bernadino, CA 92407

Lorraine McCune
Department of Education
Rutgers, The State University of New Jersey
New Brunswick, NJ 18903

Vonnie McLoyd
Department of Psychology
University of Michigan
Ann Arbor, MI 48109

Anthony D. Pellegrini
Department of Elementary Education
University of Georgia
Athens, GA 30602

Debra Pepler
Earlscourt Child and Family Centre
46 St. Clair Gardens
Toronto, Ontario
Canada M6E 3V4

Elizabeth Phyfe-Perkins
Childcare Services
University of Massachusetts
Amherst, MA 01003

Mary S. Rivkin
Child Development
Prince Georges Community College
Largo, MD 20772

Kenneth H. Rubin
Department of Psychology
University of Waterloo
Waterloo, Ontario
Canada N21 3G1

Eli Saltz
The Merrill-Palmer Institute
Wayne State University
Detroit, MI 48202

Rosalyn Saltz
Department of Education
University of Michigan-Dearborn
Dearborn, MI 4812-1491

Shirley S. Schwartz
Department of Curriculum and Instruction
University of Maryland
College Park, MD 20742

Joanne Shoemaker
First Step Designs, Ltd.
1574 Centre Street
Newton, MA 02161

Brian Sutton-Smith
Department of Psychology and Education
The University of Pennsylvania
Philadelphia, PA 19174

Brian Vandenberg
Department of Psychology
University of Missouri-St. Louis
St. Louis, MO 63121

The Play of Children

GRETA G. FEIN

Even a cursory examination of Western thought from ancient times to the present reveals repeated efforts to include the playful side of human beings in a larger philosophical vision of the human condition. These efforts are found in the works of scholars who would today represent diverse disciplines spanning the humanities, the arts, and the biological, social, and behavioral sciences. Looking at the past from the perspective of our current fascination with play, contemporary scholars see continuity and connections where none were apparent before (Sutton-Smith, this volume). From Plato to Nietzsche, from Homer to Rabelais, including all things in between and around, the emerging consensus that play is a pervasive force in culture has generated an explosion of speculation, conceptualization, and empirical research.

The recent popularity of play as a topic of serious research in the social and behavioral sciences seems belated. Anthropologists once studied exotic cultures with only incidental and incomplete observations of play (Schwartzman, 1978), while sociologists analyzed societal institutions ignoring folk models that defined how these institutions would function (Simmel, 1950). Although a rather obvious, visible, and pervasive aspect of human activity, play escaped systematic scrutiny by the emerging disciplines of anthropology, sociology, and psychology for most of the 20th century.

Psychologists, perhaps, have been the most vocal in their ambivalence about whether play merits all this fuss (Vandenberg, this volume). The complaints, by now, are familiar. How can something so elusive be studied? Why should an apparently aimless activity be taken seriously? Perhaps the concept of play is too global, too murky, or too encumbered by excess meaning to permit rigorous investigation. Play provides an interesting example of a major psychological and developmental problem that seemed more managable in clinical and educational practice than in the laboratory.

Play, however, is not the only target of such complaints. Even though behavioral scientists still debate fuzzy concepts such as culture, society, altruism, representation, attachment, social dominance, communication, curiosity, and aggression, the study of these important human attributes continues, as does the study of play. As Vandenberg (this volume) notes, some psychological theorists have extended their work to include play, whereas others view play as a convenient tool to study the development of these attributes. A similar trend appears in other disciplines as well — anthropologists see play as the expression of children's dominance hierarchies (King, this volume), while sociologists who subscribe to the symbolic interactionism of George H. Mead (1934) see play as an expression of children's perspective-taking ability. The conduct of play calls forth social skill and sensitivity; play flourishes in the comprehension of self in relation to others, and it luxuriates in the expansiveness of symbolic forms. In order to play deeply and pleasurably, children must use their best capabilities. The challenge of research is to understand how this remarkable activity is put together.

The authors contributing to this volume adopt diverse theoretical and methodological approaches to this challenge. From a cognitive perspective, the development of play reflects changes in children's ability to use symbolic forms (McCune; McLoyd), one of which is spoken language (Pellegrini). From an affective perspective, play is a behavior in which the expressive component is more important than the instrumental component (Sutton-Smith; Fein & Schwartz). From the perspective of social development, play requires children to coordinate their behavior with others (Fein & Schwartz) and contend with the opinions of peers (Rubin & Howe). Peers may support sex-stereotyped behavior (Liss). Viewed more broadly, play may help us to better understand the culture of childhood (King), although as researchers and educators we must be wary of our conclusions regarding ethnic and social class differences (McLoyd). Because the means and goals of play are controlled by the players, play can be viewed as an inherently creative activity, one that cultivates flexible, divergent thinking (Pepler). Because play calls on so many aspects of thinking, feeling, and communicating, it comes as no surprise that the benefits of play are as diverse as the skills children use in its pursuit (Saltz & Saltz).

Authors contributing to this volume provide a useful overview of the many aspects of contemporary theory and research on children's play. It is clear from these chapters that no single theory dominates the effort. In play research, we are in a time of ferment, debate, and productive inquiry, with different points of view complementing rather than competing with one another. As is often the case, studies may not always yield converging findings. As theoretical issues in each domain become more refined, disagreements are likely to increase (see McLoyd and Liss for examples) before new insights and paradigms replace the old.

The purpose of this volume is to give early childhood educators a source of information about contemporary research on children's play. Many of the chapters review studies of the development of play, stressing the intricate competencies that emerge as new play forms develop. Each author was asked to comment on the implications of the material covered for teachers. The concluding two chapters (Phyfe-Perkins & Shoemaker; Frost) review the rapidly accumulating literature on factors in the preschool environment, indoors and outdoors, that govern the amount and quality of play. Although as editors we attempted to be comprehensive in our choice of topics, the final manuscript reflects our biases about what is useful and important. Because space was limited, some issues such as the contribution of parents to play, or social class differences, are covered in chapters under more general topics rather than in chapters of their own.

References

Mead, G. H. (1934). *Mind, self, and society.* Chicago: University of Chicago Press.

Schwartzman, H. B. (1978). *Transformations: The anthropology of children's play.* New York: Plenum.

Simmel, G. (1950). *The sociology of Georg Simmel.* Glencoe, IL.: Free Press.

Subjects & Predicates

To be human, and to live in a meaningful way in a culture, requires that we live in and through a very sophisticated, abstract, and symbolic system that is largely imaginary.

Part 1:
History, Theory, and Culture

Part 1 of this volume addresses larger issues in play study. In some respects, current research is a melting pot of metaphors drawn from numerous scholarly disciplines. Much of the research reported in this volume has been influenced by psychological and developmental theories. As scholars focus on the study of play, they bring different insights, perspectives, and biases. In Chapter 1, Brian Sutton-Smith offers a view of the changing ideology of play from ancient times to the present. According to Sutton-Smith, the metaphors of play evoke polarities—order/disorder, rationality/irrationality, tranquility/upheaval. These universal, dialectical themes express opposing visions of the human condition. In understanding play, one must appreciate the contrast between what is permitted or forbidden in real life, and what is permitted in play. As others have noted (Fein, 1985), play may be a cultural boundary between what is obligatory, what is permitted, and what might be freely chosen.

The next two chapters offer somewhat different views of theory and method. Brian Vandenberg (Chapter 2) provides an overview of the major theoretical strands that weave play research together. Recently, play researchers have attempted to understand play from the child's viewpoint. Nancy King (Chapter 3) explains the value of an anthropological perspective. Ethnographic studies explore children's definition of play and offer a broader view of the childhood culture of which play is so much a part.

References

Fein, G. G. (1985). Learning in play: Surfaces of thinking and feeling. In J. L. Frost & S. Sunderlin (Eds.), *When children play*. Wheaton, MD: Association for Childhood Education International.

Vivienne della Grotta

Play has been construed differently at various times in Western history. Is it irrational? Is some play good and useful, while other play is worthless? Is play the font of creativity?

CHAPTER ONE

The Spirit of Play

BRIAN SUTTON-SMITH

Conceptualizations of play

The spirit of play is something that we are all intimately familiar with — in our involvement in games of cards, chess, or ball, and in witty conversations, or in our observations of young children in their house play, their block play, or their rope jumping. Very few of us have not had some experience of such play, and therefore some idea of its spirit. Unfortunately, to know play in personal experience is not necessarily to know what it is we know when we know that. From the Greeks onward, Western philosophical history has been characterized by a struggle over the conceptualization of play. First, we must sort the local and historical part of our definition from the universal part. I hope to show that the changing fashions in definition are essential to our conceptualizations of play. I will not, however, attempt to handle the more diverse meanings that play has had in non-Western settings. But we can take it for granted that in its earlier embedment in ritual and religion, the play of other cultures and other times has borne many characteristics that we would no longer associate with it today.

In analyzing the changing conceptual fashions of play, I will focus on the bipolar characteristics of play. Here are a few of the descriptive and functional polarities that one can find in the extensive literature:

Play is	But it also is
an Apollonian moment of free self-determination	a Dionysian moment of panic and self-abandon (Fink, 1968)
an activity where the player is the lord of her or his own imagination	an activity where the player is enslaved by the demonic power of the mask (Fink, 1968)
fun, voluntary, joyous, childlike, spontaneous, and careless	tense, bloody, fatal, and illiberal (Huizinga, 1955)

Play is	**But it also is**
free and flexible with positive affect (Krasnor & Pepler, 1982, describing nursery school play)	traditional and conforming with cruelty and negative affect (Sutton-Smith, 1981, describing playground play)
functional: it socializes and it creates adaptive repertoires and communities of players	dysfunctional: it leads to accidents, death, separations, and illicit behaviors (Fagen, 1980)

These oppositions say perhaps that there is both a light and optimistic view of the spirit of play and a dark and pessimistic view of it. And one can suppose that between these contrasts there may be many other intermediate states.

Thus, when looking at the game of *Ring Around the Roses,* one can concentrate on the wonderful *order* that 5-year-olds are able to establish as they hold hands, chant the lines, and then finally fall down ("Ashes, ashes, we all fall down"); or one can look at the *disorder* that ensues when they are all over the ground laughing uproariously. Is the spirit of play found in the tranquility of their orderly accomplishment or in the riotousness of their collapse?

What this question poses is the possibility that any *spirit* we may attribute to play is usually justified by some theory, implicit or explicit, about the way play is organized or structured. Not surprisingly for one talking about the bipolar characteristics of play's spirit, I have in prior writings argued that play is most usefully characterized structurally in dialectical terms (Sutton-Smith, 1978)—it is a special kind of medium for packaging life's contradictions. For example, the order and anarchy of everyday routine in the nursery school may be expressed and represented by the novel synthesis of the order and disorder of *Ring Around the Roses.* The spirit of play may be what arises out of the tension between these two polarities. The fun is in holding the game's order together and in allowing it to fall apart; it takes considerable competence for 5-year-olds to do them each at the right time. Though it is of course sometimes just as much fun to do them at the wrong time!

Rather than proceed further with speculations about the universal characteristics of the play structure, within which I will attempt to catch the spirit of play, I want to proceed to some historical examples, in order to fulfill my contention that any play conceptualization must take into account some underlying structural considerations, as well as the rhetoric or ideology of the age in which it exists. I will present five undoubtedly oversimplified and quite schematic historical sketches. In doing so I wish to acknowledge my profound debt to Mihai Spariosu (1982) and the speakers in a symposium organized at the Center for Renaissance and Baroque Studies, University of Maryland, entitled "Forms of Play in the Early Modern Period" (1984). The least that I hope to do with these sketches is confront modern approaches to play with their quite obvious cultural relativity. The science of play cannot be advanced by a psychology that ignores the history of this domain.

Some historical conflicts about play's spirit

The play of gods and the play of humans

It is an effort for a 20th century person to take seriously the early Greek view that the gods are at play in this universe in a random way and that we are pawns in their war games. Like children, or like a divine lottery, the gods go their arbitrary, irrational, and exuberant way, regardless of the consequences to the rest of us. In this view both spontaneity and irrationality are the *spirit* of the conflict-ridden games played with us. As Heraclitus says: "Lifetime is a child at play, moving pieces on the board" (Spariosu, 1982).

We have so confined our modern notions of play to something we or children do in our spare time, that this view that we are being played with in the universe is almost beyond our grasp. Except that in a sense we do live in a modern impersonal version of this game—we are the pawns in the great thermonuclear war game constantly being rehearsed between ourselves and the Russians. The thinking of both sides in this confrontation is governed by strategic notions derived from games while our own predicament is that of being pawns to random fate. In the 1983 movie *War Games* the central character, a boy who has precipitated a final countdown, asks the computer, "Is this a game, or is it real?" "What's the difference?" replies the machine.

For the early Greeks and many tribal cultures, there appears to have been little difference. Whether metaphorically contemplating the games played by the gods, or participating in games themselves, they held the view that contestive play was part and parcel of the sacred life (Turner, 1974). The spirit of play in this historical case emphasized the characteristics of conflict or disorder (games), irrationality (chance), and spontaneity. Perhaps it is not incidental that on the one hand we engage the Russians in a play for the world (through war games), and on the other hand we have a more direct but limited conflict with them, over whether we will play on their playing field or they on ours (as in the

Olympics). Though we may have secularized the world, the magnitude of the ludic issues that contain us has apparently changed much less than we think.

In passing, one should mention the modern philosophical inheritance of Nietzsche (1871/1967). Heidegger (1927/1962), and Gadamer (1982). This earlier view of play as a kind of mediation (or language) that controls us, rather than us controlling it, has gained a new ascendancy. For these writers the conflictful or binary nature of play commands our lives, rather than the reverse. Nietzsche is the most extreme of these in his view that reality is the eternal, arbitrary succession of appearances governed by chance within which people are not only the players but also the playthings.

Good imitations versus bad imitations

In the works of Plato and Aristotle we are introduced to a distinction between two roads to truth: There is philosophy, which can model truth after God, love, and universal justice; and there is art, literature, and play, which are falsifications of truth, but which can in turn model themselves after philosophy, and become good imitations of truth. While these arguments are too intricate to present here, what issues from all of this is a distinction between some types of play which are noble pastimes and some which are not.

From the Middle Ages onward this distinction manifested itself most often in the ruling class's advocacy of its own pastimes (tournament, horseracing, fencing, archery, tennis, hawking, and hunting), which were often of some military value, and its banning of plebian play, which it saw as of no such value and often involved damage to property and people (football, skittles and quoits, or ball games against church walls) (Brailsford, 1969).

One of our best accounts of what is seen as good or bad play in earlier ages might be a history of what was legal to play and what was not. Unfortunately there is no simple distinction established by the multiple laws of the times, because they varied in time and place in what was declared out of court. Some of the difficulties of knowing what was legitimate and what was not are nicely symbolized by the controversies surrounding Bruegel's famous painting of 1560 entitled *Children's Games*. The painting contains some 240 young children engaging in some 70 pastimes. One presumes that most of these folk pastimes depicted so vividly would not rate with the ruling classes. Indeed, the most frequent 17th century interpretation of the painting was that it represents the follies of mankind. Children's play in its passionate nature, it was said, is like the folly of adult obsessions with religion, politics, and war. Protestants used the representations of children playing at baptism and marriage ceremonies as an indication of the childishness of the same kinds of rituals practiced by the Catholic Church. Catholics, on the contrary, argued that as children were nearer to God, their imitations were a sanctification of church practices (Snow, 1983).

Others saw the painting as an exhibition of the kind of uninhibited excess that Rabelais had written about, parodied, and perhaps sanctified in his novel *Gargantua and Pantagruel*, 30 years earlier (1532/ 1955). From his point of view, play in its nature is immoderate, grotesque, and obscene. In his view, we see that the irrational play of the gods has become the irrational play of the folk; the freedom of the gods has become the dangerous freedom of the players.

Further distinction between good and bad play is found in the numerous Dutch paintings of the 17th century. Commentaries on this art can also be interpreted as moralizing about games and play. For example, depicting the playing of backgammon in brothels showed it was a condemned game. The presence of cards or dice in a painted scene (say by Jan Steen) was declared a symbol of the fickleness of life. Chess, however, was accepted because of its cultivation of astuteness. Skating was permitted because of its association with physical fitness; though some moralists also used it as a metaphor for the slipperiness of life. At one time, hoops were condemned because they were a matter of running after nothing of substance; jacks were matters of chance, therefore of folly; turning a pinwheel in the breeze was a deception; riding a hobbyhorse was a kind of self-delusion, and blowing bubbles was an exercise in transitoriness (Wheelock, 1984).

In modern guise, this separation between *good* and *bad* play is presumably between play that socializes, encourages learning, or is cognitive, and those other kinds of play that are a danger or a nuisance in the household or classroom and for which children are sent outdoors. By and large, theorists of the past two centuries have concentrated on good play. Anthropologists have been industrious in showing how children's play imitates adult work life, and psychologists have been similarly industrious in seeking to demonstrate that play socializes. Imitative play has been tacitly received as a tribute to the worthiness of adult society in these disciplines.

The other view of play captured by Rabelais and perhaps by Breugel is still found in folklore. While social scientists have focused on good play (Sutton-Smith, 1979, 1980), folklorists have focused on bad play (Opie & Opie, 1968; Sutton-Smith, 1981). The first is about order and achievement, the second is about disorder and subversion.

Self as player versus self as mask

By the Renaissance, the status of play in Western society had been considerably secularized, and yet sports were still generally held, as in ancient times, to be of a much higher order than mere idleness of folkgames. What emerges as another new way of viewing play in these times relates to the issue of individuality, and to the contrast between the ceremonial mask that the person presents to the world as a serious person (Greene, 1984), and the self who lies behind that mask.

The great parodies of the 16th century by Rabelais (1532/1955), Cervantes (1605/1938), and Erasmus (1509/1969) all focus on the distance between the role that is an absurdly serious imitation of ancient or religious wisdom, and the same role played with more manipulative flexibility. In the writings of Castiglione (1528/1968) and Machiavelli (1513/1947), one is taught to play one's roles in public life for the sake of expediency. The artifices of role playing may require some desertion from morality for the sake of public or patriotic gain — whatever moralities may still be observed in one's private life. In this context, the meaning of *freedom* refers to individual choice, rather than to the random play of the gods or the uninhibited play of the folk. This is a notion of role playing, of adopting roles *as if* they are personal fictions rather than imitations of divine or ancient life. Not to be a player is to be a rigid or foolish person who mistakes her or his own mask for reality (Beaujour, 1984). This changing view of roles is usually associated with the changing military tactics of the Renaissance and the ruler's need to be at ease not only on the battlefield but also in the court manipulations of a many-sided social life (Brailsford, 1969).

One hears a faint echo of this Renaissance view in George H. Mead's (1934) modern socialization theory where the child at play is learning her or his multiple selves in degrees of increasing complexity (also Fein, 1984). What Machiavelli cynically advocates for public practice, however, Mead seriously presents as an inevitability for child play and games, and child development. Machiavelli receives a closer representation by another modern symbolic interactionist, Goffman (1959), who is often interpreted as unravelling the cynical character of social arrangements.

The dictionary's definitions of play still contain some notion of the deceptive flexibility implied by Machiavelli when the player is defined as one who:

- makes love playfully
- amuses herself or himself
- moves lightly or erratically

- has a smile playing on the lips
- treats things in a trifling way
- plays fast and loose
- pretends to be engaged in
- plays for time
- plays into the hands of
- shows off
- plays upon others' feelings
- plays on words
- plays up to someone
- plays tricks
- plays the fool
- makes a play for someone or something (Webster, 1961)

As we shall see, this view of the player as the one with great role flexibility is a major modern opponent of the usual 20th century notion of the player as childlike or childish.

Work and seriousness versus play, triviality, and childishness

The most pervasive view of play throughout the past 300 years has been labeled as a relatively trivial, frivolous activity. During the same century that disputes about the meaning of play and games in Dutch art occurred, many festivals and games were banned, and in England, the Puritans clashed with the Cavaliers who attempted to restore some of these earlier festivals. Whether we charge the decline of folkplay to 17th century Puritanism, to the 18th century's industrial revolution, or to the increasing dominance of a middle class view of work and recreation, there was a massive shift in attitude between 1600 and 1800, when play became regarded as a children's pursuit and not a pursuit of the folk. From 1750 or so, children were increasingly given their own toys, books, and clothes, and segregated in their socialization. That discontinuity between child and adult, which we now take for granted as an essential characteristic of all play, began to appear. Play became something done by children, or when done by adults, had a childish quality to it.

And yet the very process that segregated children from adult society, and segregated play from society as a childish thing, also gave rise to a sentimentality about children in the works of Rousseau, Wordsworth, and other romantics. Children's play was their special, if primitive, world. Play was not a world afflicted by the kinds of duplicities that were part of the Renaissance concept of the playing courtier. Play was a world where children were increasingly in school, privatized, and cut off from the street play of the folk or the play of the adult world. Play was also becoming more solitary.

Although Locke and Rousseau disagreed on most things about schooling and play, they both agreed schooling and play should be solitary activities (Sutton-Smith, 1985). The play of confined children could, of course, be supervised and its grosser elements eliminated. In this way, historically, play, at first trivialized, in time became idealized as children's behavior was increasingly controlled by schools, sports, playgrounds, toys, and television sets (Sutton-Smith & Kelly-Byrne, 1984). From this developed those *generational* theories of play based on the child-adult disjunction that have dominated our notions of play theory in the 20th century (Kelly-Byrne, 1983).

Play and the imagination

Modern seriousness about children's play originated with the German philosophical idealists' interpretation of play in the early 19th century. Play began to be identified as imaginative or *as if* thinking, a heuristic fiction that perpetuated hypothetical life and hence scientific life (Schiller, 1795). With this a fundamental pivoting of intellectual life occurred and the 2,000 year dominance of philosophy, logic, and science over art, literature, and play as fundamental modes of knowledge began to be questioned. From Kant to Schiller to Nietzsche there was an intellectual shift that brought the former hegemony of the sciences into question.

This shift, still in progress according to Spariosu (1982), makes it possible to consider that play in general, and children's play in particular, contains a particular kind of truth. Increasingly it was used by educators such as Pestalozzi, Froebel, and Montessori as a kind of learning. Later it was reframed in evolutionary theory as the preparatory activity of the young. In our present century it has been conceptualized variously as a form of mental health (Erikson, 1951), as a form of cognitive consolidation (Piaget, 1951), as a kind of exploratory learning (Berlyne, 1960), or as a learning of metacommunication (Bateson, 1972).

In all these cases play is viewed as a functional activity that contributes to growth and socialization. Much of this educational play is organized or arranged by adults. Some of it is a reinterpretation of irrational play (aggression and sexual play) to give it a rational outcome (as a form of socialization). But because most of this modern study of play is done in nursery schools, research laboratories, or in schoolrooms, only the supervised forms available in such places are generally studied. This play is more civilized than street play, and can therefore be described in the more positive terms that have become current in today's play definitions of play as fun, voluntary, intrinsically motivated, and flexible. It is all *good* play.

The major technique used to obscure the difference between good and bad play has been the gradual control of children so that under our supervision they can produce only *good* play. The other tacit technique has been to identify play with a variety of other good activities, such as exploration, construction, mastery, and imagination, none of which need to be play, although they can all be played with. When play is treated in this global way to include a whole variety of such intelligent and characterological values, it naturally appears to be a most useful activity. Finally, and in confirmation, attempts are made to prove empirically that those who play more imaginatively or more playfully are more creative, and better at schooling (Singer, 1973; Lieberman, 1979; Pepler & Rubin, 1982).

Play as a fulcrum for cultural conflict

In conclusion, it appears that play has been construed differently at various times in Western history. Thought about play has gone through periods when its major focus has been the irrationality or anarchy in the contestive games of the gods; periods when distinctions have been made between good or useful play and bad or worthless play; periods when the focus has been on the player as a master of the different roles and the masks to be presented in public; periods when play was held as childish and trivial; and finally periods when play was seen as the font of imaginative life and of personal and social progress. All of these views of play have some counterparts in modern play theory, even though the latter sees play largely as good, childlike, and imaginative. All Western historical periods, however, have contributed to modern play's conceptualization which includes at least the following concepts:

Contest (competition, games, sports)
Irrational play (randomness, disorder, nonsense, deep play)
Freedom (of voluntary choices or from inhibition)
Rationality (as in games of strategy, educational games, or in problem-solving play)
As if **ness** (imagination, role playing, fantasy, and idyllism)

One approach to these historical differences is simply to see them as useful rhetorics for reinforcing the power and practices of particular ruling classes (Spariosu, 1982). This view says that any current play theory is the one consonant with the hegemony of this or that ruling group. This view neglects the possibility that play is the kind of phenomenon that lends itself intrinsically to struggles for power. Whether it is the king forbidding football, or the schoolteacher forbidding *Johnny on the Pony* on the asphalt playground, play seems to be more easily fought about than many other domains of human society. Keesing (1960) observes that play is a particularly open domain of society, and as such is more easily shifted around than most other aspects of society such as the political system, the kinship system, or the educational system. In addition, the dialectical character of play, as a tension between opposites, allows it to be used as a fulcrum for such conflicts. Play becomes a cultural projective phenomenon, not merely a projective technique. Each society uses it as grounds to struggle over conflicts between social orders, men and women, parish and nation, and adults and children.

More technically, play is the kind of mediational system that allows easy interference in its own structural character. Remembering that animals also play, we see play as a very primitive and ancient form of expression and communication. It is a primeval language, but one in which the expressive component is more important than the instrumental component. It is also like language because it brings players into a community of mutual expression. Still, being a primitive form, its cognitive-carrying capacity seems limited to fairly obvious oppositions such as to and fro (Gadamer, 1982), order and disorder, approach and avoidance, chase and escape, attack and defend, accumulate and deprive, and success and failure (Herron & Sutton-Smith, 1971). Again, as Bateson (1972) has made so clear, communication about play is always paradoxical. One is invited to join the party and participate in primary process (wishful thinking or aggression, for example); but then one is required to abide by such secondary processes as careful signaling that one's intent is not serious, and that these things will be only expressed in this time and place and under these conditions. In short, one is invited to break the rules of ordinary behavior and discourse, but is then required to abide by the new rules engendered within the play. The excitement of play, its spirit, seems to arise from this dialectic between what is usually not permitted and what is permitted, and then again more specifically from the oppositions that are engendered within the play itself (chasing and escaping).

Historical interference occurs at both levels by simply not allowing some kinds of play, or by structuring play so that its oppositions are harmless. Considering play as a primitive and paradoxical grammar of expression and communication whose dialectic of rules violated and rules engendered to excite the participants helps to explain why playfulness constantly lurks at the boundaries of any form of seriousness, attracting the participants to its own antithetical forms of response. As such it is usually manipulated for public control, but is similarly always in danger of excess. The spirit of play is typically the spirit of the times. So that not only are the players caught projectively in their paradoxical self-maskings (Sutton-Smith & Kelly-Byrne, 1983), but the interpreters of play are also caught in their cultural self-maskings, by the definitions they impose upon the phenomena.

On a practical level, this analysis indicates the quite intense importance of play to the players. Although we use play in various ways in the classroom for our own purposes, we need to remember that the children have purposes of their own, and need to deal with such purposes largely by themselves (even if under distant supervision), making use of this vital and universal kind of communication.

References

Bateson, G. (1972). *Steps to an ecology of mind.* New York: Ballantine.

Beaujour, M. (1984, March). *Delayed replay: The Renaissance as "mimicry" and representation.* Paper presented at the Conference on Forms of Play in the Early Modern Period, University of Maryland, College Park.

Berlyne, D. E. (1960). *Conflict, arousal and curiosity.* New York: McGraw-Hill.

Brailsford, D. (1969). *Sport and society.* London: Routledge & Kegan Paul.

Castiglione, B. (1968). *The book of the courtier.* London: Penguin. (Original work published 1528)

Cervantes, M. (1938). *Don Quixote.* New York: Heritage Press. (Original work published 1605)

Erasmus, D. (1969). *The praise of folly.* Princeton, NJ: Princeton University Press. (Original work published 1509)

Erikson, E. (1951). *Childhood and society.* New York: Norton.

Fagen, R. (1980). *Animal play behavior.* New York: Oxford University Press.

Fein, G. (1984). The self building potential of pretend play or "I got a fish, all by myself." In T. D. Yawkey & A. D. Pellegrini (Eds.), *Child's play: Developmental and applied.* Hillsdale, NJ: Erlbaum.

Fink, E. (1968). The oasis of happiness: Toward an ontology of play. In J. Ehrmann (Ed.), *Game, play, literature.* Boston: Beacon.

Gadamer, H. G. (1982). *Truth and method.* New York: Crossroads.

Goffman, E. (1959). *The presentation of self in everyday life.* New York: Doubleday.

Greene, T. M. (1984, March). *Ceremonial play and parody in Renaissance literature.* Paper presented at the Conference on the Forms of Play in the Early Modern Period, University of Maryland, College Park.

Heidegger, M. (1962). *Being and time.* New York: Harper & Row. (Original work published 1927)

Herron, R. E., & Sutton-Smith, B. (1971). *Child's play.* New York: Wiley.

Huizinga, J. (1955). *Homo ludens.* Boston: Beacon.

Keesing, F. M. (1960). Recreative behavior and culture change. In A. F. C. Wallace (Ed.), *Men and cultures.* Philadelphia: The University of Pennsylvania Press.

Kelly-Byrne, D. (1983). Play: The child-adult connection. In B. Sutton-Smith & D. Kelly-Byrne (Eds.), *The masks of play.* West Point, NY: Leisure Press.

Krasnor, L. R., & Pepler, D. J. (1980). The study of children's play: Some suggested future directions. In K. Rubin (Ed.), *Children's play: New directions for child development* (Vol. 9). San Francisco: Jossey-Bass.

Lieberman, J. N. (1979). *Playfulness: Its relationship to imagination and creativity.* New York: Academic.

Machiavelli, N. (1947). *The prince.* New York: Crofts Classics. (Original work published 1513)

Mead, G. H. (1934). *Mind, self, and society.* Chicago: University of Chicago Press.

Nietzsche, F. (1967). *The birth of tragedy and the case of Wagner.* New York: Vintage. (Original work published 1871)

Opie, I., & Opie, P. (1968). *The lore and language of schoolchildren.* New York: Oxford University Press.

Pepler, D. J., & Rubin, K. (1982). The play of children: Current theory and research. *Contributions to Human Development, 6,* 1–158.

Piaget, J. (1951). *Play, dreams and imitation in childhood.* New York: Norton.

Rabelais, F. (1955). *Gargantua and Pantagruel.* London: Penguin. (Original work published 1532)

Schiller, F. (1965). *On the aesthetic education of man.* New York: Frederick Ungar.

Singer, J. L. (1973). *The child's world of make-believe.* New York: Academic.

Snow, E. (1983). "Meaning" in *children's games* on the limitations of the iconographic approach to Breugel. *Representations, 1*(2), 27–60.

Spariosu, M. (1982). Literature and play: History, principles, method. In M. Spariosu (Ed.), *Literature, mimesis and play.* Tubingen, West Germany: Gunter Narr Verlag.

Sutton-Smith, B. (1978). *Die dialektik des spiels.* Schorndorf: Verlag Karl Hoffman.

Sutton-Smith, B. (Ed.). (1979). *Play and learning.* New York: Gardner.

Sutton-Smith, B. (1980). Children's play: Some sources of play theorizing. In K. Rubin (Ed.), *Children's play: New directions for child development* (Vol. 9). San Francisco: Jossey-Bass.

Sutton-Smith, B. (1981). *A history of children's play.* Philadelphia: The University of Pennsylvania Press.

Sutton-Smith, B. (1985). *Toys as culture.* New York: Gardner.

Sutton-Smith, B., & Kelly-Byrne, D. (Eds.). (1983). *The masks of play.* West Point, NY: Leisure Press.

Sutton-Smith, B., & Kelly-Byrne, D. (1984). The idealization of play. In P. K. Smith (Ed.), *Play in animals and humans.* London: Blackwells.

Turner, V. (1974). *Dramas, fields and metaphors.* Ithaca, NY: Cornell University Press.

Webster's new twentieth century dictionary of the English language (Unabridged, 2nd ed.). (1961). New York: Publishers Guild.

Wheelock, A. K. (1984, March). *Games in Dutch art: Innocent pleasures or moral exemplors.* Paper presented at the Conference on the Forms of Play in the Early Modern Period, University of Maryland, College Park.

Steve Herzog

In their focus on children, ethnographers have much in common with early childhood educators. Both groups take children seriously and recognize children's activities as significant and filled with meaning.

CHAPTER TWO

Play Theory

BRIAN VANDENBERG

The amount of theory and research or play in the last decade indicates that there has been a dramatic increase in the interest in children's play. This chapter will attempt to place these recent developments in a larger historical context by briefly sketching the major developments of play theory in the 20th century. The aim is to identify important theoretical developments, and to delineate their relationship to topics of current interest, many of which are reviewed in subsequent chapters of this volume.

The first 50 years

During the first part of this century, psychology was pulled in two directions. One direction was charted by Freud, whose theories of psychopathology and its treatment arose within the medical-philosophical tradition of the European continent. Freud's emphasis on theory, and his fundamental assumption that appearances are deceiving, is a stark contrast to behaviorism — the second direction in psychology. Behaviorism is a product of the pragmatic, fact-oriented New World. Its emphasis is on learning, minimizing theory, and on the observable. These two radically different positions gave birth to very different views of play.

Freud's concept of play changed as his theory changed. In his early work, when Freud focused on the features of the id, he suggested that play provides a safe opportunity for children to vent forbidden impulses (Freud, 1959). Later, as he began to focus on ego functioning, he argued that play allows the child to master prior traumatic events (Freud, 1961). Freud's theories of play were used as a therapeutic tool for children by psychoanalytic therapists who used children's free play constructions in a way analogous to the use of free associations in therapy with adults. Thus, play came to be seen as a source of catharsis,

17

a source of mastery, a therapeutic technique, and a window into the psychodynamics of a child's personality.

These four aspects of play that emerged from Freud's work have attracted a great deal of attention. The catharsis aspect of play has been a subject of continued debate and research. Play as a source of mastery has been elaborated on in the works of other psychoanalytic theorists, most notably Erikson (1977). Play therapy has been widely accepted in the treatment of troubled children, and the development of the doll play technique has led to a large number of studies examining various aspects of children's personality (Levin & Wardwell, 1962).

One of the major questions surrounding the study of play has been how to define the term. Part of the problem stems from the fact that play has as much to do with the *way* that something is done, as it does with *what* is done; it is more like an adverb than a noun. This sujbective, adverb-like phenomenon cannot easily (if at all) be packaged into a neat operational definition. This failure led behavioral theorists to dismiss play as a viable scientific concept (Schlosberg, 1947).

While the climate of behaviorism produced a chill in American academic psychology, the study of play proceeded on several other fronts. Most of the work on play in the United States before World War II was conducted in the education and home economics traditions. Research on the effects of play environments on the structure of children's play, on sex differences, and on the development of social play was first undertaken in this era, and has continued to this day (see chapters in this volume by Frost, Liss, McLoyd, Phyfe-Perkins & Shoemaker). The work of Parten (1932) on the stages of social play is particularly noteworthy, because it has served as a foundation for much contemporary work in this area (Rubin & Howe, this volume).

The theoretical work of Isaacs (1930, 1933) is also valuable for understanding the intellectual and social value of play. According to Isaacs, the intellectual benefits of play are derived from the opportunity to transcend the here and now, to allow individuals to develop hypotheses and the *as if* consciousness. The social benefits of play emerge from the conflict and cooperation that characterize children's social play. Social conflict in play jolts children out of their egocentric world and forces them to consider others as more than mere accessories to their own fantasies. Cooperative play, on the other hand, provides a reference group that helps children to develop a morality of equals rather than the parent-child morality of unequals. Motifs of Isaacs's work can be found in contemporary thinking about play. Her emphasis on the *as if* of play is echoed in the work of Sutton-Smith (1967), and her emphasis on the importance of social conflict is similar to that proposed by Rubin (1980; Rubin & Howe, this volume).

A second front where ideas about play were developed was Europe. Piaget (1962) and Vygotsky (1967), writing in a more academic and scientific tradition than Freud, developed elaborate theories of human development that gave considerable attention to the importance of play. Because of the behavioral orientation of American psychology, their work went unnoticed in the United States until the 1960s. At that time serious problems in the behavioral perspective were identified. There was a growing realization that to fully understand human behavior it was necessary to understand the individual's cognitive activity. It was at this time that Vygotsky and Piaget were first translated into English.

Midcentury: A period of transition

Ironically, while the behaviorism of the first half century led to the conclusion that play did not exist, it was play — and its cousin exploration — that undermined behavioral theory in the mid-1950s. Hullian theory was the dominant form of behaviorism. One of its major tenets was that learning is a consequence of the association of stimuli with responses that reduce basic drives, such as hunger and thirst, that are physiologically necessary for the organism's survival. However, the need to explore a new environment was sometimes more powerful than the hunger drive, and animals would sometimes solve puzzles "just for the fun of it" (Rubin, Fein, & Vandenberg, 1983). This was a serious challenge to Hullian theory, because these behaviors were not directly associated with physiological needs and were not a means to a reward, but were a reward in themselves; they were intrinsically motivated.

Berlyne (1960, 1969) proposed a theory to explain these behaviors within a Hullian framework. He suggested that extrinsically motivated behaviors are driven by tissue needs, while intrinsically motivated behaviors serve central nervous system (CNS) functions. Thus, specific exploration reduces the arousal level of the CNS by acquiring information, and diversive exploration (or play) increases CNS arousal by generating novelty.

The distinction between exploration (specific exploration) and play (diversive exploration) is an important conceptual distinction that has been crucial in defining play. Hutt and her colleagues (Hutt, 1966; Hughes & Hutt, 1979) have identified different physiological and behavioral correlates, and growth and decay curves for play and exploration that basically agree with Berlyne's theory. This work has also led to an understanding of how play and exploration may be linked in a broader exploration-play application sequence of adaptation (Vandenberg, 1978).

Berlyne's theory about the relationship between play and arousal is an important point of departure for other theorists. Ellis (1973) suggests that play is a stimulus-seeking behavior; where Berlyne views play as a flight from an undesirable state of under-arousal, Ellis sees play as a movement toward creating stimulus variation. Ellis's point has been further elaborated on by both Schultz (1979) and Fein (1981).

Despite Berlyne's attempt to save Hullian theory, by the 1960s the time was ripe for new approaches. The strict positivistic philosophy of science that behaviorism was based on was under heavy attack in philosophical circles (Kuhn, 1962; Polanyi, 1958). This attack dovetailed with growing evidence in psychology that human behavior could not be fully understood unless human thought was also considered. Not coincidentally, the development of the transistor and the concomitant rise of the computer occurred during this period. Scientists began to use the computer to model human thought, giving rise to cognitive science. Within this framework, American psychologists began to turn to the works of Piaget and Vygotsky.

The last two decades: Piaget and beyond

Piaget's genetic epistemology is an elaborately detailed analysis of the developmental features of human cognition. His theory of play is intimately enmeshed in his broader theory. For Piaget (1962), play is an assimilatively dominated activity that consolidates and elaborates established schemas of cognition. The form that play takes reflects the child's current level of cognitive development. The three major developmental types of play are practice play; symbolic play; and games with rules that reflect the sensorimotor, preoperational, and concrete operational stages of development.

The close association between a child's play and a child's cognitive functioning has served as a guiding principle for a great deal of research on the object play of infants. Using Piaget's detailed descriptions of the growing symbolic competencies displayed in the sensorimotor period, researchers have found similar patterns in the development of object play in infants (McCune-Nicolich & Bruskin, 1982; McCune, this volume).

In contrast to descriptive studies of infant play, studies of the preoperational child frequently focus on play as an independent variable. These studies attempt to assess whether training in various types of play could enhance a child's development. They have their roots in earlier training studies that examined whether children could be given an enriched experience that would accelerate their development through Piaget's stages (what Piaget has called the "American question"). While the early play training studies primarily used Piagetian tasks as outcome measures, later studies broadened their scope to assess social and linguistic areas of development (Saltz & Brodie, 1982; Saltz & Saltz, this volume). The general success of these studies has given support to those advocating the incorporation of structured play experiences into preschool programs. However, the use of play as an independent variable implies that play is a causal agent in development; a view that contrasts with Piaget's more passive, assimilative role. Vygotsky, Bateson, Sutton-Smith, Singer, and Bruner are five theorists who have given impetus to this causal view.

Vygotsky's (1967) theory of play hinges on his analysis of the origin and role of play in development. According to Vygotsky, play is invented as a response to the development of unrealizable desires that emerge in the early preschool years. Through play, a child is able to provide imaginary realizations to unrealizable desires. The importance of play for development is not its relationship to wish fulfillment (as Freudian theory would argue); rather, it signals the beginning of the development of imagination. Fully developed thought is abstract and not anchored in the physical givens of the environment; it does not depend upon concrete objects and actions in the perceptual field as props for thinking imaginatively. The play of preschoolers, however, does depend on such props. These objects serve as pivots for meaning. An object can stand for something it is not, such as a stick for a horse, at the same time it provides support for the child's budding ability to imagine. Preschool play is thus a transitional stage between the situationally determined thought of infants and the liberated, abstract thought of adults. Play not so much reflects thought (as Piaget suggests) as it creates thought.

Bateson (1955, 1956), like Vygotsky, focuses on the relationship between play and communication, but where Vygotsky's theory centers on meaning, Bateson's centers on metacommunication—communication about one's communication. In social play, individuals must somehow communicate that their behavior is not *real*, but only *play*. The failure to communicate that *this is play* would result in a misreading of the act's intent and would result in social discord. Bateson emphasizes that what is learned in play is the ability to frame and reframe roles through metacommunication. The individual is not learning about the particular roles they enact as much as they are learning about the concept of roles.

Bateson's work has led investigators to examine the ways humans and other species communicate *this is play* in their social play. Garvey's (1974) charming descriptions of the playful interactions of preschoolers is a detailed analysis of the metacommunicative aspects of play. Garvey's work focuses on the text of children's play. Schwartzman (1978) and Sutton-Smith (1983), however, have argued that the context of children's play is important in determining whether an individual is likely to assume that *this is a place for play*. What may constitute toys and a play environment in one culture may be an alien environment in another, and a full understanding of playful activity must incorporate both the text and the context of play (King, this volume).

While most of the other theorists discussed to this point have examined play within a broader framework of their theory, Sutton-Smith has generated a number of theories that are focused exclusively on play. His published exchange with Piaget about the role of play in development has undoubtedly been a factor in the increased attention given to play during the past 2 decades (Piaget, 1966; Sutton-Smith, 1966). In this exchange, Sutton-Smith took exception to Piaget's assimilative model of play, and argued that a divergent view of cognitive functioning would place play in a more central role in development. He argued that the production of novelty in play is not a "distorting assimilation" as Piaget suggests, but is the source of new directions for adaptive thought. The *as if* attitude that characterizes play provides the freedom to generate new meanings that may later be used in more serious contexts (Sutton-Smith, 1967). This work resulted in research investigations on the contribution of play to divergent thinking (Pepler, this volume).

Much of Sutton-Smith's work on play has addressed areas largely ignored by other theorists. He was one of the first to examine the cross-cultural influences on children's games (Avedon & Sutton-Smith, 1971), and has emphasized the importance of historical factors on children's play and adult play theorizing (Sutton-Smith, 1980). This appreciation of cultural and historical factors is reflected in his analysis of sex differences in children's play, where he argues that changing sex differences in children's play reflects changes in the values and life styles of the culture (Sutton-Smith, 1979). More recently, Sutton-Smith (1986) has turned his attention to the neglected topic of toys, suggesting that they are as much cultural artifacts as they are children's playthings.

Two other important contemporary perspectives of play can be traced to developments during the midcentury. One perspective emerged from the research of learning theorists. Paired associative learning was one of the methodological cornerstones of early learning theorists; the influence of various factors on an individual's ability to learn was assessed using the individual's ability to learn and remember pairs of words. An important discovery in the early 1960s showed that individuals could use imagery to drastically increase their ability to learn word pairs in one trial (Pavio, 1971). These results pointed to the power of *image-anation*, and contributed to the shift from the study of learned behaviors to the study of cognitive functioning.

Singer (1973) was one of the first to apply this perspective to children's play. He argued that fantasy play is instrumental in developing the capacity for using imagery, which is necessary for thinking about the past (memory) and the future (imagination), and for developing linguistic skills. He also discussed the potential contributions of fantasy play to social and emotional development, and the ways parents may enhance children's make-believe play (Singer, 1977).

The second area of play theorizing can be traced to the work of ethologists, who examined the behavior of animals in their natural habitat, with remarkable results. The significance of this work is reflected in the fact that several of these researchers have been awarded a Nobel prize; one of the few times this distinction has been bestowed on behavioral scientists. The effects of this research on play research have been twofold. First, it has prompted some psychologists to apply the observation methods of the ethologists to children in their natural play settings (for example, Blurton-Jones, 1967).

The second, more theoretically important effect is evidenced in the work of Bruner (1972). Drawing on the work of ethologists and other reseachers of nonhuman animal behavior, Bruner suggested that play provides the behavioral flexibility that makes tool use possible. In play, an organism plays with its own behaviors, creating novel combinations by splicing together behavioral subroutines that have functional utility in other contexts. Bruner's formulations have led to research and further theorizing on the relationship between play, tool use, and problem solving in humans (Pepler, this volume; Vandenberg, 1980).

A playful future

During the past 25 years, play theory in American psychology has blossomed. This ripening of play theory is not only the result of psychological research, but a consequence of broader cultural factors. The rigid adherence to a positivistic philosophy of science, with its prag-

Robert Koenig

The greater the children's control of an activity, the more likely it was to be called play. Lack of adult involvement appears to be a necessary ingredient of kindergarten children's definition of play.

matic overtones coupled with a strain of Calvinistic abhorrence of play, led to the near neglect of play in American psychology in the first part of this century. Growing attention to play and European theorists is evidence of a shift in epistemology that is no doubt related to a more general shift in the values of American culture. If this trend continues, it bodes well for play theory. However, predicting the future can be a rather presumptuous, if not humbling, endeavor and it is with the spirit of play that I offer the following suggestion.

One striking feature of much current play theorizing is the need to justify the importance of play by linking it to the development of cognitive, social, emotional, or linguistic skills and abilities. Play is not an important behavior in itself, but becomes important as its ability to enhance other (more valued?) aspects of development becomes recognized. This orientation indirectly draws on Darwinian theory, where the survival of a species is dictated by its ability to adapt (develop a range of skills related to problem solving).

An alternative perspective would be to see humans as fundamentally myth-making creatures, and reality as a set of trusted myths (including Darwinian theory) that are shared by the members of the culture (Miller, 1974). To be human, and to live in a meaningful way in a culture, requires that we live in and through a very sophisticated, abstract, and symbolic system that is largely imaginary. To be incapable of fantasy is to be barred from human culture. Thus, the importance of play and fantasy is not found in indirect stimulation of cognitive, social, educational, and problem-solving skills. Rather, play and fantasy are central features of what it means to be human, and these other skills are spinoffs of the ability to imagine.

This is one possible scenario where play theory might move. What is important is not the form that future theory might take, but the enthusiasm and playfulness of its efforts.

References

Avedon, E. M., & Sutton-Smith, B. (Eds.). (1971). *The study of games*. New York: Wiley.

Bateson, G. (1955). A theory of play and fantasy. *Psychiatric Research Reports, 2*, 39–51.

Bateson, G. (1956). The message "This is play." In B. Schaffner (Ed.), *Group processes* (pp. 145–246). New York: Josiah Macy.

Berlyne, D. E. (1960). *Conflict, arousal and curiosity*. New York: McGraw-Hill.

Berlyne, D. E. (1969). Laughter, humor and play. In G. Lindzey & E. Aronson (Eds.), *The handbook of social psychology* (Vol. 3, pp. 795–852). Reading, MA: Addison-Wesley.

Blurton-Jones, N. G. (1967). An ethological study of some aspects of social behavior of children in nursery school. In D. Morris (Ed.), *Primate ethology.* London: Weidenfeld & Nicholson.

Bruner, J. S. (1972). The nature and uses of immaturity. *American Psychologist, 27,* 687–708.

Ellis, M. J. (1973). *Why people play.* Englewood Cliffs, NJ: Prentice-Hall.

Erikson, E. H. (1977). *Toys and reasons.* New York: Norton.

Fein, G. G. (1981). Pretend play: An integrative review. *Child Development, 52,* 1095–1118.

Freud, S. (1959). Creative writers and daydreaming. In J. Stackey (Ed.), *The standard edition of the complete psychological works of Sigmund Freud* (Vol. 9). London: Hogarth. (Original work published 1905)

Freud, S. (1961). *Beyond the pleasure principle.* New York: Norton.

Garvey, C. (1974). Some properties of social play. *Merrill-Palmer Quarterly, 20,* 163–180.

Hughes, M., & Hutt, C. (1979). Heart-rate correlates of childhood activities: Play, exploration, problem-solving and day dreaming. *Biological Psychology, 8,* 253–263.

Hutt, C. (1966). Exploration and play in children. *Symposium of the Zoological Society of London, 18,* 61–81.

Isaacs, S. S. (1930). *Intellectual growth in children.* London: Routledge.

Isaacs, S. S. (1933). *Social development in young children: A study of beginnings.* London: Routledge.

Kuhn, T. S. (1962). *The structure of scientific revolutions.* Chicago: University of Chicago Press.

Levin, H., & Wardwell, E. (1962). The research uses of doll play. *Psychological Bulletin, 29,* 27–56.

McCune-Nicolich, L., & Bruskin, C. (1982). Combinatorial competency in symbolic play and language. In D. J. Pepler & K. H. Rubin (Eds.), *The play of children: Current theory and research.* Basel, Switzerland: Karger.

Miller, S. N. (1974). The playful, the crazy and the nature of pretense. *Rice University Studies, 60,* 31–51.

Parten, M. B. (1932). Social participation among preschool children. *Journal of Abnormal Psychology, 27,* 243–269.

Pavio, A. (1971). *Imagery and verbal processes.* New York: Holt, Reinhart & Winston.

Piaget, J. (1962). *Play, dreams, and imitation in childhood.* New York: Norton.

Piaget, J. (1966). Response to Brian Sutton-Smith. *Psychological Review, 73,* 111–112.

Polanyi, M. (1958). *Personal knowledge.* Chicago: University of Chicago Press.

Rubin, K. (1980). Fantasy play: Its role in the development of social skills and social cognition. In K. Rubin (Ed.), *Children's play.* San Francisco: Jossey-Bass.

Rubin, K. H., Fein, G. G., & Vandenberg, B. (1983). In E. M. Heatherington (Ed.), *Handbook of child psychology* (Vol. 4, pp. 694–774). New York: Wiley.

Saltz, E., & Brodie, J. (1982). Pretend-play training in childhood: A review and critique. In D. J. Pepler & K. H. Rubin (Eds.), *The play of children: Current theory and research.* Basel, Switzerland: Karger.

Schlosberg, H. (1947). The concept of play. *Psychological Review, 54,* 229–231.

Schultz, T. R. (1979). Play as arousal modulation. In B. Sutton-Smith (Ed.), *Play and learning*. New York: Gardner.

Schwartzman, H. B. (1978). *Transformations: The anthropology of children's play*. New York: Plenum.

Singer, J. L. (Ed.). (1973). *The child's world of make-believe: Experimental studies of imaginative play*. New York: Academic.

Singer, J. L. (1977). Imagination and make-believe play in early childhood: Some educational implications. *Journal of Mental Imagery, 1*, 127–144.

Sutton-Smith, B. (1966). Piaget on play: A critique. *Psychological Review, 73*, 104–110.

Sutton-Smith, B. (1967). The role of play in cognitive development. *Young Children, 22*, 361–370.

Sutton-Smith, B. (1979). The play of girls. In C. B. Kopp & M. Kirkpatrick (Eds.), *Becoming female: Perspectives on development*. New York: Plenum.

Sutton-Smith, B. (1980). Children's play: Some sources of play theorizing. In K. H. Rubin (Ed.), *Children's play*. San Francisco: Jossey-Bass.

Sutton-Smith, B. (1983). Piaget, play and cognition revisited. In W. Overton (Ed.), *The relationship between social and cognitive development* (pp. 229–249). Hillsdale, NJ: Erlbaum.

Sutton-Smith, B. (1986). *Toys as culture*. New York: Gardner.

Vandenberg, B. (1978). Play and development from an ethological perspective. *American Psychologist, 33*, 724–738.

Vandenberg, B. (1980). Play, problem-solving and creativity. In K. H. Rubin (Ed.), *Children's play: New directions for child development* (pp. 49–68). San Francisco: Jossey-Bass.

Vygotsky, L. S. (1967). Play and its role in the mental development of the child. *Soviet Psychology, 12*, 62–76.

Merrie L. Murray

The importance of play and fantasy is not found in indirect stimulation of cognitive, social, educational, and problem-solving skills. Rather, play and fantasy are central features of what it means to be human.

CHAPTER THREE

Play and the Culture of Childhood

NANCY R. KING

Educators who study children's culture are beginning to realize that a thorough understanding of play events requires the open-ended, in-depth study of small groups of children in natural settings. Because experimental research techniques are not useful in such inquiry, there is a growing interest in and enthusiasm for qualitative research methods. Ethnography is one of several qualitative methodologies education researchers have borrowed and adopted for their own use.

Though relatively new to education, ethnography has a long tradition in the field of anthropology. Anthropologists seek to understand patterns of human behavior through the description and analysis of particular situations and events. They do not ordinarily design experimental studies, reduce their data for statistical analysis, or display their findings numerically. Instead, anthropologists attempt to convey a richly detailed description of the life of a particular group or culture. Their understanding of events is based on the participants' viewpoints, and their goal is to share that understanding with the reader.

The ethnography of play

There are both similarities and differences between current ethnographies of play and the work of most anthropologists. The most important difference has to do with the locus of study. Anthropologists study activities and cultures foreign to most readers. Ethnographers of play, on the other hand, usually study children living in familiar social settings and participating in familiar activities.

The study of familiar settings creates difficulties for ethnographers of children's play that are no less serious than the problems encountered by ethnographers studying foreign cultures. Because the observed activities are familiar, researchers may overestimate their understanding of the children. Ethnographers working in familiar settings may unwittingly impose reconstructed recollections of their own childhood activities on their analyses of children's behaviors. Some researchers may overemphasize the continuity between childhood and adulthood and may interpret children's play *solely* as preparation for adult tasks. Other researchers, seeing childhood as entirely separate from adulthood, may consider children's play primitive and savage.

To protect themselves from the familiarity of the setting, children's play researchers must recognize children's culture as separate and distinct from adult culture. Further, they must believe that children's culture is in and of itself worthy of study. Children's activities become interesting, then, because they teach adults about children and their social reality.

There are three important similarities between the work of anthropologists and the ethnographers of children's play. First, anthropologists and the ethnographers of children's play have a common goal. They want to understand the participants' perspectives in the situations studied and to share that understanding with other outsiders. The children's activities, and their thoughts about those activities, are vital to the ethnographer's analysis; the children produce both the observed events and an interpretation of those events. Though the children's perceptions may seem incomplete or inaccurate from an adult perspective, they are not devalued as immature. The children are experts on the meaning of their play—the researchers are the novices.

Second, like anthropologists, ethnographers of children's play insist on studying play in the context where it naturally occurs. They recognize that the meaning of behavior is embedded in a complex network of social relations, institutional constraints, and material surroundings. Consequently, an understanding of children's play must include an understanding of the physical and social setting. Further, ethnographers realize that the more familiar and undisturbed the context, the more natural and spontaneous children's play.

A final important similarity between anthropology and ethnographies of children's play is the way findings are shared. Ethnographers present their findings in richly detailed, vividly descriptive reports that graphically portray participants and events. Ethnographic reports move from a consideration of specific situations in local contexts to discussions of the general issues that the analysis illuminates. The description forms the basis of the ethnographer's analysis and permits readers to assess the adequacy of the ethnographer's evidence and the logic of her or his interpretation.

In summary, ethnography is a research model borrowed from anthropology. The issues ethnographers of children's play explore are best studied in small settings, but the setting itself is not the ultimate object of study (Geertz, 1973). Play events are interesting because they facilitate the study of social relationships and the culture of childhood. It is during play that children have the opportunity to shape their social interactions and to create and maintain a cultural context. Consequently, children's culture is particularly visible during play.

Methods and techniques

Play ethnographers hope to understand children's social reality from the children's perspective and to share that understanding with other adults through detailed descriptions and carefully reasoned analyses. Such a goal requires ongoing, firsthand familiarity with children and their play. Ethnographers have developed a variety of techniques for studying social situations so that an in-depth understanding is achieved. Ethnography, however, cannot be reduced to the research methods ethnographers typically choose. It is the *goal* of ethnography that differentiates it from other approaches to research.

Ethnographers select research methods that help them understand people in social contexts. They use a great variety of techniques, including two procedures that are part of virtually every ethnographic undertaking. First, ethnographers rely heavily on personal observations. This can sometimes be accomplished by videotaping or observing from a hidden booth, but ordinarily ethnographers prefer to be present in the research setting. They may be unobtrusive, choosing not to participate in the flow of activities, but their presence and interest in events is not disguised. Children at play quickly become accustomed to the presence of a nonparticipating adult, and researchers report that their observing appears to have little or no effect on children's activities. An ethnographer must spend considerable time observing interaction among participants in the research setting. The meaning of events observed becomes clear only as their consequences unfold, and a wide variety of encounters must be observed before the researcher can assess the importance of any of them.

In addition to observing interaction, ethnographers interview participants. The participants' responses are essential to the researcher's understanding of the meaning of observed events. Young children are ordinarily honest and straightforward in interview situations; they are also accurate and insightful analysts of their social reality.

Researchers record their observations and interviews in writing and/or on tape. These data are the source of the categories the ethnographer generates to interpret and explain the behaviors and perceptions of participants. The result is a description of the regularities of behavior in a social setting (Erickson, 1984). It is detailed and vivid so that concrete events and particular individuals emerge from the written report. The reader can then see the major issues unfold in the particulars of a specific case.

Interpretive structures and conceptual categories become evident as the ethnographer moves from description to analysis. Because the analytic framework is directly tied to the detailed description, the reader can easily assess the adequacy of the ethnographer's interpretation and explanation.

In summary, then, ethnographers study naturally occurring social events without interfering *in* the event. They attempt to understand the participant's social reality and to convey their understanding to outsiders through description and analysis. They do not approach the social setting with predetermined categories or coding devices. Rather the explanatory categories that emerge are suggested by the social setting and developed by the researcher.

Ethnographers are particularly capable of sharing a richly textured understanding of a social context. They illuminate large issues by bringing us very close to small instances. The ethnographer's effort is to understand, not to predict, control, or evaluate.

Several areas of study highlight ethnography's potential to reveal important aspects of children's play. Because ethnographic techniques permit researchers to capture the participants' perspectives, ethnographers are able to explore children's perceptions and definitions of play activities. Ethnographic techniques do not alter the flow of events and, consequently, ethnographers can study children's participation in child-supervised games and investigate the ways children create and sustain fantasy play. Finally, ethnographers can study children's culture as it develops on playgrounds and during periods of unsupervised (or loosely supervised) play. We will now briefly consider examples of current ethnographic research in each of these areas.

Children's definitions

Educators have defined play in various ways and assigned it various functions, but children are rarely asked to define play or to describe its function in their lives. In order to explore the definition of play held by the participants themselves, children in four kindergarten classrooms were observed and interviewed during a series of morning sessions and a record of their activities was written (King, 1979). An interview schedule was prepared for each child listing the child's activities. These observed activities included academic experiences, such as participating in math games, as well as other daily experiences such as lining up to leave the room, running races, and eating a snack. The children were asked to categorize each activity as work or play, and to rank the relative importance of the activities listed.

Neither an analysis of the intrinsic characteristics of activities labeled play nor an analysis of the children's personal responses to these activities provided clues about the criteria children use to differentiate work experiences from play experiences. It is the context in which the activity occurs that provides the differentiating criteria.

The single most important criterion that separated play from work in the minds of these children was that play was voluntary. All assigned activities were called work, and the category of play was reserved for those activities the children chose for themselves. Further, the greater the children's control of an activity, the more likely it was to be called play. Lack of adult involvement appears to be a necessary ingredient of school play in kindergarten.

The children spoke spontaneously and enthusiastically about their play activities, and play seemed extremely important to them. However, they believed that their work activities were more significant to their teachers; the children did not believe that their play had an educational function in the classroom.

The kindergarten teachers participating in this study were surprised by the children's responses primarily because the teachers' definitions of play included a criterion of pleasure the children did not use. While the children certainly enjoyed their play, they also enjoyed most of the activities they called work, and the element of pleasure did not, then, differentiate between the categories. An ethnographic understanding of the participants' point of view about their play showed teachers the limitations of adult recollections in understanding the play of children (King, 1979).

Children's games

Ethnographers study children's games by observing the games themselves and by interviewing the players. These methods enable researchers to see the subtle techniques children use to enter and exit group games, although the players themselves may not be able to articulate the etiquette of such situations (Sutton-Smith, 1971). Observations also reveal that the seemingly inviolate rules of many games actually have an unexpected flexibility. Players debate and negotiate the application of the rules to particular situations until the game becomes the one they want to play, rather than the one described in the rule book (Hughes, 1983; Borman, 1979). Ethnographic accounts thus prevent us from confusing a description of game rules with the actual experience of playing the game.

Goldstein (1971) studied a game activity known as counting out which children use to choose teams and assign roles for group games. Goldstein observed and interviewed 67 children, ages 4 to 14, for a period of 6 months as they participated in eight separate neighborhood play groups.

Young children learned counting out rhymes such as "One Potato, Two Potato," from older children and believed that the outcome of any counting out activity depended solely on chance. Still, some younger children were perplexed when it seemed that the counter was in control. In one case, for example, they noticed that the counter's brother was never chosen to be *It*.

Older children also described counting out as a game of chance, but Goldstein's observations did not support their idealized versions of game conduct. In fact, older children used a variety of techniques to control the outcomes of counting out games, and, in the hands of a sophisticated counter, counting out was anything but a game of chance. Counters controlled the game by selecting a rhyme based on the number of children in the group, by extending the rhyme, and by deciding where to start each successive round. Children used various methods to conceal their strategies, and they admired their own skill in controlling the game while maintaining the illusion that the outcomes were a matter of luck alone.

Children's games also teach the astute observer about the larger cultural context in which the children live. For example, Farrer's (1977) ethnography of tag played by young Mescalero Apache children reveals important aspects of the culture of the community. The game is usually played by groups of cousins, indicating the importance of family ties in community activity. The children organize their game on a jungle gym which gives a circular configuration to their play and encourages close physical contact. There is little talking during play, and children are expected to learn the game by observing. Even when game rules are violated, the children simply stop playing and reorganize the game without verbal interaction. Thus their play stresses important aspects of the children's culture including contact, circularity, and teaching by example.

Pretend play

Ethnographers study pretend play as it occurs spontaneously in natural settings. Ordinarily, such studies, which take place in nursery schools, elementary schools, and child care centers, focus on the ways children create and sustain a shared imaginative narrative. Corsaro and Tomlinson (1980) use micro-sociolinguistic analysis to study children's use of talk in structuring fantasy play. They base their analysis on the utterance of 31 children involved in six episodes of pretend play taken from 25 hours of videotape recorded during a 1-year study of spontaneous play in a nursery school.

Corsaro and Tomlinson believe that "spontaneous play can be viewed as the continual practice of reality production" (Corsaro and Tomlinson, 1980, p. 105). Consequently, it is the children's view of their social world that becomes available through the analysis of the basic communicative patterns and interpretive techniques they exhibit during fantasy play.

A close analysis of the six episodes selected reveals how children's verbalizations serve as cues to other players. First, declarative statements are used to convey information and control the actions of peers. Without any understanding and analysis of the context in which these statements occur, this talk can be mistaken for a running commentary without communicative intent. This, however, is not the case. By pointing to and highlighting aspects of the play context, these statements create shared meanings among participants. Children also use questions, responses, and other verbal and nonverbal conversational devices to generate topics, sequence interaction, organize turn allocations, and control the conduct of others.

Giffin (1984) also observed children involved in fantasy play, and analyzed their use of metacommunication to organize the flow of events. She found that children tried to negotiate their play with the least possible attention to the play frame. Whenever possible, the children chose to direct their activity from within the play frame, thus emphasizing the unfolding action and strengthening their mutual commitment to the shared fantasy. For example, children asked questions during play which contained implicit answers and served to shape the play episode. When one boy Giffin observed announced to the group that he planned to call someone on the telephone, one of the girls in the group asked (and thus suggested), "The police?" He used her suggestion and the police were introduced and incorporated into the developing fantasy.

Children also subtly referred to materials and distributed roles from within the play frame. In one instance, a girl called out to another child, "Gramma, come and save me." She thus automatically assigned the role of the grandmother without interrupting the play episode.

When they had difficulty directing their play, children resorted to sharing cues in a quick low voice so that the play itself was not obviously interrupted. When absolutely necessary, the children stepped out of the play frame to announce the meaning of particular objects or to direct the actions of other children. Such communication was needed when their fantasy characters could not reasonably communicate the message they needed to share or when more subtle communication had gone unnoticed. If such action was needed repeatedly, the integrity of the play frame was likely to be jeopardized and the play episode often disintegrated into negotiation and dispute.

For more than 1 year, Schwartzman (1978) studied fantasy play as a participant observer in a Chicago child care center; she observed the children's play, the social structure of the classroom, the children's preferred playmates, and the quality of their friendships. In addition to studying the communication strategies children used to structure their fantasy play, she analyzed her data in light of the children's positions in the social hierarchy of the classroom.

Children are aware of themselves as participants in a social reality that exists beyond their play episodes, and they must inevitably take that reality into account as they play. Researchers are extremely handicapped when analyzing the meaning of children's play if that reality is not available to them, or if they pretend that it does not exist or is not important. Schwartzman's discussion, on the other hand, is immeasurably enriched by her understanding of the children's social positions and the influence of their social reality on the roles they choose and the situations they negotiate during pretend play.

Schwartzman found nine different categories of verbal and nonverbal statements children used to organize their dramatic play. Different children used these statements differently depending on the context of the play group and its relationship to the larger context of the classroom. The roles the children adopted reflected both the authority structure within the play group and the social hierarchy outside the context of the play episode.

Schwartzman used the example of one child in particular to illustrate the importance of the status hierarchy in the development of play episodes.

There was one child in the day-care center who turns out to have been the most dominant kid in the center on the basis of sociometry — my observations, kids' reports, what not — and was very adept at creating situations where she would play and then say that she was not playing. She would end up being out of the so-called defined play space and say that she wasn't playing, or she would define herself in a subservient role and abstract herself from the situation, but everyone knew that she was in fact leading the group. When they would want to play with that particular group they wouldn't go to the two little girls, or whoever was in the defined play space; they would go to Linda (which is what I call her) and ask if they could play, and she would say, "I'm not playing; why are you asking me? Go ask so-and-so. She's the one that's the mother," or something like that. But of course she was defining the person in that role, so that everyone knew she was the leader and the one you had to check out. (1979, p. 247)

The children's fantasy play reflected their concerns with issues such as dominance and control in the classroom as a whole, and served as both a challenge to and corroboration of the authority structure in the children's network of social interactions. As Schwartzman points out ". . . the 'pretense' of equality [is] maintained in the classroom by the teacher(s), while the 'reality' of the hierarchy is reflected only in the 'pretense' of play, where the children are in control" (Schwartzman, 1978, p. 245). Children's play is thus a form of critique, an exploration of their social network, and an art form.

Playground culture

An outstanding example of the ethnography of children's play has recently become available in Sluckin's (1981) study of playground activity. Sluckin studied children's culture by systematically observing and interviewing children on two school playgrounds in Britain. During the first year of his study, he observed approximately 100 five- to eight-year-olds on the playground of a primary school serving working class children. For the first month he noted all activities. The next 3 months were spent watching each child for a period of 3 consecutive minutes in order to observe their interactions in detail. Finally, he focused on 10 children for the remainder of the year. Sluckin followed the oldest children to a middle school the following year and observed playground activity there during the second year of his study. The length of time he spent observing, interviewing, and reflecting on his data permitted the meaning of events and the social order of playground life to become clear.

Sluckin observed organized games, quiet conversations, fights, teasing, scatological taunts, crude rhymes, and power struggles. As his study progressed, he became particularly interested in the children's strategies for coping with the stream of social problems that arise during play. His observations reveal that children use a variety of rituals to prevent or solve many social problems. For example, *bagsee*, a word widely used by children throughout Britain, was used by the children Sluckin observed. As he relates:

I heard *bagsee* used not only to gain possession, claim precedence and avoid a rule, but also to state extra rules in a game. In all these contexts, the ritual makes life more predictable and acts to the advantage of the child who invokes it. If you are repeatedly chased by the *bulldog* in "British bulldog," it helps to shout "bagsee-no-following" so that he can't keep coming after you. If you want to bide time before running across, it helps to claim "bagsee no guarding" so that he can't stand over you till you leave the circle. But in return the bulldog might invoke "bagsee counting" and if you haven't left the safety of the ring by the time he reaches ten, then he can come in and tig you. And if you are about to be caught, then jump up and shout "bagsee no tigging in the air." (1981, p. 33)

There are verbal formulas to claim time out, to state extra rules, and to gain possession of an object. Used correctly, these words enable children to avoid disputes, organize games, cope with exclusion, limit aggression by playmates, and control the power of dominant children.

One of the dominant children, Neill, was known as the boss of the playground. He could enter any game without permission, control the participation of other children, bend rules in his favor, and defuse challenges to his authority. Sluckin's observations reveal that Neill simply declared himself boss and the other children tolerated his reign. Neill was careful to avoid direct confrontations and fights, and maintained his leadership largely through teasing and harrassment.

When Neill moved up to the middle school and became one of the younger children on the playground, he seemed unsure of himself. None of the children acknowledged him as a boss, and he deferred to older boys when challenged. Neill was observed asking permission to join games, and suffering exclusion on occasion. His general style of interaction did not change, however. He boasted of his athletic prowess, and was anxious to win at races; he was intolerant of opposition during games, but continued to be careful to avoid physical confrontation.

After a year at middle school, Neill seemed subdued; he no longer claimed to be boss, and others no longer acquiesced to his self-styled leadership. He was less likely to be involved in disputes and more likely to be ignored by other children. Though he lost his position and reputation, Neill did not lose his desire to be in control. His interview responses reveal a nostalgia for the days when he was one of the biggest boys on the playground.

Neill's reputation did not follow him to middle school, and his lack of size and status mitigated the possibility of his reasserting his leadership position on the playground. Further, as Neill's primary school classroom teacher noted, he seems to have lacked genuine leadership skills.

Neill wanted to be accepted as a leader but he didn't really have the character to be like that. He tried to buy it, to some extent, with sweets. They said, in effect, "Well, he wants to be leader, so we'll let him and accept him as such." He wasn't a natural leader, the others found him amusing, which wasn't quite the respect that he wanted. He pushed for leadership by organizing them, but the others didn't take too much notice of him unless they wanted to. (Sluckin, 1981, p. 95)

Because of Neill's size, status, and skills, he was unable to establish himself as an important person among his middle school peers. Sluckin concludes his discussion of Neill, however, with the prophecy that Neill will again be a prominent power on the playground when he becomes one of the older boys. Neill has not lost his ambition to be the boss, and when size and status again favor him, he may well be able to reassert himself.

Sluckin asked children why their playground activities were important. The response of one child, Jon, seems particularly insightful.

Author: What do you think playtime's for?
Jon (5 years): I think it's to make me grow up a bit.
Author: How?
Jon: Well, I think running around and playing hopscotch and lying down make me grow up a bit. Well, I mean I get a bit more excited in the playground.
Author: You say it helps you to grow up?
Jon: No, that doesn't mean anything. I can't think of anything else what it's for.
Author: What about playing hopscotch, do you think it's a very grown-up thing to do?
Jon: No, of course not.
Author: I thought you said playing hopscotch makes you grow up?
Jon: It doesn't make you grow up right to the ceiling!
Author: What does it do?
Jon: It makes me grow up extremely slowly. (Sluckin, 1981, p. 1)

Other children answered similarly; they recognized the intrinsic merit of playtime, but they also indicated a connection between the skills they use on the playground and the skills that adults use in social settings. Sluckin also sees this link and points to the combination of regulated competition, voluntary participation, and negotiated rules as particularly relevant to the social and economic reality these children will encounter in adulthood.

When Sluckin asked teachers the purpose of playground activity, they responded by pointing out that children need opportunities to let off steam and relax. They also stressed the social skills children learn as they participate on the playground. When pressed for details, however, the teachers had very little idea what children actually do during playtime. A study such as Sluckin's permits these teachers and other adults to become aware of both the children's activities and the meaning of those activities in the context of the children's social culture.

Implications for teachers

Bauman (1972) defines ethnography as ". . . the process of constructing through direct personal observation of social behavior, a theory of the working of a particular culture in terms as close as possible to the way members of that culture view the universe and organize their behavior within it" (p. 157). The culture that interests ethnographers of children's play is the culture of childhood, and their goal is to develop a theory reflecting the children's point of view. Ethnographic techniques do not interrupt or intrude upon the children or their activities. Consequently, the freshness and authenticity of the children's natural behaviors are captured and shared in ethnographic reports. A good children's play ethnographer must be an astute observer and a careful listener, patient enough to spend considerable time gathering and reflecting on data, receptive enough to permit children's perceptions to take precedence over adult notions, and insightful enough to analyze and explain the results. In their focus on children, ethnographers have much in common with early childhood educators. Both groups take children seriously and recognize children's activities as significant and filled with meaning.

Ethnographers also focus on social contexts. The importance of context as a source of meaning is emphasized, and all behavior is analyzed in terms of the setting in which it naturally occurs. Ethnographers of play ordinarily study classroom and playground settings, and consequently, their findings are particularly relevant to teachers who design these settings.

Bolster (1983) recently stated that most educational research is useless to classroom teachers because researchers do not look at educational issues the way teachers do. In order to produce relevant studies, Bolster said, researchers must conceptualize teaching as a process and the classroom as a miniculture. He then recommended that researchers use ethnographic techniques to produce *thick, critical descriptions* of what naturally occurs in educational settings, and to develop analyses and explanations based on a thorough understanding of the descriptive data.

Findings of such studies are useful to teachers because the researcher has self-consciously adopted the teacher's perspective as one important element in understanding the setting. Further, sharing the children's perspectives is relevant to teachers who realize that the better a teacher understands the learners, the more likely that the curricular experiences planned for them will be educational. The goal of the research project, then, is similar to the goals of teachers who want to improve the quality of the experiences in their classes. In both cases, the undertaking begins with a search for understanding.

Though ethnography is a difficult and time-consuming mode of research, the field of education needs ethnographers. As Geertz (1973) has pointed out, it is not possible to understand people we do not know. Ethnographers are in a unique position to introduce us to the people we would like to understand.

References

Bauman, R. (1972). An ethnographic framework for the investigation of communicative behavior. In R. D. Abraham & C. Troike (Eds.), *Language and cultural diversity in American education*. Englewood Cliffs, NJ: Prentice-Hall.

Bolster, A. S., Jr., (1983). Toward a more effective model of research on teaching. *Harvard Educational Review, 53*, 294–308.

Borman, K. (1979). Children's interactions on the playgrounds. *Theory Into Practice, 18*, 251–257.

Corsaro, W. A., & Tomlinson, G. (1980). Spontaneous play and social learning in the nursery school. In H. B. Schwartzman (Ed.), *Play and culture*. West Point, NY: Leisure Press.

Erickson, F. (1984). What makes school ethnography "ethnographic"? *Anthropology and Education Quarterly, 15*, 51–66.

Farrer, C. R. (1977). Play and inter-ethnic communication. In D. F. Lancy & A. B. Tindall (Eds.), *The study of play: Problems and prospects*. West Point, NY: Leisure Press.

Geertz, C. (1973). Thick description: Toward an interpretive theory of culture. In C. Geertz (Ed.), *The interpretation of cultures*. New York: Basic.

Giffin, H. (1984). The coordination of meaning in the creation of a shared make-believe reality. In I. Bretherton (Ed.), *Symbolic play: The development of social understanding*. New York: Academic.

Goldstein, K. S. (1971). Strategy in counting out: An ethnographic folklore field study. In E. Avedon & B. Sutton-Smith (Eds.), *The study of games*. New York: Wiley.

Hughes, L. A. (1983). Beyond the rules of the game: Why are Rooie rules nice? In F. E. Manning (Ed.), *The world of play*. West Point, NY: Leisure Press.

King, N. R. (1979). Play: The kindergartners' perspective. *The Elementary School Journal, 80*, 81–87.

Schwartzman, H. B. (1978). *Transformations: The anthropology of children's play*. New York: Plenum.

Schwartzman, H. B. (1979). The sociocultural context of play. In B. Sutton-Smith (Ed.), *Play and learning*. New York: Gardner.

Sluckin, A. (1981). *Growing up in the playground*. Boston: Routledge & Kegan Paul.

Sutton-Smith, B. (1971). Boundaries. In R. E. Herron & B. Sutton-Smith (Eds.), *Child's Play*. New York: Wiley.

Steve Herzog

Whether at home or in a child care center, children have opportunities for play that include variations in floor freedom, available objects, and other children or adults as play partners.

Part 2:
The Symbols and Language
of Play

The ability to mentally represent objects and events is a prerequisite for the use of symbols and for the acquisition of language. Piaget's view that pretense signals a major achievement in the development of symbolic thought forms the basis of Lorraine McCune's (Chapter 4) discussion of this emerging behavior in infants and atypical children. According to this author, pretense reflects one aspect of children's representational knowledge of objects. Because pretend play depends on a child's cognitive maturity, developmentally delayed and normally developing children matched on mental, rather than chronological age, play at the same developmental level. Given an opportunity, developmentally delayed children will engage in pretense when they reach the appropriate level of cognitive maturity.

A major aspect of children's play development involves the ability to substitute one object for another — to treat a piece of wood as if it were a telephone, plate, or sandwich. Vonnie McLoyd (Chapter 5) discusses the development of preschool children's ability to represent imagined objects. The role of low- and high-realism toys is especially important in encouraging preschoolers' pretend play.

Pretend play reflects children's symbolic abilities, but it also provides a vehicle for these abilities to be practiced and extended. In Chapter 6, Anthony Pellegrini describes the sophisticated language children spontaneously use in sociodramatic play. The opportunity to engage in pretense enhances many of the language skills valued in school. The symbolic character of play, especially pretend play, provides a natural occasion for talking about thoughts and feelings.

43

Susan D. Shilcock

In play, the child is the leader and should be able to express meanings and feelings freely.

CHAPTER FOUR

Symbolic Development in Normal and Atypical Infants

LORRAINE McCUNE

Play is a reflection of and a contributor to every child's cognitive and emotional growth. This assertion, so long understood by those who interact closely with infants and young children, has been the subject of intensive investigation during the past 10 years. In 1976, Weisler and McCall noted that despite the increasing number of articles appearing yearly, there was little real increase in knowledge about the nature, function, and developmental course of play. They attributed this to a lack of comprehensive theory and precise definition of concepts, but encouraged continued study of the behavior in its observable form. They recommended increased attention to conceptual issues, which would hopefully lead to more comprehensive knowledge of play development. Findings and conceptualizations that have emerged since that time, particularly with respect to pretend play, indicate that this strategy has been followed with fruitful outcomes (Fein, 1981; McCune-Nicolich, 1981).

The rationale that has emerged for the study of play is, at one level, the simple fact that infants engage in such activities, and thus we need to know more about them. Are there steps or stages babies pass through as their capacity to play evolves? The related, more complex, question has been: If there are such steps, in what way do they relate to cognitive growth or other developing skills such as language?

As early as 1962, Piaget's thesis relating play development to cognitive development was widely available to American readers. However, only in the past 10 years has considerable progress been made in defining the developmental sequence of play skills, and the relationship of play to other variables, based at least partly on the impetus of Piagetian theory. Detailed reviews of this literature can be found in Fein (1981); McCune-Nicolich (1981); and Rubin, Fein, and Vandenburg (1983).

The primary focus of this chapter is on the development of pretending that begins as early as 12 months and is in full flower by age 3. However, certain steps prior to and parallel with pretending need to be mentioned to give full flavor to the range of infant play activities. This chapter also includes discussion of the relationship of pretending to cognitive development. Parents and educators who interact with children can have a significant impact on their play, so some issues and guidelines for enhancing children's play are noted. Recent studies of play in developmentally delayed babies are also included in this review.

Sensorimotor exploration and play

From the time an infant is able to take an object in hand, and bring it before the eyes or to the mouth (about 7 months), play, broadly defined, begins. Even earlier, babies' social interactions with parents and siblings show a playful character. Object and social play are integrated in some interactions, such as games of giving and taking objects that 1-year-olds enjoy initiating with adults. Throughout the first 2 years children pretend more frequently in the presence of their mothers than when alone, and often invite adults to join in pretend play. So, although we often think of play as the child's activity, social factors are important from the beginning, and continue to be influential as the infant develops play partnerships with parents and other caregivers, and as the toddler begins to enjoy the play potential of peers.

From Piaget's (1952, 1954, 1962) viewpoint, the activities termed play all require the interaction of at least two sensory and/or motor systems. Some of these activities are exploratory in nature, as the child attempts to learn more about the world. Others are more clearly done for fun such as gleefully banging a block repeatedly on a surface. For purposes of this discussion, an infant who interacts with objects using at least two sensory and/or motor systems is considered to be playing. Even prior to visual exploration, infants learn to bring objects to their mouths and actively explore them with their lips and tongue. Recent work by Rose, Gottfried, and Bridger (1978) has demonstrated that such mouthing is not merely an offshoot of teething or of the desire to suck. Rather, infants learn enough through such buccal exploration to discriminate between the object previously mouthed and an unfamiliar object when both are presented visually for the first time. Soon after the beginning of exploratory mouthing, babies begin to bring objects before their eyes and subject them to serious visual scanning. Ruff (1984) has also observed spontaneous alternation of mouthing with looking at an object, as the infant apparently attempts to coordinate the information from these two sensory systems.

Belsky and Most (1981) provided a concise review of literature concerning early infant behaviors with objects. They noted that varieties of simple manipulation follow the development of mouthing and visual examination. In general, infants' handling of objects proceeds from a less discriminant approach, where all objects are treated similarly, to more discrete processes of manipulation appropriate to the physical (and later the social) characteristics of the objects. Thus when children are most involved in mouthing, all objects, regardless of their nature, are brought to the mouth.

Later, when the baby has more skills available (banging, turning the object over for visual exploration), all objects are subjected to the available strategies. Infant mental tests such as the Bayley Scales of Infant Development (Bayley, 1969) reflect the gradual development of strategies suited to particular objects by assessing the baby's ability to deal discriminantly with, for example, a string by twisting and fingering, paper by crumpling and wrinkling, and noise-making objects by banging or shaking.

Tests such as the Bayley Scales are presented in a manner similar to intelligence tests for older children. The child is asked to respond to various items graded in difficulty. However, many items for the 8- to 24-month age range involve giving the baby a toy and either watching the behavior or encouraging some specific activity. In addition to the gradual development of object-appropriate strategies, the child also makes a transition from interacting, at first, with only a single object in a global fashion, to making both part-whole distinctions and relating one object to another. Early handling of single objects involves mouthing, turning for visual exploration, and banging. Later the child begins to examine the object more closely, and will often isolate an interesting part by pointing with the index finger (Ruff, 1984). This early pointing for self has sometimes been interpreted as an early indication that the child sees the object world as out there, separate from the self (Werner & Kaplan, 1963).

With respect to multiple object contacts, at first the child can only hold one object at a time. Later, two objects may be held, but only one attended to. Occasionally as the baby looks away from one object to the other, the first object is inadvertently released—its absence often unnoted. Some babies explore one object with great care, while another object rests, unnoticed, in the other hand. The first instances of relating objects to one another often appear accidental. The child may bring the two hands, each containing an object, to midline so they touch. Later increasingly complex relational activities have been observed. At a simple level, one object may be banged on another. Later infants place one object in or on another, and engage in such activities as filling and dumping a container of small toys, or repeatedly completing a puzzle or form board.

Throughout the course of these activities the infant is learning about defining attributes of objects: sensory properties, as well as manipulative possibilities. These sensorimotor activities contribute to the development of representational knowledge of objects which is later reflected in pretend play and other play activities, such as grouping like objects and fitting together pieces that match.

Development of pretend play

A 10- to 12-month-old infant, seated on the floor, surrounded by such common objects as a drinking cup, a comb, a spoon, and a doll bottle are likely to pick up each object in turn, and demonstrate by gesture, that its meaning is familiar. This behavior termed the *presymbolic scheme* or *enactive naming* (Nicolich, 1977; Piaget, 1962) is the harbinger of true pretend activities that follow during the next 12 months of development. Table 4.1 includes a summary of the five levels of pretend play that I have defined (McCune-Nicolich, 1981; Nicolich, 1977) based on Piaget's original description of the development of symbolic play.

Presymbolic scheme: Level 1

The infant's first socially meaningful actions with objects are termed presymbolic. Instead of the child's action representing a particular meaning, the action is apparently identical with that meaning. The child who touches a cup to the lips or a comb to the hair has an attitude of recognition ("Oh yes, I know what that is!"), rather than an attitude of pretend play. The child's manner is serious and the gestures are brief, not embellished with sound effects and exaggerated gestures as later true pretend acts will be.

Self-pretend: Level 2

When the child shows an awareness of the pretend nature of an activity by making drinking noises with a cup to the lips, grinning broadly when pretending to sleep, or looking meaningfully at the mother and seeking audience appreciation, a transition to symbolic activity has been made. Werner and Kaplan (1963) emphasized the gradual nature of symbolic development. The distinction between Level

	Levels and criteria	Examples
Sensorimotor Period	**Level 1 Presymbolic scheme:** The child shows understanding of object use or meaning by brief recognitory gestures. No pretending. Properties of present object are the stimulus. Child appears serious rather than playful.	The child picks up a comb, touches it to her or his hair, drops it. The child picks up the telephone receiver, puts it into ritual conversation position, sets it aside. The child gives the mop a swish on the floor.
	Level 2 Auto-symbolic scheme: The child pretends at self-related activities. Pretending. Symbolism is directly involved with the child's body. Child appears playful, seems aware of pretending.	The child simulates drinking from a toy baby bottle. The child eats from an empty spoon. The child closes her or his eyes, pretending to sleep.
Symbolic Stage 1	**Level 3 Single scheme symbolic games:** Child extends symbolism beyond her or his own actions by: **Level 3.1** Including other actors or receivers of action, such as a doll. **Level 3.2** Pretending at activities of other people or objects such as dogs, trucks, and trains.	Child feeds mother or doll. Child grooms mother or doll. Child pretends to read a book. Child pretends to mop floor. Child moves a block or toy car with appropriate sounds of vehicle.
	Level 4 Combinatorial symbolic games: **Level 4.1** Single Scheme Combinations: One pretend scheme is related to several actors or receivers of action.	Child combs own, then mother's hair. Child drinks from the bottle, feeds doll from bottle. Child puts an empty cup to mother's mouth, then experimenter, and self.
	Level 4.2 Multi-scheme combinations: Several schemes are related to one another in sequence.	Child holds phone to ear, dials. Child kisses doll, puts it to bed, puts spoon to its mouth. Child stirs in the pot, feeds doll, pours food into dish.
	Level 5 Planned symbolic games: Child indicates verbally or nonverbally that pretend acts are planned ahead. **Level 5.1** Planned single scheme symbolic acts—Transitional type: Activities from Levels 2 and 3 that are planned. Type A—Symbolic identification of one object with another. Type B—Symbolic identification of the child's body with some other person or object.	Child finds the iron, sets it down, searches for the cloth, tossing aside several objects. When cloth is found, she or he irons it. Child picks up play screwdriver, says "toothbrush" and makes the motions of toothbrushing.
	Level 5.2 Combinations with planned elements: These are constructed of activities from Levels 2 to 5.1, but always include some planned element. They tend toward realistic scenes.	Child picks up the bottle, says "baby," then feeds the doll and covers it with a cloth. Child puts play foods in a pot, stirs them. Then says "soup" or "Mommy" before feeding the mother. She or he waits, then says "more?" offering the spoon to the mother.

1 and Level 2 play, based mainly on how the child executes the activity, is an example of this. Another example is the primitive nature of the symbolic relationship at Level 2 — pretending to drink from an empty cup actually symbolizes a very similar real action, drinking liquid when the child is thirsty. This contrasts with drinking from a block or feeding a doll with a stick, both more advanced, and clearly symbolic because the symbol (stick or block) is differentiated from what is symbolized (cup or bottle).

Decentered pretend: Level 3

Piaget distinguished two forms of decentered pretend. The first involved application of the child's well-practiced pretend schemes to other animate-type toys and to people. Thus the doll or mother receives a drink, rather than the child. The second form of decentered pretend involves the child pretending at activities that are not normally part of her or his activities. For example, the child may pretend to scrub or mop the floor, or with appropriate intonation, pretend to read a book.

Considerable literature suggests that prior to this development, pretending is centered around the child's own body and daily activities (Belsky & Most, 1981; Fenson & Ramsay, 1980; McCune-Nicolich, 1981). Later pretending involves behaviors learned from observing others, or directing pretend actions to dolls or other people. Theories of symbolic development (Piaget, 1962; Werner & Kaplan, 1963) indicate that this developmental sequence is characteristic of symbolization in general, and not just characteristic of pretend play. At first the infant is cognitively egocentric, and only capable of consolidating representational knowledge confined to her or his own body. This focus is a global rather than differentiated understanding of the world. It is not clear whether the child who pretends to drink clearly understands the flexibility of the drinking act, as it might be applied to other objects or engaged in by others. Progress in such differentiation, and hence decentration, is needed before the child can, at a symbolic level, extend pretending beyond the self.

Pretend play combinations: Level 4

Related to the concept of decentration is that of integration. In symbolic development, when the child's symbolic acts become cognitively separate from the behaviors they represent, play acts can be combined. A hypothesis that has been proposed and has received some support states that the ability to combine symbolic acts in play may be based on the same underlying cognitive skill that allows combinations in language (McCune-Nicolich, 1981; McCune, in press). Several forms of combination have been observed in play. Nicolich (1977) distinguished between single-scheme sequences, where only a single action is played out with others who participate in or receive action, and multi-scheme combinations where two different actions are connected (such as combing a doll's hair and then covering the doll with a blanket). Fenson and Ramsay (1980) made the further distinction between sequences that were ordered (such as pouring from a pot to a cup and then drinking) and those that were not. In general, single-scheme sequences develop earlier than multi-scheme combinations.

Planned pretend: Level 5

All of the pretend behaviors described so far involve actions that seem to rely on the particular situation, and the particular objects at the infant's disposal. As symbolic activities, none of these pretend behaviors are very far removed from the realistic activities they represent. For some theorists (Huttenlocher & Higgins, 1978; Ungerer & Sigman, 1981; and others), these are not symbolic activities. Rather, the term *symbolic play* is reserved for activities where the symbolic element is clearly different from what it represents. The most commonly cited example is pretending with a substitute, rather than with a realistic object. Fein (1975), for example, reported that children were much more likely to feed a toy horse from a cup, than to feed it if a stick were the only prop available.

Piaget also emphasized the special nature of activities where it was clear that the child had formed a mental symbolic image before performing an action with the object. His clearest example of this was announced substitution of one object for another. However, this process of substituting one object for another is also identified with other activities. In my work I have called this *planning* and tried to be alert for various forms of evidence that a pretend game was planned prior to action. The criteria we used were announcement, search for needed materials, and preparatory activity such as removing the doll's hat prior to combing its hair. In addition, when a child pretended that a doll performed an active role in pretend play, it seemed that the prior symbolic designation doll = agent could function as a plan. The doll was considered active when the child moved its legs and walked it to bed, placed a cup in its hand rather than to its lips, and otherwise emphasized the doll's role as an agent.

Contexts for symbolic play research

When play is broadly defined to include all of a baby's freely chosen encounters with objects, a large proportion of the child's waking time is playtime. Whether at home or in a child care center, children have opportunities for play that include variations in floor freedom, available objects, and other children or adults as play partners. Most research concerning the free play of children under 2-years-old has been conducted in the home (Belsky & Most, 1981; Nicolich, 1977) or in a home-like laboratory environment (Fenson & Ramsay, 1980; Ungerer & Sigman, 1981). Typically, the experimenter provides the child with a set of toys appropriate to the investigation and leaves the child to play, in the presence of the mother, who may or may not be allowed to interact actively with her child in any given study. Often the play interaction is videotaped for later coding. Some studies (Field, De Stefano, & Koewler, 1982) have used a checklist procedure and studied children during free play in a child care environment.

Modeling

Often, when investigators have been interested in how a particular play skill develops, they have demonstrated the relevant behaviors to the child and noted after the demonstration what types of play occur with what objects and at what ages, rather than completely relying on free play (Watson & Fischer, 1977). When free play and modeling techniques have been used in the same study (Fenson & Ramsay, 1981), children have shown slightly more advanced behavior following modeling, but they have not skipped any of the steps children develop when playing naturally. For example, a child who showed only self-pretend play spontaneously might show decentered pretend play after it was modeled, but would not show sequenced pretend without also showing the prior step, decentered pretend. These results suggest that modeling can be a very powerful technique for studying play capability. While some might argue that activities following modeling are more correctly considered imitation than play, the skills needed for play can be isolated and studied in this fashion.

Maternal participation in play

A baby's play can be greatly influenced by the social aspects of her or his environment. Dunn and Wooding (1977) observed that when children engaged in pretend play at home, they were likely to bring the toys to their mothers and demonstrate the activities for her. Nonpretend activities did not seem to lead to this behavior. Sorce and Emde (1981) noted that the mothers' emotional availability, not merely their presence, significantly enhanced babies' play activities. Thus when mother read a magazine, baby was likely to fuss, ask for attention, and stay near her. When mother watched and responded verbally, babies vocalized more and spent more time engaged with toys.

I have designed a mother-child play procedure where mother and child are seated on the floor with a standard set of toys placed near them. Mothers, although instructed to let the baby take the lead in play, observe, interact, or attempt to direct the child's activities in a variety of ways. Our reason for suggesting mothers be responsive rather than leading is to counteract their tendency to make the baby perform all of the skills they think we would be interested in seeing. In addition we hope to have a sufficient sample of child activities to assess the child's particular capability without maternal suggestion or modeling. In this situation children show slightly greater levels of play capability following mothers' demonstrations and suggestions than they do independently (McCune, in press). In addition, our subjects, compared to subjects of our colleagues who more strongly inhibit the maternal role, are willing to play longer, usually 30 minutes as opposed to 10 or 15 minutes. From a research point of view such maternal participation muddies the water, but for adults who wish to encourage the play of children in their care, the message is clear. Sit down beside the child on the floor, and try to observe and support the child's activities as much as possible, reacting when asked, playing when invited, and giving an occasional gentle suggestion or demonstration.

As more children spend time in child care, where children as young as 9- to 12-months-old have a peer group, it becomes important to consider the effects of social interactions on these infants' play. It is rare for two children to engage in sustained joint pretend play before 31 months of age. By the age of 36 months, such play, at a simple level, is common. However, Brenner and Mueller (1982) have demonstrated that children as young as 12-months-old engage in interactive social games, where they share meanings to the extent that they can alternate observer and actor roles, sustain a number of mutually imitative play rounds, and are competent play partners at a social and sensorimotor level. Young children that play with older peers can also participate, somewhat passively, in pretend roles beyond their expected capacity.

Play objects

The toys used in play research are also appropriate for playing with babies for fun and learning. Table 4.2 lists the toys I use. These are presented to the child in a large dishpan with intriguing parts of toys

Table 4.2   Toy list

Blanket	Covered matchbox with sliding
Blocks	compartment
Baby's thing book	Small mirror
Pat the bunny book	Toy mop
Small brush	7-inch stuffed monkey
Large comb	Cloth napkin
Small comb	Bottle cover
Toy cup	White plastic necklace
Toy saucer	Round nesting cups
Baby doll	Table tennis ball
Baby doll's clothes: diaper, jacket,	Popbeads snapped in necklace
and bonnet and wrapped in	Toy purse
blanket	Puzzle with five pieces: chicken,
9-inch dressed doll, girl or boy doll	pig, mule, cow, duck
9-inch doll's clothes: blue pants, red	Scrub brush
jacket with hood, red shoes	Women's slippers
Doll bottle with soft nipple	Sponge
Brown stuffed dog	Child's sunglasses with lenses
Drum with bell inside	removed
Small jack-in-the-box	Toy teapot
Clear plastic dumping bottle	Toy teapot cover
Dumping bottle pieces: apple,	Teaspoon
grapes, banana, lemon, doll bottle,	Toy telephone
two fish, butter, milk, orange	Toy toolbox
juice, red bottle, corn	Toy tools: hammer, screwdriver,
Finger puppets	wrench, saw, pliers
Toy iron	12-inch truck
Toy jeep	2-inch man
Mailtruck	

emerging from the top. This elicits an initial period of exploration, where the child takes toys out, one at a time, often presenting them to the mother, briefly manipulating the toy, or showing knowledge of its function by enactive naming (Level 1). After this exploratory period, the children usually settle down and begin either more detailed explorations or extensive pretending, depending on their level of development.

This toy list was designed to include opportunities for sensorimotor, symbolic, and relational or logical play. Toys that are useful in symbolic play later, are useful in manipulative play earlier. Thus a child will manipulate the truck wheels and throw the ball at a young age. At an older age dolls are given rides, and the ping-pong ball becomes an egg cooked for breakfast. Similarly the tool chest is, at first, something to open and close, later it is the focus of repair games and grooming games (saw = comb, pliers = tweezers). This toy list includes a few ambiguous objects, such as oddly shaped blocks, that might elicit frequent object substitution. Addition of some of these, especially with older children, is a good plan.

Although the focus here is on pretend play, logical or relational play is preferred by some children (Shotwell, Wolf, & Gardner, 1980). These children, called *patterners,* prefer to complete puzzles, arrange toys in patterns, and nest series of cups rather than engage in the pretend play of the *dramatists.* Both types of play are used by all children to some extent, and it is unclear how stable or how distinctive these two play styles are. Balanced observation of a child's play should take in both sets of skills, although this has been rarely done in the literature. When offering a choice of toys to children, toys for both types of play should be included.

Play and cognitive development

Play has been considered facilitative of cognitive development, and a number of studies have found positive relationships between play experience and such variables as problem solving, perspective-taking, and the development of conservation skills, although findings have not been entirely consistent (e.g., Pepler & Ross, 1981). Recent reviews of these topics include Brainerd (1982); Cheyne (1982); Pepler (1982); Rubin, Fein, and Vandenburg (1983); and Saltz and Brodie (1982).

Play has also been considered to reflect increases in cognitive development (Piaget, 1962) as well as contributing to specific skills and cognitive growth in general. Most often with normally developing populations, this relationship has been inferred from age changes in the frequency and maturity of children's play. A few studies have addressed this question directly by assessing play in relation to mental age in handicapped children and in relation to intelligence test scores in normal children. Wing, Gould, Yeates, and Brierly (1977) found that a minimum mental age of 20 months was required for developmentally delayed children to show symbolic play. Jeffree and McConkey (1976) compared groups of 10 normally developing and 9 developmentally delayed children for developmental age. They found no difference in maturity of play between the two groups, although the normally developing children were chronologically younger than the developmentally delayed children. Play was significantly correlated with developmental level in both groups. Hill and McCune-Nicolich (1981) reported a higher correlation of play level (described in this chapter) with mental age than with chronological age in their sample of 30 Down Syndrome children with mental ages between 12 and 26 months.

A number of studies have reported that developmentally delayed children play at a level of maturity appropriate to their mental rather than chronological ages. Hill and McCune-Nicolich (1981) found that play levels previously observed in normal samples also occurred at mental-age appropriate levels in the Down Syndrome children.

Carroll (1983) compared a sample of 10 autistic boys ranging from 2.8- to 6-years-old with a group of subjects matched for mental age (chronological ages ranged from 12 to 30 months) and with a group matched for chronological age. Across a number of play tasks the general pattern of results was that the autistic subjects did not differ from the normal children who formed the mental-age matched group, but did differ from children of their own chronological age. Some exceptions were noted: The autistic children engaged in less self-pretend than both the mental-age and chronological-age matched samples. These two nonautistic groups did not differ in frequency of self-pretend.

Ungerer and Sigman (1981) reported that 4 of their 16 autistic children produced symbolic play spontaneously, and an additional 3 responded to modeling. Their play was less frequent than normally developed children's play, particularly in the more mature forms.

Prior to these studies there was some controversy in the literature concerning whether or not autistic children were capable of pretend play (De Myer, 1979; Rutter, 1970). It is clear from recent research that autistic children do pretend in a manner consistent with their mental age. A comparison of methodology in the Carroll versus Ungerer and Sigman studies suggests that the active presence of the mother in a relatively freely structured play session led to increased and higher level performance in the Carroll study. Mothers in this study sat on the floor with their children and were encouraged to respond to their children's overtures as they normally would, but to let the child take the lead in play activities. These mothers were quite active in the sessions, particularly in their attempts to help focus their children on play. In Carroll's structured play task, where a fairly long play sequence was modeled for the child followed by free play with the same toys, modeling by the experimenter led to increased frequency of a number of different play categories. However, free play with the mother was more useful because children participated more fully in play and showed a broader range of play activities.

In summary, results from play studies conducted in several categories of developmentally delayed and normal children support the relationship of play to cognitive development. Findings that involve modeling suggest children may improve their play capability through this form of intervention. Handicapped children *do* play spontaneously, at a cognitively appropriate level. A number of correlational studies involving normally developing preschool and kindergarten children also support a relationship between play maturity and measured intelligence (Bese-vegis, 1983; Clune, Paolella, & Foley, 1970; Johnson, Ershler, & Lawton, 1982; Tizard, Phillips, & Plewis, 1976).

Implications for educators

As kindergartens succumb more and more to formal teaching ap-proaches, and the preschool curriculum becomes increasingly task-oriented, we should consider the special qualities of free play that make it a highly suitable learning mode for children. By definition, play activities are freely chosen; hence they follow the child's interests and are likely to be chosen in a manner appropriate to the child's develop-mental level. A child engaged in pretending often shows long spans of concentrated activity, belying the notion of short attention span in children.

How can teachers of young children help to preserve and enhance children's play? Time is of the essence. Children need freedom from structured curricular activities to develop comfortable modes of play in the classroom. Objects are also critical, especially for young children. For infants and young children, supportive participation by adults particularly facilitates pretend play.

Johnson, Dowling, and Wesner (1980) described a technique that provides a framework for play participation with children between the ages of 1 and 3. This technique, Infant and Toddler Centered Activity, is based on a few strategies that separate the play mode from the care-taking mode of interacting with a young child. In play, the child is the leader and should be able to express meanings and feelings freely. Play sessions conducted with one or occasionally two children on a weekly basis can help the caregiver learn more about the children and enhance the human relationship between child and teacher.

Johnson et al. suggest defining an area that is relatively childproof. This could be a small room in a child care center, or it could be a floor space defined by a large square of carpeting. The play session should last from 15 to 30 minutes, depending on the schedule and the child's continued interest in participating. During the session there should be no need to prohibit the child from any activity—hence the childproof-ing suggestion. The adult should assemble a few toys to form a focus for the session. For encouraging pretend, the toys listed in Table 4.2 are ideal. Because the child takes the lead, it is best not to have specific expectations for the child's performance. The adult sits on the floor near the child, watching and waiting for an invitation to join in play.

Children Naturally

During early pretense, when the fields of meaning and vision have only begun to diverge, very young children may need the material support provided by high-realism toys to bolster their newly emerging representational skills.

The adult tries to become aware of the child's goals and to facilitate these intentions without taking over, remaining in the role of supportive partner. The adult stays aware that the play session is a special situation, not typical of routine teacher-child interactions, so if the adult finds it necessary to resume a directive role, the session ends. As play proceeds, the adult can tentatively extend play activities initiated by the child. Children are as fascinated by watching an adult demonstrate pretend play as they are with listening to stories.

By virtue of the relationship of play to cognition, cross-fertilization is bound to occur. The child who plays well and enjoyably is likely to learn from play; learnings derived from play are likely to influence intellectual growth.

References

Bayley, N. (1969). *The Bayley Scales of Infant Development*. New York: Psychological Corporation.

Belsky, J., & Most, R. (1981). From exploration to play: A cross-sectional study of infant free play behavior. *Developmental Psychology, 17*, 630–639.

Besevegis, E. (1983). *The development of dramatic and constructive play in preschool children*. Unpublished doctoral dissertation, Rutgers University, New Brunswick, NJ.

Brainerd, C. J. (1982). Effects of group and individualized dramatic play training on cognitive development. In D. J. Pepler & K. H. Rubin (Eds.), *The play of children: Current theory and research*. Basel, Switzerland: Karger.

Brenner, J., & Mueller, N. (1982). Shared meanings in boy toddlers' peer relations. *Child Development, 53*, 380–391.

Carroll, S. (1983). *Modes of symbolic functioning in autistic boys*. Unpublished doctoral dissertation, Rutgers University, New Brunswick, NJ.

Cheyne, J. A. (1982). Object play and problem-solving: Methodological problems and conceptual promise. In D. J. Pepler & K. H. Rubin (Eds.), *The play of children: Current theory and research*. Basel, Switzerland: Karger.

Clune, C., Paolella, J., & Foley, J. (1979). Free play behavior in atypical children: An approach to assessment. *Journal of Autism and Developmental Disorders, 9*, 61–72.

De Myer, M. (1979). *Parents and children in autism*. New York: Halsted Press.

Dunn, J., & Wooding, C. (1977). Play in the home and its implications for learning. In B. Tizard & D. Harvey (Eds.), *Biology of play*. Philadelphia: Lippincott.

Fein, G. (1975). A transformational analysis of pretending. *Developmental Psychology, 11*, 291–296.

Fein, G. (1981). Pretend play in childhood: An integrative review. *Child Development, 52*, 1095–1118.

Fenson, L., & Ramsay, D. (1980). Decentration and integration of play in the second year of life. *Child Development, 51*, 171–178.

Fenson, L., & Ramsay, D. (1981). Effects of modeling action sequences on the play of twelve-, fifteen-, and nineteen-month-old children. *Child Development, 52*, 1028–1036.

Field, T., De Stefano, L., & Koewler, J. (1982). Fantasy play of toddlers and preschoolers. *Developmental Psychology, 18,* 503–508.

Hill, P., & McCune-Nicolich, L. (1981). Pretend play and patterns of cognition in Down's Syndrome children. *Child Development, 52,* 611–617.

Huttenlocher, J., & Higgins, E. T. (1978). Issues in the study of symbolic development. In W. A. Collins (Ed.), *Minnesota symposium on child psychology.* Hillsdale, NJ: Erlbaum.

Jeffree, D., & McConkey, R. (1976). An observation scheme for recording children's imaginative doll play. *Journal of Child Psychology and Psychiatry, 17,* 189–197.

Johnson, F. K., Dowling, J., & Wesner, D. (1980). Note on infant psychotherapy. *Infant Mental Health Journal, 1,* 19–33.

Johnson, J. E., Ershler, J., & Lawton, J. (1982). Intellective correlates of preschoolers' spontaneous play. *Journal of General Psychology, 106,* 115–122.

McCune, L. (in press). Symbolic play: Developmental sequences in the first three years.

McCune-Nicolich, L. (1981). Toward symbolic functioning: Structure of early pretend games and potential parallels with language. *Child Development, 52,* 785–797.

Nicolich, L. McCune (1977). Beyond sensorimotor intelligence: Measurement of symbolic maturity through analysis of pretend play. *Merrill-Palmer Quarterly, 23,* 89–99.

Pepler, D. J. (1982). Play and divergent thinking. In D. J. Pepler & K. H. Rubin (Eds.), *The play of children: Current theory and research.* Basel, Switzerland: Karger.

Pepler, D., & Ross, H. (1981). The effects of play on divergent and convergent problem-solving. *Child Development, 52,* 1202–1210.

Piaget, J. (1952). *Origins of intelligence.* New York: International Universities Press.

Piaget, J. (1954). *The construction of reality.* New York: Basic.

Piaget, J. (1962). *Play, dreams and imitation.* New York: Norton.

Rose, S., Gottfried, A., & Bridger, W. (1978). Cross-modal transfer and information processing by the sense of touch in infancy. *Developmental Psychology, 17,* 90–98.

Rubin, K., Fein, G., & Vandenburg, B. (1983). Play. In E. M. Hetherington (Ed.), *Handbook of child psychology: Social development.* New York: Wiley.

Ruff, H. (1984). Infants' manipulative explorations of objects: Effects of age and object characteristics. *Developmental Psychology, 20,* 9–20.

Rutter, M. (1970). Autistic children: Infancy to adulthood. *Seminars in Psychiatry, 2,* 435–449.

Saltz, E., & Brodie, J. (1982). Pretend play training in childhood: A review and critique. In D. J. Pepler & K. H. Rubin (Eds.), *The play of children: Current theory and research.* Basel, Switzerland: Karger.

Shotwell, J., Wolf, D., & Gardner, H. (1980). Styles of achievement in early symbol use. In M. Foster & S. Brandes (Eds.), *Symbol as sense: New approaches to the analysis of meaning.* New York: Academic.

Sorce, J., & Emde, R. N. (1981). Mother's presence is not enough: Effect of emotional availability on infant exploration. *Developmental Psychology, 17,* 737–745.

Tizard, B., Phillips, J., & Plewis, I. (1976). Play in preschool centres: Play measures and their relation to age, sex & I.Q. *Journal of Child Psychology and Psychiatry, 17,* 251–265.

Ungerer, J., & Sigman, M. (1981). Symbolic play and language comprehension in autistic children. *Journal of the American Academy of Psychiatry, 52,* 318–337.

Watson, M. W., & Fischer, K. W. (1977). A developmental sequence of agent use in late infancy. *Child Development, 48,* 828–836.

Weisler, A., & McCall, R. (1976). Exploration and play: Resume and redirection. *American Psychologist, 31,* 492–508.

Werner, H., & Kaplan, B. (1963). *Symbol formation.* New York: Wiley.

Wing, L., Gould, J., Yeates, S. R., & Brierly, L. M. (1977). Symbolic play in severely mentally retarded and in autistic children. *Journal of Child Psychology and Psychiatry, 18,* 167–178.

Betty Ford

Teachers should provide high-realism toys to preschoolers, especially those younger than 4-years-old, to support and sustain pretend play. As children grow older, they increasingly are able to enact pretend sequences without high-realism toys.

CHAPTER FIVE

Scaffolds or Shackles? The Role of Toys in Preschool Children's Pretend Play

VONNIE C. McLOYD

Toys, whether they are highly realistic or unstructured, manufactured or natural, figure prominently in the lives of preschool children. It has been estimated that in home settings, preschool children spend about 25% of their waking time or about 4 hours a day playing with manufactured toys, household objects, such as kitchen utensils, and natural materials such as rocks and sticks (Giddings & Halverson, 1981). Children play with manufactured toys almost 3 times as frequently as they play with materials not intended for play (Giddings & Halverson, 1981). Most of these manufactured toys are highly realistic and appear to serve conventional functions.

Observations of the ways children use toys during pretend play and the changes that occur in pretend play when different toys are present have opened a window on the development of children's representational thought. The role of pretend play in the cognitive and social development of children has been of major theoretical interest to prominent scholars for decades (El'Konin, 1966; Piaget, 1962; Vygotsky, 1967), but systematic and thoughtful attempts to verify and extend these theoretical analyses have been made only recently.

In this chapter, I will review empirical work on the nature of object pretense in children who vary in age and social class. Also reviewed is a complementary set of studies that examines ways in which the degree of toy realism and the presence of props affect children's pretend play. Toys vary along several dimensions, but it is the dimension of toy realism that has attracted most attention among researchers who study pretend play. Finally, I will consider the educational implications of this research.

The development of object pretense

Vygotsky (1934/1967) and El'Konin (1966) provided particularly focused and detailed analyses of the development of object pretense during the preschool years. Vygotsky contended that prior to the emergence of pretend play, the child's understanding of meaning is primarily visually mediated (the perception of an object predominates over its meaning and, thus, determines the child's actions). This fusion between meaning and what is seen renders the child unable to act independently of what she or he sees.

In Vygotsky's view, the emergence of pretend play profoundly alters this relationship. The fields of meaning and vision gradually diverge and the child begins to operate with meanings other than those usually attached to an object or action. Complete separation of thought from objects is preceded by a transition period during which the child uses a concrete object or pivot (e.g., stick) as a substitute for the imagined object (e.g., horse). According to Vygotsky, when a stick is used as a pivot (e.g., a horse), the meaning of the word *horse* is severed from a real horse and meaning predominates over the object. In a similar way, prior to complete detachment of the meaning of an action from the real action, the young child requires a pivot in the form of a substitute action (e.g., stamping the feet to represent riding a horse).

El'Konin (1966) extended Vygotsky's analysis by focusing on the role of socialization in pretend play and charting developmental changes in the nature of pivot objects. He believed that pretense originates during the course of joint adult-child activity when adults model and instruct children about the use of high-realism toys. The actions (such as feeding animals) demonstrated to children with different toys are later reproduced with similar toys. As El'Konin observed, children feed not only those specific toy animals they fed together with adults, they also feed other toy animals. Later, the child spontaneously transfers actions to categories of objects not part of the adult-modeled behavior.

In early acts of transfer, the child demands that the substitute object physically resemble the imagined object. Gradually, this demand is lifted and the child represents objects with substitutes that bear little similarity to the imagined objects and without any concrete object or pivot. Similarly, the motoric behavior associated with imagined objects is gradually curtailed and transformed into a scheme that gives only the general sense of the activity by denoting its results or its general method of enactment.

In his analysis of the development of pretend play, Piaget (1962) also noted the gradual separation of thought from objects that occurs during the preschool years. Unlike El'Konin (1966), however, he contended that pretense originates during the sixth sensorimotor stage when, for the sake of pleasure, the child applies familiar action sequences to objects other than those to which they are usually applied. This ludic assimilation marks the gradual separation of the signifier (the substitute object and the make-believe actions applied to it) from the signified (the schema as it would develop if completed seriously with the object to which it is usually applied). Initially the substitution of one object for another is inseparable from the set of actions that gave rise to the substitution. Later, the act of substitution occurs spontaneously and itself gives rise to pretend action. With development, the child becomes capable of constructing entire pretend scenes instead of merely assimilating one object to another. Symbolic acts eventually become completely independent of actions and material support and occur internally in representational thought.

The relationship between age and object pretense

Recent intense study of children's use of objects in pretend situations has resulted in strong empirical support for certain elements of the analyses provided by Vygotsky, El'Konin, and Piaget, and insight into issues not previously examined. Several studies concur with these theorists in documenting an increase with age in the ability of preschool children to represent imagined objects with physically dissimilar objects and without concrete signifiers altogether (Elder & Pederson, 1978; Jackowitz & Watson, 1980; Johnson & Ershler, 1981). In an often cited and well-designed study of this issue, Elder and Pederson (1978) asked 2½-, 3-, and 3½-year-olds to pretend to perform actions (e.g., combing the hair) conventionally associated with specific objects (e.g., comb) first using *no object,* then using a *substitute object* whose physical dimensions were *similar* to those of the referent (imagined) object and had no defined function (e.g., rectangular piece of wood), and then using a *substitute object* that was physically *dissimilar* to the referent object and had a conventional use of its own (e.g., rubber ball). Among the 2½-year-olds, performance was significantly better in the similar condition than in the no object condition, which was significantly better than performance in the dissimilar condition. However, 3½-year-olds performed the pretend actions equally well in all of the conditions and significantly better than the 2½-year-olds, except in the similar condition. Thus, sometime during the third year of life, children's mental representations of common personal and household objects are established well enough that they can represent these objects without pivots and with high-realism objects whose physical appearance and function conflict with those of the referent objects.

Pretense that calls for two concurrent substitutions with low-realism toys may exceed the limits of the budding representational skills of very young children. Fein (1975) asked 2-year-olds to make either a high-realism toy horse (a detailed plush toy horse) or a low-realism toy horse (a metal horse shape) drink from either a high-realism toy cup (a plastic egg cup) or a low-realism toy cup (a clam shell). When one of the toys was low in realism and the other was high in realism, more than one half of the children enacted the pretend sequence. However, when both of the objects were low in realism, only about one third of the children were able to do so.

These findings suggest, in line with Piaget (1962), Vygotsky (1967), and El'Konin (1966), that very young children are restricted in their ability to enact pretend sequences that are even modestly complex, without the presence of anchor supports from objects in their perceptual field. Also in keeping with these observations are reported increases with age in the tendency to play with natural, low-realism objects (e.g., rocks, sticks) (Giddings & Halverson, 1981) and to symbolically represent objects and events without spontaneously performing actions appropriate to the imagined object or situation (Lowe, 1975; Ungerer, Zelazo, Kearsley, & O'Leary, 1981).

While not inconsistent with the fundamental principles of Piaget (1962), El'Konin (1966), and Vygotsky (1967), other developmental changes in object pretense not examined by these scholars have been identified. Ungerer et al. (1981), for example, found that substitution with objects whose functions are unambiguous (high-realism objects such as cups) and in conflict with those of the referent object, occurs relatively frequently only during later development. This type of substitution is preceded by substitution with objects whose functions are ambiguous (low-realism objects such as blocks). Bretherton, O'Connell, Shore, and Bates (1984) found differences in this direction in their short-term longitudinal study of 20- and 28-month-olds, though the differences were small and statistically insignificant.

Substitution with high-realism objects also appears to be preceded developmentally by representation without the use of concrete objects (Elder & Pederson, 1978). Satisfying the requirements inherent in high-realism substitution (namely, ignoring or overriding salient, conflicting perceptual and functional cues, Ungerer et al., 1981) appears to require representational skills beyond those needed in representation without pivot objects.

The perceptual cues of objects appear to have no more influence than functional cues on children's ability to use them as substitutes. Jackowitz and Watson (1980) found that when substitute objects differed from referent objects (e.g., toy telephone) in function but not form (e.g., toy banana), they elicited as much referent-appropriate pretense in 1- to 2-year-olds as those that differed in form but not function (e.g., walkie-talkie). This finding must be regarded as provisional because, as Jacko-witz and Watson acknowledged, they were not altogether successful in separating the form dimension from the function dimension in the objects used in their study, and as a result an extreme dissimilarity in one often resulted in a dissimilarity in the other.

However, certain functional and perceptual cues from high-realism objects may combine to evoke conventional object-related actions more readily than others, making it extremely difficult for an object to be used as a substitute. Pederson, Rook-Green, and Elder (1981) reported that children younger than 3-years-old experienced considerable diffi-culty using high-realism objects that were associated with a distinctive action sequence as substitutes (e.g., a ball is associated with a bouncing action; a toy car with a rolling action), compared to high-realism objects that are less restricted to particular actions (e.g., toy watch, dustpan). They suggested that this difficulty arises because the former objects elicit actions that are incompatible with the desired pretend actions. This study provides particularly compelling support for Vygotsky's (1967) and El'Konin's (1966) claim that objects determine meanings and actions in the young child.

Studies of object representation in school-age children are virtually nonexistent. We do know from self-reported data, however, that during the primary school years the use of props to assume the identity of a person and the belief that toys are necessary for play decline with age. Conversely, the use of action and imagination to assume the identity of a person and to define a toy by its use rather than by the object increases with age (Chaillé, 1978).

In summary, numerous changes occur in object pretense during the preschool years that indicate a progressive separation between thought and object. Preschool children show an increased ability with age to represent imagined objects with physically dissimilar objects, without concrete signifiers, and without spontaneously performing actions ap-propriate to the imagined object. Evidence strongly suggests that chil-dren initially make substitutions with objects that are ambiguous in function and only later are able to make substitutions with objects that are highly realistic and have functional and perceptual cues that con-flict with those of the imagined object. These developmental trends hold for both boys and girls.

Relationship between social class and object pretense

Though there are few relevant studies, the onset and very early development of pretense appear to be similar in children from different socioeconomic backgrounds. Neither White (1978) nor Kagan, Kearsley, and Zelazo (1978) found that pretense was related to social class during the first 2 years of life. However, in her extensive but qualitative study of 3- to 6-year-olds, Smilansky (1968) reported that middle-class Israeli children of European descent, compared to lower-class children of Asian-African descent, engaged in more sociodramatic play, enacted a greater variety of roles and richer episodes, made more pretend verbalizations, and, particularly relevant to our discussion, showed a stronger preference for low-realism toys and a lesser preference for high-realism toys.

Subsequent work on this issue has yielded conflicting findings. In keeping with Smilansky's claim for advanced representational skills in middle-class children, there is evidence that middle-class preschoolers are more likely than working-class and lower-class children to perform substitutions and represent imaginary objects without a substitute object during pretend play and less likely to use objects in conventional ways (Griffing, 1980; Smith & Dodsworth, 1978). However, other researchers have found social class to be unrelated to these measures (Fein & Stork, 1981; Stern, Bragdon, & Gordon, 1976). McLoyd (1982) has provided an extensive and critical review of research on social class differences in pretend play.

The effects of toy realism and environmental supports on pretend play

High- versus low-realism toys

Smilansky (1968) contended that children find high-realism toys extremely satisfying emotionally because they help the child to portray more exact, detailed action or role pretense, and contribute to the sense that they are really performing the action or behaving like the adults being portrayed. Notwithstanding the positive affect that they produce, high-realism toys are limiting, argued Smilansky, because the child can only use them in conventional ways. Other writers concur with Smilansky in suggesting that the detail and realness of a replica toy can hinder free creative play (Caplan & Caplan, 1973; Singer, 1966; Sotamaa, 1980). On the one hand, repetitive enactment of themes congruent with high-realism toys (e.g., enactment of a healer-patient theme using a medical kit) may lead to boredom. On the other hand, the difficulty and low probability (McLoyd, 1983; McGhee, Ethridge, & Benz, 1981) of violating distinct perceptual and function cues (e.g., using a medical kit as a substitute for a truck) or contravening the laws of usage in the adult world (Smilansky, 1968) may subvert interest in pretend themes incongruent with high-realism toys.

Low-realism toys, it is argued, are more conducive to creative and rich fantasy (Caplan & Caplan, 1973; Singer, 1966; Sotamaa, 1980). Because they are free of embellishments that dictate a rigid purpose, they are thought to be easier to incorporate into preconceived play plans and easier to hold the child's interest for longer periods of time as new ideas are tried out. A major problem with this line of reasoning is that it lacks a developmental perspective that takes into account different levels of representational skill in preschool children. During early pretense, when the fields of meaning and vision have only begun to diverge, very young children may need the material support provided by high-realism toys to bolster their newly emerging representational skills. Moreover, if El'Konin (1966) is correct, high-realism toys are more familiar to very young children because they are more likely to be used by adults when modeling pretend play. That is, joint adult-child pretend activities most often center around everyday objects that have strict functions (e.g., eating utensils) or "playthings similar to those" (El'Konin, 1966, p. 37). In early independent pretend activity, the child performs action primarily with objects used previously by adult models.

As their representational skills become more advanced and proficiency increases in the use of language as a vehicle for the communication of symbolic meaning, children's dependency on high realism objects for the communication of symbolic meaning is minimized (El'Konin, 1966). This leads to the prediction that pretend play in older preschoolers may be as frequent in the presence of low-realism toys as in the presence of high-realism toys. Alternatively, on the basis of the claims that low-realism toys are easier to incorporate into preconceived play plans and do not inhibit free creative play (Caplan & Caplan, 1973; Singer, 1966; Sotamaa, 1980), we might even predict that among older preschoolers low-realism toys will elicit more and richer pretend play than high-realism toys.

A number of studies have examined the effects of toy realism on general solitary and social pretend play but, taken as a whole, they do not clearly support any of these hypotheses. In these studies, children are observed during at least two play sessions, one in which high-realism toys are available, and one in which low-realism toys are present. In studies with very young children (3½ and younger), the experimenter models pretend sequences with the toys (Jeffree & McConkey, 1976) or makes play suggestions without demonstrating the suggested play theme (Fein & Robertson, 1974). Generally, the high-realism toys are detailed, miniature replicas of common objects that have specific functions (home furnishings, fully outfitted dolls, vehicles, eating utensils) whereas the low-realism toys are relatively lacking in detail and in most cases are ambiguous with respect to function (cardboard boxes and tubes, blocks, pipecleaners). These studies differ from those reviewed earlier because the primary dependent variable is the frequency, quality, or diversity of nonspecific solitary or social pretend play, rather than performance of specific object-related actions. With one exception (McLoyd, 1983), the children observed have been from predominantly middle-class homes. There are no studies that examine the differential effects of toy realism on middle-class versus lower-class children.

Considerable disagreement is evident in the findings of these studies. Olszewski and Fuson (1982) and Phillips (1945) found no effect of toy realism on the frequency of solitary pretend doll play in children 3- to 5-years-old. In line with these findings is evidence that training with low-realism props facilitates the growth of symbolic skills (e.g., divergent thinking, story recall) no more than training with high-realism props (Mann, 1984). However, other studies report differences in favor of high-realism toys, especially in toddlers and young preschool children.

In their study of a group of 18- to 41-month-old children, Jeffree and McConkey (1976) found that high-realism toys elicited significantly more solitary pretend doll play than low-realism toys. Fein and Robertson (1974) reported a similar effect on solitary pretend play for 20-month-old children, but among 26-month-old children this effect held only for girls. Pretense with low-realism toys increased between 20 and 26 months in both sexes.

Observations of children in a group setting agree with this general pattern of effects. McLoyd (1983) found that high-realism toys significantly increased noninteractive (solitary and parallel) pretend play in 3½- but not 5-year-old triads. She also reported that these toys increased associative and total pretend play (solitary, parallel, associative, and cooperative combined) in both age groups, but failed to increase cooperative pretend play.

Toy realism is unrelated to the richness of fantasy (i.e., number of imaginary items present in fantasy production, distance of fantasy production from daily reality, organization, and plot development) (Pulaski, 1970), but significant effects on play diversity, albeit inconsistent, have been reported. In McLoyd's (1983) study of preschool triads, high-realism toys evoked significantly more pretend themes than low-realism toys among boys but not girls. Fein and Robertson (1974) reported that high-realism toys resulted in more diverse pretend themes than low-realism toys in boys and girls at 20 months but only in girls at 26 months. Contradicting these findings is the work of Pulaski (1970) and Phillips (1945), which indicate that low-realism toys elicited more thematic variation in 3- to 7-year-olds. Low-realism toys also have been found to elicit fantasy role enactment more frequently than high-realism toys in 3½- to 5-year-old boys (McLoyd, Warren, & Thomas, 1984).

Several methodological factors may contribute to the discrepant pattern of findings from these studies. First, some studies contrast effects in different-age children (Fein & Robertson, 1974; McLoyd, 1983; Olszewski & Fuson, 1982), whereas others pool data across a relatively wide age span with the result that interaction effects of age and toy realism may be masked (Phillips, 1945; Pulaski, 1970). Second, though the nature of high-realism toys is relatively consistent across studies, there is considerable variation across studies in the degree of realism of the toys in the low-realism category, as well as in the extent to which these toys differ from those in the high-realism category. Indeed, both Pulaski (1970) and Olszewski and Fuson (1982) speculated that the toys they chose to represent the two categories may have been too similar to provide adequate tests of effects.

McLoyd (1983) sought to increase the dissimilarity between high-realism and low-realism toys by excluding any object resembling a human form from the low-realism category, but in other studies, low-realism dolls ranged in character from stuffed cloth figures with movable arms and legs (Phillips, 1945) to wooden cylinder figures with painted eyes and mouths (Olszewski & Fuson, 1982). In Phillips's (1945) study, low-realism doll furniture (e.g., sink, bathtub) was represented by different sizes and combinations of wooden blocks with pen lines to designate hollow areas but, in other studies, plain blocks were used in the low-realism condition (Jeffree & McConkey, 1976; McLoyd, 1983; Pulaski, 1970). Particularly problematic are disparities in the categorization of the same kind of toys. For example, dress-up clothes were categorized as low-realism toys by Pulaski (1970) (they were contrasted with ready-made costumes representing specific occupations and roles) but as high-realism toys by McLoyd (1983) because of their unambiguous function.

Finally, some reported effects may be artifacts of the scoring procedures. Phillips (1945) gave theme credit for all organizational behaviors that appeared to construct a background for an impending story, even if the story never actually materialized. She acknowledged that low-realism toys required children to spend more time organizing, leading to a spurious association with thematic variation.

Obviously, definitive conclusions about the effects of toy realism on the frequency and richness of children's pretend play are not yet in order. Studies are too few and findings too varied. We can conclude tentatively that when significant effects have been found in American samples, they have been in favor of high-realism toys for very young children (Fein & Robertson, 1974; Jeffree & McConkey, 1976; McLoyd, 1983). Reported effects on thematic diversity are decidedly discordant and do not permit even provisional conclusions. This issue merits further study in view of its important theoretical and educational implications. In the interests of comparability of results and, ultimately, resolution of the issue, researchers need to use similar procedures and toys and devise more explicit and rigorous measures of thematic variation. Short-term longitudinal studies also are needed to determine the long-term effects of differential exposure to high-realism versus low-realism toys.

Presence versus absence of ancillary toys

Researchers have also shown interest in determining the effects on doll play of the presence and absence of ancillary toys (environmental supports) intended to accompany doll play. Like studies of the relationship between toy realism and the frequency of pretend play, studies tend to indicate positive effects for environmental supports, but only in very young preschoolers.

Olszewski and Fuson (1982) found that environmental supports (e.g., doll furniture, vehicles) increased fantasy play utterances (p < .10) and role-taking speech (p < .05) in the doll play of 3-year-olds, giving support to the claim that young preschoolers need pivot objects during the early stages of vision-meaning divergence. Olszewski and Fuson suggested that the props prompted pretend themes by facilitating retrieval of scenarios from the child's memory.

On the other hand, these environmental supports decreased pretend play in 5-year-olds who tended to act out nondomestic themes, even though the ancillary toys were largely domestic in nature. This discrepancy inhibited pretend play although it demonstrated advanced representational skills. Nevertheless, the nondomestic pretense that was produced tended to be repetitive and unelaborated, leading Olszewski and Fuson to suggest that nondomestic props may have enriched the pretend play of the 5-year-olds.

Pursuing a similar query, Jeffree and McConkey (1976) reported that a toy set comprised of a high-realism doll and high-realism environmental supports (e.g., doll furniture, eating utensils) increased pretend doll play in 18- to 41-month-olds, compared to a toy set comprised of a high-realism doll and low-realism environmental supports (e.g., box, wood, tin can) which, in turn elicited more doll play than a toy set comprised of a low-realism doll (a piece of material tied around a ball of cloth) and low-realism environmental supports.

Educational implications

The facilitation effect of high-realism toys on the frequency of pretend play found in some studies suggests that teachers should provide high-realism toys to preschoolers, especially those younger than 4-years-old, to support and sustain pretend play. However, there is reason to believe that it may be advantageous to include a few low-realism toys along with high-realism toys. The latter set the broader context for pretense by suggesting to young preschoolers thematic scenarios that generally call for role and situational transformations. High-realism toys rarely will be used as substitutes for other objects. Low-realism toys play a complementary role by encouraging object substitution and, thus, presumably facilitate the child's progression toward complete separation of meaning and object. Without the material support provided by high-realism toys, however, the potential for such object pretense is lessened in young preschoolers.

As children grow older, they increasingly are able to enact pretend sequences without high-realism toys. To accurately gauge this development, it may be necessary for the teacher to demonstrate and then elicit from the child relatively complex pretense sequences because children's free play behavior understates their symbolic competence (Watson & Fischer, 1980). As children mature in their representational skills, they should be encouraged to make greater and, eventually, exclusive use of low-realism toys. In most cases, however, this level of maturity probably will not be reached until the child approaches completion of preschool, because children as old as 5 appear to benefit from the presence of high-realism toys (McLoyd, 1983).

Teachers need to monitor changes in children's thematic preferences and provide high-realism toys that are compatible with these preferences. Older preschoolers, especially boys, show more interest than younger preschoolers in nondomestic themes (McLoyd et al., 1984; Olszewski & Fuson, 1982), undoubtedly reflecting expanded contacts with nonfamily members in nondomestic settings and increased expo-

Subjects & Predicates

Children as young as 3 are capable of sustaining their own play. They do not seem to need teacher guidance. Teachers may be needed, however, to provide children with a play theme.

sure to mass media. These findings suggest that different kinds of high-realism toys may be optimal at different ages. High-realism toys that are incongruous with thematic preferences may undermine the frequency and quality of pretend play (Olszewski & Fuson, 1982).

The quality of sociodramatic play in older preschoolers seems to be enhanced by limited access to toys (where children are required to ask teacher for permission to check out toys and prompted to return toys not in use), compared to free access (where children freely select toys). Montes and Risley (1975) observed 4- and 5-year-old children in the housekeeping area (equipped with child-size household furniture) of a preschool and found that limited access to ancillary toys resulted in greater make-believe with regard to actions and situations and more pretend verbalizations. Perhaps controlled access directed children's attention to the planning and elaboration of pretense and encouraged subordination of concrete toys to mental imagery. This kind of procedure also has the advantage of prompting child-initiated interaction with teachers that can be used as an occasion for incidental teaching (Montes & Risley, 1975) and/or as an opportunity to make suggestions for the elaboration of an ongoing pretend episode.

On the other hand, controlled access to individual toys may require a degree of long-range planning beyond the capacities of very young children and also may demand more time and responsiveness from teachers than is feasible. In a modified version of the controlled access procedure, sets of high- and low-realism toys representing diverse themes might be readily available to children, with other sets on rotation or available on request.

References

Bretherton, I., O'Connell, B., Shore, C., & Bates, E. (1984). The effect of contextual variation on symbolic play: Development from 20 to 28 months. In I. Bretherton (Ed.), *Symbolic play: The development of social understanding.* New York: Academic.

Caplan, F., & Caplan, T. (1973). *The power of play.* Garden City, NY: Anchor.

Chaillé, C. (1978). The child's conceptions of play, pretending, and toys: Sequences and structural parallels. *Human Development, 21,* 201–210.

Elder, J. L., & Pederson, D. R. (1978). Preschool children's use of objects in symbolic play. *Child Development, 49,* 500–504.

El'Konin, D. (1966). Symbolics and its functions in the play of children. *Soviet Education, 8,* 35–41.

Fein, G. (1975). A transformational analysis of pretending. *Developmental Psychology, 11,* 291–296.

Fein, G., & Robertson, A. R. (1974). *Cognitive and social dimensions of pretending in two-year-olds.* Unpublished manuscript, Yale University.

Fein, G., & Stork, L. (1981). Sociodramatic play: Social class effects in integrated preschool classrooms. *Journal of Applied Developmental Psychology, 2,* 267–279.

Giddings, M., & Halverson, C. F. (1981). Young children's use of toys in home environments. *Family Relations, 30,* 69–74.

Griffing, P. (1980). The relationship between socioeconomic status and socio-dramatic play among Black kindergarten children. *Genetic Psychology Monographs, 101,* 3–34.

Jackowitz, E. R., & Watson, M. W. (1980). Development of object transformations in early pretend play. *Developmental Psychology, 16,* 543–549.

Jeffree, D. M., & McConkey, R. (1976). An observation scheme for recording children's imaginative doll play. *Journal of Child Psychology and Psychiatry, 17,* 189–197.

Johnson, J. E., & Ershler, J. (1981). Developmental trends in preschool play as a function of classroom program and child gender. *Child Development, 52,* 995–1004.

Kagan, J., Kearsley, R. B., & Zelazo, P. R. (1978). *Infancy: Its place in development.* Cambridge, MA: Harvard University Press.

Lowe, M. (1975). Trends in the development of representative play in infants from 1 to 3 years: An observational study. *Journal of Child Psychology and Psychiatry, 16,* 33–47.

Mann, B. L. (1984). Effects of realistic and unrealistic props on symbolic play. In T. D. Yawkey & A. D. Pellegrini (Eds.), *Child's play: Developmental and applied.* Hillsdale, NJ: Erlbaum.

McGhee, P. E., Ethridge, O. L., & Benz, N. A. (1981, April). *Effect of level of toy structure on preschool children's pretend play.* Paper presented at annual meeting of the Association for the Anthropological Study of Play, Fort Worth, TX.

McLoyd, V. C. (1983). The effects of the structure of play objects on the pretend play of low-income preschool children. *Child Development, 54,* 626–635.

McLoyd, V. C. (1982). Social class differences in sociodramatic play: A critical review. *Developmental Review, 2,* 1–30.

McLoyd, V. C., Warren, D., & Thomas, E. A. C. (1984). Anticipatory and fantastic role enactment in preschool triads. *Developmental Psychology, 20,* 807–814.

Montes, F., & Risley, T. R. (1975). Evaluating traditional day care practices: An empirical approach. *Child Care Quarterly, 4,* 208–215.

Olszewski, P., & Fuson, K. (1982). Verbally expressed fantasy play of preschoolers as a function of toy structure. *Developmental Psychology, 18,* 57–61.

Pederson, D. R., Rook-Green, A., & Elder, J. (1981). The role of action in the development of pretend play in young children. *Developmental Psychology, 17,* 756–759.

Phillips, R. (1945). Doll play as a function of the realism of the materials and the length of the experimental session. *Child Development, 16,* 123–143.

Piaget, J. (1962). *Play, dreams and imitation in childhood.* New York: Norton.

Pulaski, M. (1970). Play as a function of toy structure and fantasy predisposition. *Child Development, 41,* 531–537.

Singer, J. (1966). *Daydreaming: An introduction to the experimental study of inner experience.* New York: Random House.

Smilansky, S. (1968). *The effects of sociodramatic play on disadvantaged preschool children.* New York: Wiley.

Smith, P. K., & Dodsworth, C. (1978). Social class differences in the fantasy play of preschool children. *Journal of Genetic Psychology, 133,* 183–190.

Sotamaa, Y. (1980). Criteria for children's playthings and play environments. In P. F. Wilkinson (Ed.), *In celebration of play*. New York: St. Martin's.

Stern, V., Bragdon, N., & Gordon, A. (1976). *Cognitive aspects of young children's symbolic play*. Unpublished manuscript, Bank Street College of Education.

Ungerer, J. A., Zelazo, P., Kearsley, R., & O'Leary, K. (1981). Developmental changes in the representation of objects in symbolic play from 18 to 34 months of age. *Child Development, 52*, 186–195.

Vygotsky, L. S. (1967). Play and its role in the mental development of the child. *Soviet Psychology, 5*, 6–18.

Watson, M. W., & Fischer, K. W. (1980). Development of social roles in elicited and spontaneous behavior during the preschool years. *Developmental Psychology, 16*, 482–494.

White, B. (1978). *Experience and environment* (Vol. 2). Englewood Cliffs, NJ: Prentice-Hall.

Elaine M. Ward

The teacher's role in children's play is to create an environment that invites children to play. Children's explicit language is encouraged when children use dramatic play centers or enact stories read to them.

CHAPTER SIX

Communicating in and About Play: The Effect of Play Centers on Preschoolers' Explicit Language

ANTHONY D. PELLEGRINI

The language of children

A common element in preschool and primary school curricula today is the stress on children's proficiency in oral and written language. In school, children are expected to produce and comprehend standard forms of English. At the preschool level, psychologists and anthropologists from a variety of theoretical perspectives have advocated the stimulation of children's language proficiency. For example, the Talk Reform program (based on behavioral learning theory) attempts to facilitate children's use of standard syntactic and phonological forms through modeling and reinforcement (Gahagan & Gahagan, 1970). At the opposite end of the theoretical spectrum is the belief that children become language proficient by using language in many different situations, with many different people. In this model, the educational goal is to have children become communicatively competent. That is, children learn to use the forms of language appropriate to specific situations.

Language variation in different contexts is known as *register* (Halliday, 1966). For example, the appropriate register for talking about a basketball star among peers is different from the classroom register of student-teacher discourse on the same subject. When discussing a TV interview with Boston Celtics' star Larry Bird, a child may say to her or his peers, "That was cool." When talking to the teacher about the same interview, the child is expected to use a different register, and say for example, "He really knows about the game."

A number of researchers have suggested that, through play, children learn and practice aspects of language that help them become more effective communicators. Garvey's (1977) observations of children's language and play suggest that children learn to manipulate aspects of the language system while playing. Children first play with the phonological, or sound, aspect of language. As infants babble in early solitary play, they practice sounds that are appropriate to their native language. Older children also play with the phonological aspect of language when they use rhymes (e.g., jump rope songs) and onomatopoeia (e.g., saying "ruff-ruff" to represent a barking dog). Older children, according to the observations of Garvey (1977) and Keenan (1974), also learn about the pragmatic, or communicative, aspects of language while playing with their peers. For example, during play children learn and practice the rule that speakers must take turns during conversation and not interrupt other speakers.

Experimental researchers have provided additional support for the notion that sociodramatic play can help children master aspects of language. Griffing's work is particularly relevant here. Exposing children to structured sociodramatic play results in more effective communication during play (Griffing, 1980; Griffing, Stewart, McKendry, & Anderson, 1983). Further, children who engage in sociodramatic play tend to be better storytellers.

These findings have important educational implications. They suggest that by encouraging children to engage in sociodramatic play, teachers can have a positive impact on children's ability to master important school tasks. For example, in school, children are expected to read and talk about stories in a very specific way (Michaels, 1981; Pellegrini, 1985). When writing and talking with teachers they are also expected to use this school register (Pellegrini, Galda, & Rubin, 1984).

The Georgia Project

Sociodramatic play centers, such as housekeeping areas, provide excellent instructional settings where children can use a variety of registers. Exposure to such contexts should therefore improve children's communicative competence. In Table 6.1, I have outlined the communicative forms children tend to use while engaging in sociodramatic play. I have labelled these forms *explicit language*.

In this section, I discuss a research program at the University of Georgia where we are attempting to identify those play contexts and aspects of sociodramatic play that elicit explicit language from children. A more technical description of this report can be found in Pellegrini (1986). In the following discussion, I will examine the ways two play contexts frequently found in preschool classrooms, blocks and dramatic centers, elicit explicit language.

Table 6.1   Forms of explicit language

Form	Definition	Example
Elaborated language		
Endophoric reference	Two textual elements tied to each other	*Joe* is here. *He*'s fun to be with
Nominal groups	Composed of a *noun*, *modifiers* (precede the noun), and *qualifiers* (follow the noun)	The *brown* (modifier) *house* (noun) *there* (qualifier) is new
Metacognitive verbs	Verbs denoting mental processes	think, mean, decide, understand
Metalinguistic verbs	Verbs denoting linguistic processes	talk, say, speak, tell
Language of absence		
Past tense verbs	Verbs referring to past events	The boy *slept* all day.
Future tense verbs	Verbs referring to future events	The car *will come* today
Third person pronouns	Pronouns referring to an absent party	they, them, he, she

Explicit language

Explicit language conveys information primarily through words; there is minimal reliance on shared knowledge and gestures among communicators to convey meaning. In our work we have defined explicit language on two levels: elaborated language, and language that takes people away from their immediate surroundings, such as the language of absence. These two attributes of explicit language — elaboration and reference to physically absent phenomena — are seen as critical to the school register (Cook-Gumperz, 1977; Olson, 1977; Pellegrini, 1985). Elaborated language has been extensively described by English sociologists and linguists (Bernstein, 1971; Cook-Gumperz, 1977; Halliday, 1966; Hawkins, 1973). Elaborated language is marked linguistically by the presence of endophoric reference (Halliday & Hasan, 1976), elaborated nominal groups (Hawkins, 1973), and metacognitive and metalinguistic verbs (Torrance & Olson, 1984).

Endophoric reference. Endophoric reference is established by ties between two linguistic elements underlying the same referent (e.g., a noun defining a pronoun). Predominantly endophoric statements are relatively independent of context and shared assumptions in the conveyed meaning. For example, compare the two sets of utterances

1. The car is red. It's mine.
2. It is red. It's mine.

In Number 1, an endophoric tie exists between the *car* and *it*. A listener or reader will be able to understand the meaning of *it* by way of the tie between *it* and *car*. In Number 2, on the other hand, *it* is ambiguous because that word has not been tied to a particular referent. *Exophora* is the label given to statements that have no contextual ties. The only way a listener or reader could understand the meaning of *it* in Number 2 is by sharing knowledge or a physical context with the speaker/writer. For example, by seeing the speaker point to a car, the listener might understand that *it* means car.

Children tend to use endophoric reference when engaging in dramatic play (Pellegrini, 1982, 1986). For example, in defining a play role, children use endophora, "I'll be Batman." Children engaging in dramatic play, compared to children engaging in constructive play, use significantly more endophora (Pellegrini, 1982, 1986), thereby avoiding the ambiguity inherent in dramatic play. How else would other players know a block represents a make-believe piece of cheese?

Nominal groups. The nominal group is a noun phrase comprised of an obligatory head (i.e., a noun or pronoun) and optional modifiers (which immediately precede the head) and qualifiers (which immediately follow the head). For example, in the sentence, *The big yellow dog over there is mine; dog* is the head, *big* and *yellow* are modifiers, and *over there* are qualifiers. The extent to which a nominal group is elaborated depends on the number of modifiers and qualifiers used to elaborate the noun. Elaborated noun groups, like endophora, indicate that speakers are using words, rather than gestures or shared knowledge, to convey meaning. For example, in *The big old house across the river burned down*, the speaker is relying more on a verbal description of the house than someone saying, *You know that old house? It burned down.* Children use more elaborated noun phrases in dramatic play than in constructive play, presumably to give fantasy objects and roles new characteristics that fit into play themes.

Metalinguistic and metacognitive verbs. Encoding of metalinguistic (language) and metacognitive (thinking) processes is marked by linguistic (talk, say, tell) and cognitive (think, mean, decide) verbs. When children use these verbs, it indicates that they are thinking consciously about the processes they use to communicate and solve problems. Children use these verb forms to plan and negotiate different aspects of dramatic play episodes (Pellegrini, 1986). For example, children in our studies used metalinguistic verbs to negotiate play roles. One child began an episode by saying, "I'll be him." Because *him* was ambiguous to the other player, that player asked for clarification, saying "I can't understand you. Say that again." In this case, the child used both metacognitive *(understand)* and metalinguistic *(say)* verbs to clarify an interaction. Again, presence of these *meta* verbs indicates that children are using explicit language, rather than shared assumptions and gestures, to communicate about the process of playing.

Language of absence

Language that takes people away from their immediate surroundings also occurs in dramatic play. This form of language is marked by past and future tense verbs, and by third person pronouns (Sigel, 1969; Sigel & Cocking, 1977). Children typically use these language forms in play to evoke imaginary people or objects (Scarlett & Wolf, 1979). These linguistic forms indicate that children are talking about physically absent phenomena. Because they cannot rely on the physical attributes of props to convey their play meaning, children must use explicit language to transform the identity of a prop or a player. For example, by saying, "You be Batman," the child transforms a peer into an imaginary play character. In addition, *you* is defined by *Batman*.

These aspects of elaborated language and the language of absence are found in school language. A primary goal of school is to teach children to use explicit language to convey their meanings in words. In reading and writing, they are expected to comprehend and produce language, with minimal reliance on pictures and gestures. Eventually children are expected to read text without pictures. When writing, they cannot use gestures to convey information. Further, in reading lessons, children are expected to answer questions from information derived from the text. Similarly, in writing tasks children are expected to convey meaning to unfamiliar readers (Pellegrini, Galda, & Rubin, 1984), mainly through the text itself, minimizing reliance on shared knowledge with the reader. Even during kindergarten sharing time, children are expected to use explicit oral language (Michaels, 1981). In short, school language is typified by the ability to convey and comprehend meaning from text alone.

The language of play

Not surprisingly, children's elaborated language changes during the preschool period. In the remainder of this section, I will describe the ways children used elaborated language in two play centers and how the use of elaborated language changed in children from 4- to 5-years-old.

A recent study of children enrolled at the University of Georgia laboratory preschool (see Pellegrini, 1986) involved two age groups of children (4- and 5-year olds) in same age, same sex dyads, playing either with blocks or doctor props. Two play sessions in an experimental playroom were recorded with an audio-video camera. Children were exposed to specific centers, rather than observing them during free play with a variety of centers to choose from, because I was interested in the behaviors elicited by the centers themselves. Studies describing the free play behaviors of children at various play centers in their classroom are often describing the behaviors of *children choosing to play* in certain centers, not the behaviors elicited by the centers themselves (Rubin, Fein, & Vandenberg, 1983). Observations of children's free choices of play contexts only tells us about the *play* of those children choosing a specific context.

For example, because boys prefer to play with vehicle toys (Rubin & Seibel, 1979), observations of spontaneous play with vehicle toys does not give us much information about the way girls play with these toys. As such, in natural play studies, we are observing the effects of the self-selection of toys and the toys themselves on children's behaviors. I chose to manipulate the children's exposure to centers to avoid this problem. Generally, in this study I was interested in the forms of elaborated language elicited by each play center and how these language forms varied with age.

The results of this study generally supported previous observational work (e.g., Pellegrini, 1982, 1983, 1984a) which indicated that children produce more elaborated language in dramatic play centers than in constructive centers. Children generated more linguistic verbs, physically absent tenses, and less exophora in the dramatic center than in the blocks center. Elaborated language was also used to represent perceptually absent phenomena. Children used language to transform players and props into other roles and identities.

Children in the dramatic center often used third person pronouns and past and future tense verbs to represent the perceptually absent people and events. Children often used third person pronouns in the dramatic center to represent imaginary players (e.g., "The nurse gave her a shot.

She hurt her."). Similarly, they often used future and past tense verbs to orient a current play episode in terms of related past and future events. For example, future tense verbs were used to plan play episodes ("I'll do that, then you can do it."). This form of planning language which is important in sustained sociodramatic play (Sachs, Goldman, & Chaillé, 1984), is also important for more traditional school tasks, such as math problems. Using language to plan has been shown to be a good predictor of elementary schoolchildren's achievement (Peterson, Wilkinson, Spinelli, & Swing, 1984).

The dramatic center also elicited verbs describing linguistic processes (metalinguistic verbs). One possible explanation for children talking about language in the dramatic center may be that they used linguistic verbs to clarify ambiguous language (e.g., "No, I said start now."). In this example, the use of the metalinguistic verb *said* indicates that this child is explicitly reflecting on a linguistic process. In this case, the child is restating an utterance.

Piagetian-oriented research (e.g., Sinclair, 1978) suggests that children reflect on their linguistic processes, and consequently use metalinguistic terms, when they encounter conceptual conflict, such as ambiguity. Conceptual conflict arises in play when children's intended meanings are not conveyed successfully to other players. At that point, statements must be clarified if the interaction is to be maintained (e.g., "Say that again."). If the ambiguity is not clarified, the play episode would probably break down. Other descriptions of preschoolers' peer play (McLoyd, Thomas, & Warren, 1984) support this position. McLoyd et al. found that children used metalanguage to maintain play episodes. Further, the use of metalanguage seems to indicate that children are considering the perspective of other players (see Rubin, this volume). Children need metalanguage to make their strategies understood by others.

To summarize, our data suggested that in the constructive center children used less elaborated language than when in the dramatic center. For example, in the constructive center children tended to refer to the blocks as *this*, *that*, and *those* without linguistically defining these terms; that is, these terms were not endophorically defined. When these same children played in the dramatic center, they used explicit language to communicate about perceptually absent phenomena and to reflect on their language and cognitive processes. In the dramatic center, children tended to verbally elaborate on play props. For example, the doll became *a very sick girl* and the hypodermic needle became *a big, bad needle*. In these cases, children used elaborated noun phrases to further describe the props. Thus, the dramatic center seemed to facilitate certain types of elaborated language.

The use of elaborated language increased with age. First, older children talked more than younger children, especially in the dramatic center. Second, older children used more elaborated language. That is, older children, more frequently than younger children, talked about perceptually absent phenomena (i.e., used third person pronouns, and past and future tense verbs) and verbally embellished (i.e., used modifiers) the nouns they encoded. Younger children, on the other hand, seemed to talk more about themselves (first and second person pronouns) than about perceptually absent others.

These results suggest that, with age, children use language to put distance (Sigel, 1969) between themselves and their immediate environments during dramatic play. Such uses of language indicate that 5-year-olds use language to go beyond their immediate environment. Going beyond perceptually present stimuli is a necessary skill for other, more complex, cognitive tasks. For example, in order to classify objects paradigmatically (i.e., classify by function rather than by perceptual similarity), children must be able to put psychological distance between themselves and the stimuli (Bruner, 1973). Further, Flavell (in press) makes the point that children who represent past and future events also have metacognitive knowledge. That is, children who look both backward and foward in time also are conscious of their thoughts. In our study, which supported this claim, 5-year-olds used both past and future tense verbs and cognitive verbs. These age-related abilities to view events in temporal perspective and to monitor one's own thought processes, are important components in the execution of planned behavior (Flavell, in press).

Implications for teachers

This research suggests that children's use of elaborated language can be stimulated by interactions in centers that elicit dramatic play. Housekeeping or dress-up areas encourage children to practice forms of language they will be expected to produce (in talking with teachers and in writing) and comprehend (in reading) throughout their school careers. Further, it should be noted that research has found that many young children (as young as 3-years-old) are capable of sustaining sociodramatic play themselves (Garvey, 1977; Pellegrini, 1984c; Rubin, Fein, & Vandenberg, 1983). They may not need adults to direct their play for it to be sustained.

The teacher's role with these competent players is to provide centers that encourage dramatic play. Teachers can also intervene in children's play when they want to familiarize them with a specific topic. For example, before a visit to the doctor's office, a teacher might first read the children a related story. Next, the teacher might provide children with play props relevant to the story. The teacher might then become involved in the children's story dramatization as a player or as a director of the play episode (Smilansky, 1968). For example, in helping children enact a doctor-patient scene, a teacher playing the role of a nurse might help children enact a forgotten part of the story by saying "Take this pill," as she or he hands the child an imaginary pill.

A variant of Smilansky's procedure has been shown to be an effective facilitator of young children's explicit language. Pellegrini and Galda (1982) used the adult-as-director variant of the procedure to help primary schoolchildren enact folktales. Different groups of children reconstructed stories by drawing pictures, discussing, or enacting stories. All children then retold the stories they reconstructed. They found that the stories retold by children who enacted the stories were more complete and explicit than the stories retold by children in other groups (Pellegrini & Galda, 1982; Pellegrini, 1984b). Saltz and his colleagues (Saltz & Johnson, 1974; Saltz, Dixon, & Johnson, 1977) have also used this procedure with lower socioeconomic preschool children. They, too, found that adult-guided play strategies facilitated children's story knowledge.

In a later study, Pellegrini (1984b) compared teacher-directed play episodes with episodes that had no adults involved. Kindergarten and first-grade children were the players. Again, children's ability to reconstruct the stories they enacted was measured. Results from this study suggested that both procedures were equally effective in facilitating story reconstruction. As noted previously, it seems children as young as 3 are capable of sustaining their own play. They do not seem to need teacher guidance. Teachers may be needed, however, to provide children with a play theme.

We have suggested that the teacher's role in children's play is to create an environment that invites children to play (e.g., provide play props and encourage play) and to participate in play episodes (as players or as directors). Teachers are encouraged to participate in children's play when they want children to enact a specific story in a specific way. If children are familiar with the stories to be enacted, minimal adult direction will be required. Children's cultural backgrounds may affect their familiarity with stories. As a result, teachers should be sensitive to children's cultural background when choosing stories to be enacted (Schwartzman, 1984).

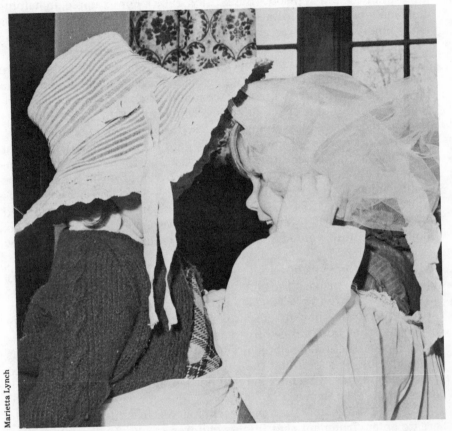

Marietta Lynch

Sustained peer play begins to appear at 2 years of age and by 4 years of age, children play elaborate pretend games with one another.

In this chapter I have discussed two experimental studies which have shown that dramatic play centers facilitate preschoolers' use of explicit language. This is the form of language children are expected to use in school. Such a strategy is effective in stimulating a basic skill: school language. Teachers can further encourage children to use school language by using dramatic play centers and/or by having children enact stories read to them. Thus, the intrinsic behavior required and encouraged in play helps children master important aspects of communicative competence.

References

Bernstein, B. (1971). *Class, codes and control* (Vol. 1). London: Routledge & Kegan Paul.

Bruner, J. (Ed.). (1973). *Beyond the information given.* New York: Norton.

Cook-Gumperz, J. (1977). Situated instructions: Language socialization of school-age children. In S. Ervin-Tripp & C. Mitchell-Kernan (Eds.), *Child discourse* (pp. 103–124). New York: Academic.

Flavell, J. (in press). Speculations about the nature and development of metacognition. In R. Kline & F. Weinert (Eds.), *Metacognition, motivation, and learning.*

Gahagan, D., & Gahagan, G. (1970). *Talk reform.* Beverly Hills: Sage.

Garvey, C. (1977). *Play.* Cambridge, MA: Harvard University Press.

Griffing, P. (1980). The relationship between socioeconomic status and sociodramatic play among Black kindergarten children. *Genetic Psychology Monographs, 101,* 3–34.

Griffing, P., Stewart, L., McKendry, M., & Anderson, R. (1983). Sociodramatic play: A follow-up study of imagination, self-concept, and school achievement among Black school-age children representing two social-class groups. *Genetic Psychology Monographs, 104,* 249–305.

Halliday, M., (1966). Notes on transitivity and theme in English, Part 2. *Journal of Linguistics, 3,* 177–274.

Halliday, M., & Hasan, R. (1976). *Cohesion in English.* London: Longman.

Hawkins, P. (1973). Social class, the nominal group and reference. In B. Bernstein (Ed.), *Class, codes, control* (Vol. 2, pp. 81–92). London: Routledge & Kegan Paul.

Keenan, E. (1974). Conversational competence in children. *Journal of Child Language, 1,* 162–183.

McLoyd, V., Thomas, E., & Warren, D. (1984). The short-term dynamics of social organization in preschool triads. *Child Development, 55,* 1051–1070.

Michaels, S. (1981). "Sharing time": Children's narrative styles and differential access to literacy. *Language in Society, 10,* 423–442.

Olson, D. (1977). From utterance to text. *Harvard Educational Review, 47,* 257–287.

Pellegrini, A. (1982). The generation of cohesive text by preschoolers in two play contexts. *Discourse Processes, 5,* 101–108.

Pellegrini, A. (1983). Sociolinguistic contexts of the preschool. *Journal of Applied Developmental Psychology, 4,* 397–405.

Pellegrini, A. (1984a). The effects of classroom play centers on children's functional uses of language. In A. Pellegrini & T. Yawkey (Eds.), *The development of oral and written language in social contexts* (pp. 129–144). Norwood, NJ: Ablex.

Pellegrini, A. (1984b). The effect of dramatic play on children's generation of cohesive text. *Discourse Processes, 7,* 57–67.

Pellegrini, A. (1984c). Identifying causal elements in the thematic fantasy play paradigm. *American Educational Research Journal, 21,* 691–703.

Pellegrini, A. (1985). The relations between symbolic play and literate behavior: A review and critique of the empirical literature. *Review of Educational Research, 55,* 207–221.

Pellegrini, A. (1986). The effect of play contexts on preschoolers' imaginative language. *Discourse Processes, 9,* 115–125.

Pellegrini, A., De Stefano, J., & Thompson, D. (1983). Saying what you mean: Using play to teach "literate language." *Language Arts, 60,* 380–384.

Pellegrini, A., & Galda, L. (1982). The effects of thematic-fantasy play training on the development of children's story comprehension. *American Educational Research Journal, 19,* 443–452.

Pellegrini, A., Galda, L., & Rubin, D. (1984). Context in text. *Child Development, 55,* 1549–1555.

Peterson, P., Wilkinson, L. C., Spinelli, F., & Swing, S. (1984). Merging the process-product and the sociolinguistic paradigms: Research on small group processes. In P. Peterson, L. C. Wilkinson, & M. Hallinan (Eds.), *Instructional groups in the classroom: Organization and processes* (pp. 126–132). New York: Academic.

Rubin, K., & Seibel, C. (1979). *The effects of ecological setting on the cognitive and social play behaviors of preschoolers.* Paper presented at the ninth Annual International Interdisciplinary Conference on Piagetian Theory and the Helping Professions, Los Angeles.

Rubin, K., Fein, G., & Vandenberg, B. (1983). Play. In E. M. Hetherington (Ed.), *Handbook of child psychology: Vol. 4. Socialization, personalities and social development* (pp. 693–774). New York: Wiley.

Sachs, J., Goldman, J., & Chaillé, C. (1984). Planning in pretend play: Using language to coordinate narrative development. In A. Pellegrini & T. Yawkey (Eds.), *The development of oral and written language in social contexts* (pp. 119–128). Norwood, NJ: Ablex.

Saltz, E., & Johnson, J. (1974). Training for thematic fantasy in culturally disadvantaged children: Preliminary results. *Journal of Educational Psychology, 66,* 623–630.

Saltz, E., Dixon, D., & Johnson, J. (1977). Training disadvantaged preschoolers on various activities: Effects on cognitive functioning and impulse control. *Child Development, 48,* 367–380.

Scarlett, W., & Wolf, D. (1979). When it's only make believe: The construction of a boundary between fantasy and reality in storytelling. In E. Winner & H. Gardner (Eds.), *Fact, fiction, and fantasy in childhood* (pp. 29–40). San Francisco: Jossey-Bass.

Schwartzman, H. (1984). Imaginative play: Deficit or difference. In T. Yawkey & A. Pellegrini (Eds.), *Child's play: Developmental and applied* (pp. 49–62). Hillsdale, NJ: Erlbaum.

Sigel, I. (1969). Language of the disadvantaged: The distancing hypothesis. In C. Lavetelli (Ed.), *Language training in early childhood education* (pp. 60–76). Champaign, IL: National Council of Teachers of English.

Sigel, I., & Cocking, R. (1977). Cognition and communication: A dialectical paradigm for development. In M. Lewis & L. Rosenblaum (Eds.), *Interaction, conversation, and the development of language* (pp. 207–226). New York: Wiley.

Sinclair, H. (1978). Conceptualizations and awareness in Piaget's theory and its relevance to the child's conception of language. In A. Sinclair, R. Jarvella, & W. Levelt (Eds.), *The child's conception of language* (pp. 191–200). New York: Springer-Verlag.

Smilansky, S. (1968). *The effects of sociodramatic play on disadvantaged preschool children*. New York: Wiley.

Torrance, N., & Olson, D. (1984). Oral language competence and the acquisition of literacy. In A. Pellegrini & T. Yawkey (Eds.), *The development of oral and written language in social contexts* (pp. 167–182). Norwood, NJ: Ablex.

Elaine M. Ward

Kindergarten children who engaged in relatively high frequencies of solitary-dramatic play were rated by their Grades 1 and 2 teachers as socially incompetent; furthermore, these kindergarten solitary-dramaticists demonstrated poor social problem-solving skills in Grades 1 and 2.

Part 3:
Social Perspectives
and Social Encounters

Infants play alone and often with their mothers. While they have a keen interest in peers, young children's ability to sustain social play in the absence of a sensitive, supportive adult or older child is strikingly limited during the first and second years of life.

Sustained peer play begins to appear at 2 years of age and by 4 years of age, children play elaborate pretend games with one another. As Greta Fein and Shirley Schwartz note (Chapter 7), the coordination of social and conceptual skills needed to manage these complex encounters develop gradually and eventually culminate in the pattern of individual differences discussed by Kenneth Rubin and Nina Howe (Chapter 8). Young children's ability to take another's perspective is crucial in the social management of shared pretend episodes. At the same time, children refine these perspective-taking skills as they play, learning how to form agreements, negotiate disagreements, and deal with views different from their own. Rubin and Howe suggest that the 5-year-old who pretends alone in a group situation may need help from a sensitive teacher.

Observations of sex-stereotyped behavior in children's play appeared in the 1930s and continued to appear in studies of play during the following decades. Marsha Liss (Chapter 9) reviews these studies of play preferences of boys and girls, examining the different ways parents, teachers, and peers maintain them. According to Liss, traditional patterns may be changing as parents and teachers encourage children to experiment with a wider variety of activities and play materials. An important issue is whether this experimentation in early childhood will alter the way boys and girls perceive their roles and capabilities later in life.

Barbara Rios

Rather than break into play to correct a misconception, teachers need to be careful observers. Armed with information about children's apparent misunderstandings, teachers can plan the curriculum to help children gain more knowledge about events that interest them.

CHAPTER SEVEN

The Social Coordination of Pretense in Preschool Children

GRETA G. FEIN AND SHIRLEY S. SCHWARTZ

Sociodramatic play, an activity in which children jointly construct pretend episodes, requires considerable conceptual, symbolic, communicative, and social skill. Each player must be able to integrate social-interactive and social-representational abilities and coordinate these with the ideas and intentions of other children in a common enterprise (Forys & McCune-Nicolich, 1984). Children involved in this play seem to understand that pretend play can be a social endeavor with shared rules about the production and communication of symbolic representations (Fein, 1984). When we consider the inherently ambiguous, personal quality of pretend constructions, its emergence as a socially coordinated activity merits respect and attention from those interested in the education and development of young children.

In pretend play, children make assertions about important aspects of experience, some real and some imaginary. Unlike other forms of cognitive activity, these assertions are nonliteral; the players know that they are untrue or counterfactual (Ariel, 1984). A 2-year-old who uses a toy mop as a fishing pole, then a few minutes later uses the mop as an oar, knows that the toy mop is a replica of a real mop used to wash floors. In pretense, a child asserts that objects or people in the immediate situation are other than what the child knows them to be; they are, at that moment, what the child imagines them to be. When the same 2-year-old pretends to row a boat or catch a fish, the child claims an achievement that might have been observed but not yet attained and a level of competence disparate from what the child knows to be true. When a child pretends about monsters, death, marriage, and other emotionally charged, exotic events, or adds these events to seemingly benign, mundane occasions, the child makes a claim about events that may have never been directly experienced. Pretense illustrates children's ability to explore invented worlds not constrained by the immediate situation or by actual experience.

In an important analysis of the logic of pretend play, Ariel (1984) argues persuasively that the thematic meaning of pretense (the signified) consists of ideas and images retrieved from long-term memory and of novel combinations of these ideas and images. On the one hand, the player makes mental claims about the reality and tangible presence of these images, denies that they are memories or invention, and insists that "they actually exist in the concrete, external reality now, at the very time this claim is being made" (Ariel, Carel, & Tyano, 1985, p. 49). On the other hand, the player simultaneously affirms the playfulness of these claims and says, "I know they are nonsensical. I am not making them seriously" (Ariel et al., 1985, p. 50).

Because of these seemingly paradoxical claims, pretense differs from other expressive symbolic activities. Unlike storytelling, pretense involves a claim about the here and now; unlike biography, the events portrayed in pretense might never have happened; unlike delusional thinking, pretense is playful. As Ariel (1984) notes, pretend play most resembles dramatic playacting, except that sequences are invented by the players as exchanges unfold; there is no formal script, only a general theme or setting. Because the process of construction is bottom-up, not even the players know exactly what is going to happen next (Fein, 1986).

Despite its complexity, some preschool children become expert pretend players. As pretense becomes more social, its structural characteristics become more differentiated. Pretend sequences may be shared before being executed, and children may discuss others' roles and the activities being enacted. Their role representations reflect intricate systems of complementary relationships, and their themes give evidence of shared improvisation. In this chapter, we trace the development of socially organized pretense using actual play episodes whenever possible to illustrate the research literature. We begin with play activities that form the basic skills of socially organized pretense, as well as those pretend activities that fail to become socially integrated. Next, we discuss component skills that seem necessary in the evolution of socially organized episodes. Finally, we offer some suggestions that might be useful to teachers of young children who wish to promote this play in the classroom.

Early peer encounters

The infant and young toddler are acutely interested in peers. During the second year of life, children watch peers, imitate them, and seek proximity to them (Eckerman, Whatley, & Kutz, 1975). However, differences may exist between the social skills needed for peer exchanges and the toddler's social interest. Interactions, when they occur, tend to be brief and often unreciprocated. Brief, one-round encounters characterize about 58% of the social encounters among 2-year-olds, while sustained, extended reciprocal sequences characterize only about 13% (Bronson, 1981).

Peers are most attractive when they are using a toy, but the outcome of toy-engendered interaction is often negative. One child might offer another a toy, but the offer might be ignored. If the toy is accepted, the recipient may play with the toy, ignoring the giver. Generally, small toys reduce child-to-child interactions because the toys themselves become the focus of activity, while large sharable toys (steps, wooden rocking boats) encourage social interaction (Mueller & Brenner, 1977).

Although extended interaction sequences are infrequent, they are nevertheless interesting. The following transcript of an exchange between two 22-month-old boys illustrates the kind of spontaneous game children sometimes discover at this age:

David approaches the overturned doll carriage. After exploring the spokes of the wheel, he discovers that the wheel can be made to spin. Sam wanders over, watching David's motion on the wheel and the resulting spin. David looks up at Sam, grinning. The wheel is no longer spinning, and Sam timidly puts his hand on it, giving it a push. He laughs, looks at David, who is smiling broadly. As the spin slows down, David gives it a push, and when it slows again, looks at Sam who again makes it spin. The children continue to take turns, but soon they begin to overlap. After five turns, Sam moves the wheel continuously, studying its motion. David fingers the spokes, then wanders off to another toy. (Fein, observational data)

This game was marked by turn-taking, repetition, imitation, and mutual awareness. The game began with David's experimentation with the wheel, an object-centered activity. The spinning wheel attracted Sam's attention, an attraction that again was object-centered rather than person-centered. The important moment came when David smiled at Sam. Here was the social signal, interpreted tentatively by Sam as an invitation to participate in the activity. As the encounter became a game, turns were regulated by the wheel's deceleration and by mutual glances that signaled role changes from spinner to watcher. These roles were imitative, rather than complementary (an action such as catching, related to the partner's action of throwing) or reciprocal (a reversal of complementary roles). In younger toddlers, games involving mutual awareness require more social coordination and social purpose than children can muster at this age. In somewhat older children, games are more likely to involve role complementarity (one child runs while the other chases) or role reversal (Ross, 1982). By 3 years of age, games involving social awareness and reciprocity occur more frequently and last longer (Garvey, 1977).

Games played by younger children build on sensorimotor actions coordinated by partner-sensitive behaviors such as social signaling, turn-taking, visual regard, and the ability to produce complementary and reciprocal roles. In these early sensorimotor games, children exhibit some of the skills needed in socially organized pretense. However, in order to initiate and maintain pretend exchanges, these simple invitational and attentional signals must become messages about the simulative nature of the activity. Turns must become less ritualized or object-cued. For social pretense to develop, these sensorimotor or functional activities must be replaced by symbolic activities understood equally well by both partners. Play roles must express social complementarity rather than physical or instrumental complementarity, play actions must represent personally meaningful experiences, and mutual awareness must include sensitivity to the thoughts and intentions of other players in addition to their overt behavior.

The beginnings of social pretense

Interest and understanding. Sustained social interactions in playful functional activities precede socially organized pretense (Fein, Moorin, & Enslein, 1982). By age 2 children may have interactional skills they are unable to apply to pretense and pretend skills they are unable to share. Even when potential partners are present, pretend play is likely to be a solitary activity among well-acquainted 2½-year-olds:

(Alan sits on a chair, a mop extended over the edge of the table. Richard, another child, is sitting on the floor nearby reading a book. Richard occasionally glances at Alan, but there is no interaction between them.)

Alan: "I'm gonna get a fish." (He raises the mop, commenting on his catch and the wetness of the sea water. Taking the mop with him, he crosses the room [and] picks up the broom.) "I want to row." (He crosses the mop and broom over his head.) "I got my boat over here." (Walks back to the table.) "Eee, ooh. I'm in my boat. . . . I'm gonna get two fish, fish." (He extends both mop and broom over the edge of the table.) "A fish!" (Fein, 1984, p. 130)

Two-year-olds may have grasped the essential properties of pretense, and still be uninterested in negotiating a shared activity. Alan's play illustrated sophisticated substitution behavior. The mop was first a fishing pole and then an oar. The broom, too, became an oar, while the chair-table combination was a boat being rowed, even though the gestures of rowing occurred in what moments before was claimed to be water. We know about Alan's object transformations and the scene he enacted because his actions are vividly organized and because he talked about his actions. But his comments were addressed to no one in particular. He expressed no interest in Richard as a partner; Richard, in turn, showed no interest in participating. Although a potential partner is available, Alan's pretense is solitary.

Unlike Alan, some children this age display an interest in sharing pretend episodes with peers. However, more than interest is required for a collaborative effort. At the very least, interest must be reciprocated. A lack of mutual understanding rather than a lack of social interest characterizes this episode between two acquainted children of the same age:

(Barb is sitting on the floor, holding the doll in her lap. Sandy has been putting trucks in and out of the buggy. The two children occasionally glance at one another.)

Barb (whispers to the doll): "There's dad working." (Puts the doll on the floor and covers it with a blanket.) "Cover you up. Night-night, night-night. Don't cry . . . will you children go to sleep." (Walks to toy shelf.)

Barb (to Sandy): "Dad, do you want to stay with . . . ?" (Sandy and Barb are looking at one another.) "Cover her up, all right, dad?" (Sandy pokes at the truck in the buggy. Barb picks up the broom and the rake, drops the rake, sweeps, drops the broom, picks up the rake.) "Get that one, that one." (Rakes floor, then rug.) "I'm brushing." (Sandy, watching Barb, follows her as she rakes).

Barb (referring to the broom): ". . . your brush. Sandy, will you watch my baby?" (Falls next to doll.) "Uuh! Will you watch my baby so she's not gonna cry?"

(Sandy sits next to the doll, looking at it, as Barb gets up and continues her raking. After a few seconds, he picks up a doll bottle and feeds the doll. Barb approaches Sandy.)

Barb: "Thank you, dad. Thank you. Get up now."

(Remaining seated, Sandy continues to feed the doll.) (Fein, 1984, p. 131)

Barb actively sought the participation of a partner, but the encounter she envisioned failed to materialize. Socially coordinated pretense makes certain demands on the players. First, it requires a partner who understands the meaning of pretend roles. In this example, Sandy had to grasp the basic idea that he could be himself and dad too, and that the role of dad bore some relation to Barb's role of mom and the doll's role of child. Sandy had to unpack Barb's gestures and conversation and interpret them as a playful claim about the immediate reality of people and things not actually present. Second, Barb had to know how to announce, prepare, and maintain pretend exchanges. Whereas a more comprehending partner might have recognized her signals, they may have been too subtle for Sandy. Between 2 and 3 years of age, the development of pretense is uneven, with some children better able than others to pursue collaborative ventures with peers (Cole & LaVoie, 1985; Field, De Stefano, & Koewler, 1982).

As this episode illustrates, children's play is affected by the presence of a partner. While Barb was not able to induce Sandy to participate at her level of attainment, the stimulation she provided induced a level of play more advanced than Sandy might have attained alone. Mature play behavior is more evident when children play with peers than when they play alone (Rubenstein & Howes, 1976). If the peers are friends, the effect is even more favorable (Doyle, Connolly, & Rivest, 1980). Activities conducted with the assistance of more capable collaborators — more mature peers, adults, or older siblings — enable children to achieve more than they would on their own (Dunn & Dale, 1984; Fenson & Ramsey, 1981; Miller & Garvey, 1984; O'Connell & Bretherton, 1984). Particularly with younger children, the presence of a partner — whether the same age or older — elevates and increases the complexity of play behavior.

The Barb-Sandy episode also illustrates another research finding. What children gain from more competent partners might be limited to what they already understand. Children pick and choose which suggestions and forms of activity to respond to, depending on their age and ability. Several studies indicate that children imitate a modeled activity at a level only slightly beyond that which they will produce spontaneously and ignore those that are too difficult (Belsky, Garduque, & Hrncir, 1984; Fenson & Ramsey, 1981; O'Connell & Bretherton, 1984). Further, even though an activity may be imitated immediately, young toddlers forget it only 10 minutes later (Abravenel & Gingold, 1985).

In contrast to 2-year-olds, older preschoolers' interest in peers matches their social capability. Because play partners are likely to have comparable skills, pretend episodes are more sustained and elaborate. The nature of these skills is described in the next section.

The orchestration of collaborative pretense

Between 2 and 5 years of age, children engage in more associative and cooperative play, and the frequency and duration of sociodramatic play increases (Cole & LaVoie, 1985; Fein, 1981; Rubin, Watson, & Jambor, 1978; Smilansky, 1968). In the following example, a group of acquainted 5-year-olds coordinates pretend dramas.

(In the housekeeping area of their kindergarten classroom, Sally is clearing the table as Susan crawls over to her.)

Susan: "Find something for me. Pretend you have to feed me."

Sally: "The baby food isn't ready yet. Pretend you are playing."

Shawn (coming into the area): "Roar, roar, roar."

Sally: "Stop it, monster." (She raises her hands as if to ward off the roaring monster. Shawn continues to roar and reaches for baby Susan.) "Stop it, monster! You're not good company around this baby. If you can't behave, you can't have any chocolate."

(As this exchange progresses, Susan clutches Sally's dress and sucks her fingers, her eyes wide in mock fright. Shawn continues to make menacing noises and chases both girls.)

Sally: "You can't take this baby." (To Susan) "Hide, baby, hide under here, under here." (She points under the table.) "Fast, fast, under the table." (She pushes Susan under the table.) "Be quiet so the monster doesn't get you." (To Shawn) "Get out that door, monster!"

(Shawn stops and considers Sally's orders, as Susan crawls out from under the table.)

Shawn (to Sally): "You know what I am really? A standing dog that growls."

Sally: "OK, standing dog. But stop growling so much so I can get the baby food ready." (To Susan) "Your food is ready, baby. It's time to get in your highchair." (Schwartz, observational data)

As pretense becomes more social, its structural characteristics become more differentiated. Children discuss the activities they and others will enact. Their role characterizations are richly detailed, although not always enacted. In their themes, the possible and the impossible are juxtaposed, with each receiving its due. Several specific aspects of this behavior — communications about play, the way role relations are established, and the socioemotional content of dramatic themes — have received systematic attention.

Metacommunication

In his theory of play as comunication, Bateson (1955) contended that social play could only occur if participants were capable of some degree of metacommunication — communicating about communication — and were able to signal others that *this is play.* These communications, in the form of smiling, laughter, and eye-to-eye contact, are evident in early sensorimotor games. They serve to frame the situation as play, rather than some other serious activity. The metacommunications used in pretense are considerably more intricate and diverse. First, they must signal that the kind of play is pretense, and then they must indicate what the pretense will be about. In socially organized pretense, *framing* refers to communications about the play setting and its themes. It involves communications about coparticipants and their roles, about what objects are present, and about what events are transpiring (Goncu & Kessel, 1984).

Following Bateson, Giffin (1984) proposed a taxonomy identifying the way children use metacommunicative statements to construct a shared metaphoric system and interact within that system during their joint pretend activity. Giffin believes that for all its flexibility, shared pretense is rule-governed, and that children use their metacommunicative options to preserve the illusion of reality, or in Ariel's (1984) terms, to protect the mental claims that constitute the logic of pretense. Children use a variety of metacommunicative options, verbal and nonverbal, to conjointly represent events and transform meaning. These metacommunicative options convert personal symbols into shared collective symbols.

The metacommunicative options children choose range on a continuum from those outside the play frame to those within it. When Susan said, "Pretend you have to feed me," she stepped outside the play frame to describe her status within the frame. Sally's response, "The baby food isn't ready yet," moved within the frame serving double duty as a metacommunicative message about the play food, and as a role-appropriate message to a hungry baby. Sally then stepped unambiguously out-of-frame to add, "Pretend you are playing." This statement is especially interesting because it draws attention to the paradoxical, self-referencing aspects of pretense in which it is even possible to communicate about playing about playing.

Metacommunications are not always socially directed. In Alan's play, communications about his activity accompanied his actions, but were not directed to any particular person. Barb, too, talked as she played, but when she addressed Sandy as dad, she assumed that he shared the play frame, unmindful of his need for more direct information. An important achievement in the development of sociodramatic play is the shift from egocentric play communications to those explicitly directed to a partner (Fein et al., 1982). Socially directed announcements increase steadily and become more subtle and diverse from 2 to 5 years of age.

The subtlety of these announcements in older players is illustrated in the Sally-Susan-Shawn episode. Shawn's roar simultaneously communicated a pretend role and an enactment of it. Sally identified the role as that of monster, while responding appropriately as an alarmed mother protecting her helpless infant. Shawn skillfully renegotiated this role when he asked, "Do you know what I am really?" But consider what he meant by *really*. At one level he was saying, "I am really pretending to be a dog who is pretending to be a monster by standing and growling." Yet it is semantically ambiguous whether *I* referred to the monster, the standing dog, or Shawn himself. Within the play frame, he proclaimed the reality of a pretend role, itself a mental claim. At another level, he announced an end to the threatening reality of the monster role, and a return to the domestic tranquility that began the play. Despite its ambiguity, Sally understood his multilayered message and supported the transformation by addressing Shawn in his new identity and by resuming the central episode. Because these children manage the meta-communicative language of pretense so well, play transitions can be smoothly negotiated.

According to Giffin (1984), children make decisions about their communicative options based on their desire to extend and elaborate play. Shawn might have realized that the monster role made him an alien in the play, or that the adversarial theme would be difficult to expand. Goncu and Kessel (1984) have also explored how children make decisions and frame their play. Children move implicitly in and out of play episodes with relatively few explicit invitations and termination statements. Statements about roles, objects, or situational transformations, however, are frequent and a partner's transformation suggestions are hardly ever rejected. Older children are more inclined than younger children to explicitly mention transformations to one another, a tendency that also increases when the toy set consists of less realistic objects (Olszewski & Fuson, 1982). Older children also provide more explanations about their involvement in current and forthcoming activities, thus providing information that serves to orient themselves and their partners to the play context they are creating.

Role transformations

Socially organized pretense requires a language to talk about pretense, but it also requires something to talk about. A major component of pretense, especially pretense that involves elaborate peer exchanges, requires children to conceptualize roles and relationships among different role representations (Watson & Fischer, 1980). Role play increases, both in frequency and duration, from 2 to 6 years of age. A three-step progression—from reality play, to object fantasy play, to person fantasy play—is generally supported by research (Field et al., 1982; Cole & LaVoie, 1985).

Children's ability to enact a role reflects a growing awareness of self and others, a continuation of the process of decentration that first appears between the ages of 1 and 2 (McCune, this volume). Both Alan and Barb reflected some awareness of self, but only Barb reflected an awareness of self in relation to socially defined others. While Alan was more proficient than Barb in his ability to transform objects, Barb was more proficient in her protrayal of a person other than herself. In her tone of voice and gestures, and in her reference to dad, Barb indicated that her play involved a maternal role. She talked to her child, heard her cry, and gently scolded her. By contrast, Alan seemed to play himself, albeit a more competent and mature self, able to catch a fish and row a boat.

Barb, who understood the meaning of complementary social roles, playfully claimed the existence of caregiving roles that involved mothers and children and fathers and children. Barb not only envisioned herself as a parent in relation to an animated speaking doll, she also attributed a parallel parenting role to Sandy. In Barb's view, parental roles are related, permitting fathers to substitute for mothers. At 2 years of age, some agemates are more ready than others to participate in these represented relationships. Despite Barb's efforts, Sandy seemed not to understand what Barb meant when she called him dad, or even that she was referring to him. Perhaps grasping his confusion, she finally addressed him by his real name. As Sandy, he fed the doll, even though this act seemed to have exhausted his vision of a pretend role. Sandy's social spirit was willing, but the subtlety of Barb's game eluded him.

Developmentally, the ability to designate a self-transformation occurs earlier than the ability to manage an other-transformation (Fein & Stork, 1981; Johnson & Ershler, 1981). At 3 years of age, children may initiate complementary role play in which differentiated roles are assigned, but in the actual play these roles are often enacted independently. Older children are more likely to produce integrated role structures in which the activity of each player is tied to the activity of the others and the roles express reciprocity between the players (Iwanaga, 1973). Integrative role structures are present in the episode produced by Sally, Susan, and Shawn. These children effortlessly establish complementary roles, refine the details about one another's role-appropriate actions as they go along, and add new roles as the spirit moves them.

What kinds of roles do children play? In Alan's case, the role is instrumental, built around competent adult behavior. Researchers have distinguished between real-life roles and fantastic roles (McLoyd, Warren, & Thomas, 1984; Saltz, Dixon, & Johnson, 1977). In the case of Barb, Sally, and Susan, the roles reflect real life. In Shawn's case, whether monster or standing dog, the role is based on fantasy.

In the real-life category, domestic roles can be distinguished from occupational roles. Although boys and girls may not differ in their tendency to enact roles, they differ markedly in the specific roles they choose. From the time role playing begins to emerge, girls display a preference for domestic roles. Boys, by contrast, show more diversity in the roles they choose, and domestic role play diminishes as fantastic roles increase from the ages of 3 to 6. Shawn's role diversity and flexibility appear in the continuation of the play episode described earlier:

Shawn (to Sally): "I have a good idea. We can bathe this baby."

Sally: "The sink is the bathtub." (To Susan) "Baby, it's time for your bath. Hop in." (Sally tries to lift Susan into the sink.)

Shawn: "She can't fit in there. Make the phone booth a bathtub. She'll fit in there." (The children walk to the play phone booth and put Susan in the tub.) "Pretend to close the doors. Fill it with water." (Sally returns to the sink and climbs into it.)

Sally: "This is really a better tub. Shawn, bring the baby over. Look, Susan, you can fit." (Susan leaves the phone booth, and climbs into the sink.)

Sally: "Is the water cold or warm?"

Susan: "Goo-goo." (Shawn clutches Susan around the waist. Susan protests.) "Goo-goo!"

Sally: "You're hurting her. Don't hold so hard." (She pushes Shawn away. Susan climbs out of the sink, skips over to the stove, and climbs on it.)

Sally (in alarm): "Baby, the stove is very hot! Baby, I mean it!" (Shawn pulls Susan.)

Sally: "Don't, Shawn! She's a baby. Are you the daddy?"

Shawn: "No, I'm a baby." (Crawls on the floor.)

Sally: "You're acting like a stupid dog actor."

Mickey (entering the play area): "I want to be a baby." (He finds a baby bottle and joins Susan and Shawn on the floor.)

Sally: "Only if I get another head." (Hands on hips, she surveys her disorderly babies.) (Schwartz, observational data)

The dramatic play of these children was recorded over a 10-week period. During this time, the girls played domestic roles, while the boys' roles were domestic, occupational, and fantasy (McLoyd et al., 1984). As in other studies, these pretend roles often reflected actual relationships within the group (Schwartzman, 1978). Sally had just won a power struggle with Terry (a child not present in this scenario) over who would be the play mother. Compliant Susan always played either the role of baby or small sister, while impulsive Shawn was allowed to be the gadfly, shifting roles at will, but most often cast as an aggressive character. The regular play group, which also included Mickey and one other child, tended to be exclusive. Other children who wished to join needed the support of a regular member or a teacher.

In summary, sociodramatic play draws upon children's ability to represent societal or fantasy roles and to negotiate these roles with other children. In so doing, they adopt multiple perspectives in the roles they represent, while simultaneously acknowledging the real-world perspectives of their playmates. The roles children choose reflect aspects of experience and personal dispositions. How these roles are represented in play is affected by the theme children choose to render. Different approaches to the thematic aspects of pretense are discussed in the next section.

Themes and feelings

It is often said that children reveal their views of the broader social world in pretend play. However, the nature of these views and their organization in play have been a source of considerable debate. Some theorists argue that pretend scenarios reflect children's knowledge of real-life events (Bretherton, 1984). In this view, Barb played out a familiar bedtime script, one in which adults and children regularly do the things she portrayed. Mothers and fathers talk to children who cry when put to bed. Children need to be covered by fathers and mothers who care for them. Scripted behavior is characterized by sequences that reflect either social conventions (a baby is put to bed, covered, and then told night-night) or the logic of real-life behavior (a fishing pole must be put in the water before a fish can be caught).

Critics of script theory point out that pretend episodes are far more loosely organized than script theory implies (Fein, 1986). Alan's rowing motions were disconnected from the rowboat (in a scripted sequence he would have gotten the oars, climbed into the boat, and then rowed), and Barb asked Sandy to cover a child who was already covered. While Barb knew something about what some mothers might say, how some children might respond at bedtime, and what some fathers might do, Barb's scenario may not reflect a typical bedtime routine and it may not exhaust her knowledge of bedtime routines. Rather, the elements of real life used in pretense represent emotionally vivid events (crying children, irritated mothers) selected from personally consequential experiences, whether real or invented. If so, an observer ought not to conclude from this episode that Barb herself regularly cries at bedtime, that her mother regularly goes out, or that her father regularly provides nighttime care. These events might or might not have actually happened.

A second view of the thematic content of pretense stresses thematic elements called *action plans*, a more abstract sequence than scripts (Garvey, 1977). A threatening monster requires actions to nullify the threat — a denial of chocolate, hiding the baby, or ordering the monster out of the house. The threat serves to organize play actions because a counterthreat is called for. Again, this notion suggests a more rigid level of thematic organization than may actually occur. As illustrated in the play episode involving Sally, Susan, and Shawn, action plans are flexible schemata, readily aborted as new ideas are spontaneously put into the pot.

Psychoanalytic theory, a third view, maintains that pretense reflects children's concerns rather than their objective knowledge (Fein, 1986; Peller, 1954). In this view, inferences from pretend scenarios to actual experiences are risky; Barb might be anxious about abandonment without actually having been abandoned; she might have cried or might have wanted to cry without actually having done so. While the connections between play representations and reality can be unravelled, psychoanalytic theory is more concerned about the symbolic expression of distress than about the actual life experience (Schafer, 1979).

Older children's play, which is also about mothers and children, presents even stronger affective elements. While food must be prepared before baby is fed, and sitting in a highchair reasonably precedes eating, these events establish the play roles and the setting; they are talked about but never enacted. Other, more vivid, emotionally charged events move to center stage. From the perspective of psychoanalytic theory, the most interesting features of this episode are found in the emotional meaning of a monster who threatens the child but not the mother, a mother who is protective and controlling, and a child who is frightened and vulnerable. A standing dog (not daddy), a bath, and a hot stove are expressive elements that add zest to the play. The meanings of the symbols might differ for each of the participants. For Susan, the symbols legitimize feelings of fear and vulnerability; for Sally, feelings of effective coping; and for Shawn, feelings of anger. From this play, the children draw reassurances that the monsters within can be contained. Children use this play to express deeply felt concerns that can be shared because they are widely experienced (Field, 1984; Rubin, Fein, & Vandenberg, 1983).

Each of these theoretical positions might have merit, although they address distinctively different aspects of the behavior. The eagerness with which children respond to such themes suggests that some important aspects of their inner lives are being represented. The degree to which these themes are understood by those participating suggests a shared conceptual framework. Finally, the fluidity, flexibility, and divergent productivity of these thematic constructions reveal a spirit of social tolerance without which sociodramatic play might not occur.

Implications for teachers

Pretense has been viewed by early childhood educators with both enthusiam and apprehension. The enthusiasm comes from the notion that pretense contributes to intellectual and social development. The apprehension comes from its unruliness; pretend scenarios may reveal inaccurate knowledge, social stereotyping, or fascination with the seamy side of life. Numerous suggestions for supporting the shared pretense of young children are offered in this volume. However, the timing and appropriateness of adult involvement in children's sociodramatic play involves some special considerations.

Play misrepresentations

Teachers often insist upon reality-based play representations and many adults have a low threshold for misrepresentations. However, adult interventions that press toward realism might undermine the mental claims that characterize the activity, or replace claims that make sense to the children with those that are comfortable for adults. Rather than break into the play to correct a misconception, teachers need to be careful observers. Armed with information about children's apparent misunderstandings, teachers can plan the curriculum to help children gain more factual and differentiated knowledge about events that interest them. A curriculum based on factual knowledge supplemented by theme-related props might enrich children's pretend ideas, making pretend episodes more differentiated and, perhaps, better informed.

Unacceptable themes?

Some play themes (monsters, superheroes) heighten the children's level of activity. (These themes often stir up powerful feelings in adults. How much excitement should be tolerated in the classroom?) Play themes may, at times, be cruel or in poor taste, expressing anger, anxiety, or a bleak view of life. When should the teacher intervene directly, why, and toward what end?

Teachers need to examine their own feelings and values about the content of children's pretense. Part of the benefits of pretense come from the freedom to express unpleasant thoughts. Skilled teachers can remind children, by their presence and actions, that an adult is available to support children's own efforts to maintain control. Honest appraisals by adults may help to deal with sensitive and personal matters. Discussions at staff meetings and with parents might help to clarify what expectations are realistic for children and what sorts of play will be acceptable in the classroom.

Teachers need to be careful about interpretations of children's pretense. While there is truth in the feelings expressed, events and characterizations are not necessarily true. Children from peaceful families may play about family violence and singletons (only children) may give realistic renderings of sibling rivalry. Play may have more to do with children's need to feel competent and in control than with actual events.

Social facilitation

Sociodramatic play can be viewed as an arena for the practice of social skills. Careful observation will help teachers assess children's social capabilities. Are children able to communicate about pretense? Are they able to share ideas about pretend episodes, objects, and roles? Judicious participation in dramatic play with the children provides an opportunity to model appropriate behaviors, expand a play role, or introduce metacommunicative options the children may not have discovered. However, the benefits of play are greatest when it truly belongs to the children. Children respond differently to unobtrusive and intrusive assistance. At times, children capitalize on an adult suggestion. At other times, adult proposals are ignored or might even disrupt the play. What is needed is thoughtful reciprocity between the children's own constructive processes and the form of assistance given by adults.

References

Abravenel, E., & Gingold, H. (1985). Learning via observation in the second year of life. *Developmental Psychology, 21,* 614–623.

Ariel, S. (1984). Locutions and illocutions. *Journal of Pragmatics, 8,* 221–240.

Ariel, S., Carel, C. A., & Tyano, S. (1985). Uses of children's make-believe play in family therapy: Theory and clinical examples. *Journal of Marriage and Family Therapy, 11,* 47–60.

Bateson, G. (1955). A theory of play and fantasy. *Psychiatric Research Reports, 2,* 39–50.

Belsky, J., Garduque, L., & Hrncir, E. (1984). Assessing performance, competence, and executive capacity in infant play: Relations to home environment and children's play. *Developmental Psychology, 20,* 406–417.

Bretherton, I. (1984). Event representation in symbolic play: Reality and fantasy. In I. Bretherton (Ed.), *Symbolic play: The representation of social understanding.* New York: Academic.

Bronson, W. C. (1981). *Toddlers' behaviors with agemates: Issues of interaction, cognition, and affect.* Norwood, NJ: Ablex.

Cole, D., & LaVoie, J. C. (1985). Fantasy play and related cognitive development in 2- to 6-year-olds. *Developmental Psychology, 21,* 233–240.

Doyle, A. B., Connolly, J., & Rivest, L. P. (1980). The effect of playmate familiarity on the social interaction of young children. *Child Development, 51,* 217–223.

Dunn, J., & Dale, N. (1984). I a daddy: 2-year-olds' collaboration in joint pretend with sibling and mother. In I. Bretherton (Ed.), *Symbolic play: The representation of social understanding* (pp. 131–158). New York: Academic.

Eckerman, C. O., Whatley, J. L., & Kutz, S. L. (1975). The growth of social play with peers during the second year of life. *Developmental Psychology, 11,* 42–49.

Fein, G. G. (1981). Pretend play: An integrative review. *Child Development, 52,* 1095–1118.

Fein, G. G. (1984). The self-building potential of make-believe play or "I got a fish, all by myself." In T. D. Yawkey & A. D. Pellegrini (Eds.), *Child's play: Developmental and applied* (pp. 125–142). Hillsdale, NJ: Erlbaum.

Fein, G. G. (1986). Pretend play: Creativity and consciousness. In D. Gorlitz & J. Wohwill (Eds.), *Curiosity, imagination, and play: On the development of spontaneous motivational and cognitive processes.* Hillsdale, NJ: Erlbaum.

Fein, G. G., & Stork, L. (1981). Sociodramatic play: Social class effects in integrated preschool classrooms. *Journal of Applied Developmental Psychology, 2,* 267–279.

Fein, G. G., Moorin, E. R., & Enslein, J. (1982). Pretense and peer behavior: An intersectoral analysis. *Human Development, 25,* 392–406.

Fenson, L., & Ramsey, D. S. (1981). Effects of modeling action sequences on the play of twelve-, fifteen-, and nineteen-month-old children. *Child Development, 52,* 1028–1036.

Field, T. (1984). Separation stress of young children transfering to new schools. *Developmental Psychology, 20,* 786–792.

Field, T., De Stefano, L., & Koewler, J. H., III. (1982). Fantasy play of toddlers and preschoolers. *Developmental Psychology, 18,* 503–508.

Forys, S. K., & McCune-Nicolich, L. (1984). Shared pretend: Sociodramatic play at 3 years of age. In I. Bretherton (Ed.), *Symbolic play: The representation of social understanding* (pp. 159–191). New York: Academic.

Garvey, C. (1977). *Play.* Cambridge, MA: Harvard University Press.

Giffin, H. (1984). The coordination of shared meaning in the creation of a shared make-believe reality. In I. Bretherton (Ed.), *Symbolic play: The representation of social understanding* (pp. 73–100). New York: Academic.

Goncu, A., & Kessel, F. (1984). Children's play: A contextual-functional perspective. In F. S. Kessel & A. Goncu (Eds.), *Analyzing children's play dialogues: New directions for child development.* San Francisco: Jossey-Bass.

Iwanaga, M. (1973). Development of interpersonal play structures in 3-, 4-, and 5-year-old children. *Journal of Research and Development in Education, 6,* 71–82.

Johnson, J. E., & Ershler, J. (1981). Developmental trends in preschool play as a function of classroom program and child gender. *Child Development, 52,* 995–1004.

McLoyd, V. C., Warren, D., & Thomas, E. A. C. (1984). Anticipatory and fantastic role enactment in preschool triads. *Developmental Psychology, 20,* 807–814.

Miller, P., & Garvey, C. (1984). Mother-baby role play: Its origins in social support. In I. Bretherton (Ed.), *Symbolic play: The representation of social understanding* (pp. 101–130). New York: Academic.

Mueller, E., & Brenner, J. (1977). The origins of social skills and interaction among playgroup toddlers. *Child Development, 48,* 854–861.

O'Connell, B., & Bretherton, I. (1984). Toddlers' play, alone and with mother: The role of maternal guidance. In I. Bretherton (Ed.), *Symbolic play: The representation of social understanding* (pp. 337–368). New York: Academic.

Olszewski, P., & Fuson, K. C. (1982). Verbally expressed fantasy play of preschoolers as a function of toy structure. *Developmental Psychology, 18,* 57–61.

Peller, L. (1954). Libidinal phases, ego development, and play. *Psychoanalytic Study of the Child, 9,* 178–198.

Ross, H. (1982). Establishment of social games among toddlers. *Developmental Psychology, 18,* 509–518.

Rubin, K. H., Watson, K., & Jambor, T. (1978). Free-play behaviors in preschool and kindergarten children. *Child Development, 49,* 534–536.

Rubin, K. H., Fein, G. G., & Vandenberg, B. (1983). Play. In P. Mussen (Ed.), *Handbook of child psychology* (Vol. 4, pp. 693–774). New York: Wiley.

Rubenstein, J. L., & Howes, C. (1976). The effects of peers on toddler interaction with mothers and toys. *Child Development, 47,* 597–605.

Saltz, E., Dixon, D., & Johnson, J. (1977). Training disadvantaged preschoolers on various fantasy activities: Effects on cognitive functioning and impulse control. *Child Development, 48,* 367–380.

Schafer, W. (1979). Expressive symbolism in spontaneous play before two years of age. In D. Wolf (Ed.), *Early symbolization. New directions in child development.* San Francisco: Jossey-Bass.

Schwartzman, H. B. (1978). *Transformations: The anthropology of children's play.* New York: Plenum.

Smilansky, S. (1968). *The effects of sociodramatic play on disadvantaged preschool children.* New York: Wiley.

Watson, M. W., & Fischer, K. W. (1980). Development of social roles in elicited and spontaneous behavior during the preschool years. *Developmental Psychology, 16,* 483–494.

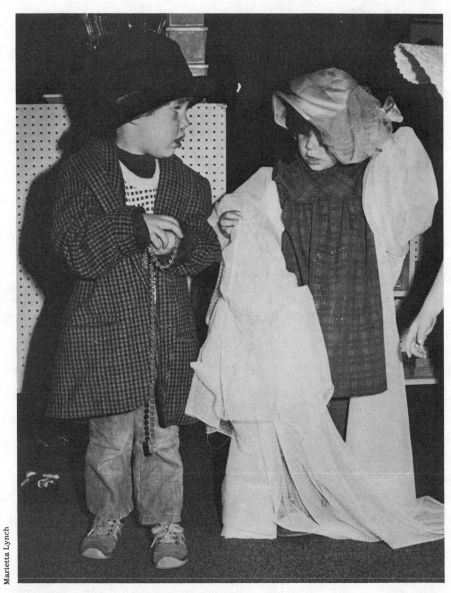

Pretend play provides a forum for children to develop, practice, and demonstrate newly emerging perspective-taking skills. Sociodramatic play in early childhood may be causally related to social-cognitive development in the early years.

Marietta Lynch

CHAPTER EIGHT

Social Play and Perspective-Taking

KENNETH H. RUBIN AND NINA HOWE

Joshua: (The 4½-year-old son of the first author approaches his friend by singing): "He-Man, He-Man, and the Masters of the Universe! Hey Cara, wanna play He-Man™?"

Cara (a 5-year-old female neighbor playing in the Rubins's sandbox): "Who's he?"

Joshua (incredulous): "You mean you don't know? Wow! He-Man is kinda like a superhero. He's Prince Adam in disguise. Don't you know anything 'bout Castle Grayskull and Skeletor?"

Cara: "Nope, don't know anything. Hey Josh, wanna build a road for these cars?"

Joshua (ignores Cara's countersuggestion): "I'll tell you 'bout He-Man. We can build Castle Grayskull and I'll be He-Man. You can be the evil Skeletor."

And so it went; another summer afternoon in the Rubin backyard with Joshua and Cara, two preschool-aged children discussing the ins and outs, good and evil, weapons and accoutrements of all characters that bear some minimal relation to He-Man and the Masters of the Universe toy collection and television series. Joshua filled this particular afternoon with vivid and minute details concerning his almost favorite toy characters (third to his Care Bears and to his life-sized doll, Steve Martin Rubin, respectively). Cara, of course, was the recipient of these detailed pronouncements and by the day's end, she could recall, for any willing listener, everything there was to know about He-Man, his friends and enemies, and his assorted collection of weapons, traveling paraphernalia, and exotic pets. Indeed, by the end of the afternoon, Cara could manage a pretty decent imitation of the evil Skeletor.

This description provides the reader with a sense for what children can learn, practice, and consolidate in and around the boundaries of a typical sociodramatic play episode. Joshua, for example, practiced and tried to perfect his communicative and tutorial skills. In directing the play episode, Joshua set the rules of He-Man, described the various roles, and then played some of the roles within an agreed upon rule-governed boundary. Furthermore, in order to get Cara to participate, he had to make sure that she received his information willingly and that there would be a reasonable give-and-take about the allocation of roles within the play frame (Cara agreed to be the evil Skeletor if she could also be the good Teela). In short, Joshua practiced the social skills of communicating, negotiating, teaching, directing, initiating, and maintaining a social interactive episode with positive affect and with a sense of fair play that summer afternoon.

Of course, Cara gained from the playful experience as well. Cara also practiced communicating, listening, and negotiating skills. She learned all about a new (for her) phenomenon that would undeniably improve her status in the community of preschool-aged He-Man aficionados. Moreover, Cara played a wide variety of roles, male and female, good and evil, and she followed numerous role-relational rules (Skeletor never gets to defeat He-Man; the reverse is always the case!) within the play frame.

In a nutshell, this brief example shows some of the many benefits of sociodramatic play for young children. Although one may wonder about the value of playing He-Man, the children were, in fact, engaging in a positive affective encounter that allowed the practice and maintenance of social skills. Implicit in all of the benefits derived from this play episode is the possibility that social pretense allows children to understand simultaneously multiple roles, cognitions, and emotions. This ability is labeled *perspective-taking*.

In this chapter, we will examine the conceptual and empirical links that psychologists and educators have made between pretend play and the development of perspective-taking skills. Our examination will involve, in sequence, (1) defining pretend play and perspective-taking, (2) noting evidence for causal and correlational linkages between play and perspective-taking, and (3) describing recent conceptual connections between the two phenomena.

Defining pretend play and perspective-taking

Definitions of *play* are not easy to come by. Philosophers, psychologists, and educators have had a long, often unsuccessful history of attempting to define it. A recent review by Rubin, Fein, and Vandenberg (1983) provides this definition. *Play* is intrinsically motivated; characterized by an attention to means rather than ends; free from externally imposed rules; laden with positive affect; and characterized by an *as if*, nonliteral set (pretense). These elements distinguish play from related activities such as exploration, construction, and games.

Perspective-taking can be defined as the ability to *simultaneously* consider, one's own, thoughts, feelings, and literal, visual views of the world along with another's. The study of perspective-taking has its roots in the earliest writing of Piaget (1926) who suggested strongly that young children were so immersed in their own viewpoints that they were incapable of imagining any other perspective. Piaget's original assumption was that young children were highly egocentric and that they became less so with age.

The connection between pretend play and perspective-taking stems from a consideration of the processes by which children become less egocentric. First, according to Piaget and others, children are socially motivated from birth. Such motivations typically lead children into social situations with adults and peers in which the participants may not share similar viewpoints or cognitive skills. These situations tend to throw children's minds into states of *cognitive conflict;* conflicts that must be resolved for productive social growth and positive interaction experiences to ensue.

Take, for example, the following situation. During fantasy play, one 4-year-old boy adopted the role of father while his same-sex, same-age companion Jesse took the role of mother:

Father: "So long. I'll see ya later. It's time to go to work."

Mother: "Hey, wait for me! I gotta go to work too!"

Father: "Hey, my mom don't work . . . you stay here."

Mother: "Well my mom works . . . lotsa womens work ya know. My mom is a perfessor at the unibersity."

Father: "O.K. then, just hurry so we won't be late. Are you sure ya wanna work?" (Rubin, 1980, p. 75)

As the reader can note, this is a social situation in which one of the play partners (the father) is challenged by a perspective different from his own. The situation forces the child to adapt his thinking to accommodate the new information. By accepting his playmate's statement that women do work, the child has broadened his knowledge of the social world and he has moved another step beyond his own egocentered perspective.

Such is the connection between pretend play and perspective-taking. Pretense allows the child to produce new roles and to practice already known roles in an anxiety-free, rule-governed social network.

In Piagetian terms, pretend play enables children to develop and practice *decentration* and *reversibility*. Decentration skills involve the ability to simultaneously consider more than a single aspect of an object or event. Reversibility is the ability to understand that a thought carried out in one direction ("I'll be He-Man") can always be inverted or carried out in the opposite direction ("Now, I'm Joshua again.") For example, in the episode just described, the father (Todd) slipped quickly out of his pretense role when mother (Jesse) queried his position that mothers do not work. Todd's response, "My mom don't work," was made after he *reversed* roles; he returned from the pretend role of father to himself. Most likely Todd realized that he was both Todd and father and that his partner was simultaneously both Jesse and mother (decentration).

The bottom line is that many theorists and researchers believe strongly that decentration is **the** critical variable underlying the child's ability to take another's perspective (e.g., Shantz, 1983). Given that fantasy play affords children the opportunity to develop decentration, it follows that psychologists and educators would posit a connection between pretense activities and perspective-taking. Indeed, a very strong contingent of psychologists have advocated training young children in sociodramatic play to help them develop decentration skills (and more particularly, to develop perspective-taking or role-taking skills).

Pretend play training studies

Smilansky (1968), in perhaps the most often cited play training study, provided low-income Israeli children with opportunities to engage in sociodramatic play centering around the themes of medical clinic and grocery store. After an intervention period, Smilansky discovered that the play-tutored children not only engaged in more dramatic play than IQ and age-matched controls (who did not receive training), but they also performed better on a measure of communicative development. Ostensibly, the ability to communicate effectively is underwritten by an understanding that the speaker must be sensitive to her or his listener's thoughts, feelings, and abilities (Piaget, 1926). Unfortunately, much of Smilansky's data was not analyzed appropriately; consequently, the findings of her landmark study must be viewed with caution.

Nevertheless, Smilansky's work directly influenced many other researchers who pursued the relation between sociodramatic play and perspective-taking skills. Much of the data clearly supports the play/role-taking link. For example, Burns and Brainerd (1979), Fink (1976), Rosen (1974), Smith and Syddall (1978), and Saltz and Johnson (1974), among others, have found that pretend play training improves young children's abilities to understand the thoughts, feelings, or literal viewpoints of others.

One puzzling fact, however, is that play training produces as many failures as successes in social cognitive advances. Moreover, play training within particular studies often improves one kind of perspective-taking (e.g., the ability to understand other's thoughts), but not other kinds (e.g., another person's feelings) (Brainerd, 1982; Connolly, 1980). These rather curious findings have led psychologists to question the efficacy of social-fantasy play training programs for young children. Perhaps foremost among current concerns is the fact that many of the training studies have been methodologically flawed; researchers have often failed to use appropriate control group comparisons, and the outcome measures of perspective-taking have, very often, been unreliable and invalid (see Rubin, 1980, for a relevant critical review). Furthermore, the target groups appear to vary from study to study; in some cases, preschoolers are the recipients of training, in others kindergartners serve as targets. In addition, sometimes children from lower socioeconomic statuses (SES) receive compensatory intervention, while at other times, middle-class children are tutored. The bottom line is that, at present, we do not know whether pretend play serves any one particular age or SES group better.

Given the problems of inadequate control group comparisons and weak measures of perspective-taking, it seems appropriate to conclude that any causal link between social pretense and perspective-taking has yet to be established empirically to everyone's satisfaction. On an optimistic note, we fully expect researchers to continue their efforts with greater methodological rigor in years to come. In the meantime, however, we should examine recent correlational data in which researchers have attempted to consider the short- and long-term relations between pretend play and perspective-taking.

Correlational studies of pretend play and perspective-taking

The inconclusive reports from play training studies have left some researchers wondering whether or not any relation, causal and otherwise, exists between pretense play and role-taking. Our introductory statements build up an expectation for a positive relation; yet, the experimental, training data are mixed.

Perhaps researchers were on the wrong track when they attempted to provide children with play training experiences. The reader should remember that we defined play as a voluntary, spontaneously produced activity laden with positive affect. Is it not possible that any children's activity led by adult tutors in a regular (daily), nonspontaneous fashion *fails* to meet this definitional criteria of play? If this is the case, might it not be reasonable to ask whether those activities that do meet our definitional criteria relate, in any way, to the development of social-cognitive skills?

In a recent longitudinal research program launched at the University of Waterloo, we examined whether spontaneous, natural pretense activity correlated either concurrently or predictively with social-cognitive indexes in kindergarten and Grades 1 and 2. We further examined whether *all* forms of pretend play were equally predictive of social-cognitive development in early childhood. This latter question derived from two factors:

(1) Even in the preschool years (ages 3 and 4), children tend to exhibit fantasy play in a group interactive context (Rubin et al., 1983). Thus, the social-contextual *norm* at this age for dramatic activity involves group-cooperative interaction.

(2) Some play training advocates offer their pretense tutorials in noninteractive settings (e.g., Golomb, Gowing, & Friedman, 1982; Guthrie & Hudson, 1979), a strategy that may encourage non-normative activity. Tutored children may instead engage in solitary dramatic play in the classroom, a form of behavior that falls outside the norm and makes a child vulnerable to adverse judgments by peers and teachers.

Briefly, our correlational analysis of children's pretend play had, as its impetus, two studies. First, in a small-scaled report, Rubin and Maioni (1975) indicated that a positive relation existed between the dramatic play produced naturally in the preschool classroom and a measure of spatial perspective-taking. Second, Connolly and Doyle (1984) found that the frequency of observed, classroom sociodramatic play correlated significantly and positively with various role-taking measures.

However, in these studies, the authors were interested in establishing whether or not a link exists between pretend play enactment and social-cognition at a given (concurrent) point in time. As such, the results of these two studies tell little about the *causal* relation between play and social-cognitive development. In short, the results may as easily indicate that perspective-taking skills are prerequisite to the production of fantasy play as they indicate the reverse.

Our more recent longitudinal research allowed us to examine whether various forms of naturally and spontaneously produced pretense in kindergarten predicts social and social-cognitive skills in Grades 1 and 2 (Rubin, 1986). From the outset, we should note strongly that our data do not support the contention that all forms of dramatic play are predictive of competence.

For example, kindergarten children who engaged in relatively high frequencies of solitary-dramatic play (as opposed to those who engaged in relatively high frequencies of sociodramatic play) were rated by their Grades 1 and 2 teachers as socially incompetent; furthermore, these kindergarten solitary-dramaticists demonstrate poor social problem-solving skills in Grades 1 and 2! Social problem-solving skills, which involve the ability to solve dilemmas in one's social milieu (e.g., making friends, getting a desired object from another child, seeking help. See Rubin & Krasnor, 1986, for a relevant review), reportedly require prerequisite perspective-taking abilities (Spivack, Platt, & Shure, 1976).

Similarly, when kindergarten pretense is exhibited near, but not with, others (parallel-dramatic play), it is predictive of peer rejection, teacher ratings of social maladaptation, and social problem-solving deficits in Grades 1 and 2. It is important to note, however, that even in kindergarten, both solitary- and parallel-pretend play correlate negatively with index of social competence and social problem-solving skills. Thus, one cannot assume that these forms of dramatic play *cause* later difficulties; we simply do not have the data to suggest that this is the case. Rather, it is likely a high frequency of nonsocial pretense in classroom settings reflects a more general lag in the development of social skills (see also, Rubin, 1982). The cause of this lag is, as yet, unknown; we hope to address this issue in future research efforts. At any rate, given our data, it would appear important for researchers and teachers not to encourage children to play dramatically in ways that are known to relate to negative developmental indexes.

The good news is that sociodramatic play, the most common form of pretend enactment observed during naturalistic, kindergarten free play periods, does not correlate negatively with social and social-cognitive developmental indexes in kindergarten and Grades 1 and 2. Instead, it correlates significantly and positively with measures of perspective-taking (in kindergarten and Grade 1) and social problem-solving skills (Grades 1 and 2). However, kindergarten measures of social competence and social-cognition do not predict the production of observed sociodramatic play in Grades 1 and 2. Moreover, observations of sociodramatic play in Grades 1 and 2 are not significantly related with concurrent measures of social competence and social cognition. These data suggest a possible causal link between sociodramatic play in kindergarten and subsequent social-cognitive development.

Finally, in addition to our significant empirical, correlational data, we would like to offer a conceptual analysis that should make clear the inextricable link between perspective-taking and pretend play.

Play and perspective-taking: A conceptual analysis

In previous sections of this chapter, we have argued that some forms of play involve perspective-taking. We have suggested further that practicing sociodramatic play may help advance and strengthen these social-cognitive skills. In this section, we try to describe the qualitatively different types of perspective-taking that may be implicated in developmentally different forms of play.

One of the more comprehensive and creative models of perspective-taking has been developed by Selman (1980). Basically, Selman argues that role-taking in childhood is not an all-or-none phenomenon (it is too simplistic to think that children either can or cannot take another's perspective). Rather, perspective-taking is viewed as a multidimensional, multistage construct that ranges from the very young child's inability to comprehend that any view other than her or his own exists to the adolescent's understanding of how a society or a generalized other would perceive a given social situation.

To assess his hierarchical model of perspective-taking, Selman relied on interviews with children about hypothetical social dilemmas. Such interviews may be problematic for inferring **when** children first develop particular types of perspective-taking skills because they are heavily reliant on children's ability to express their thoughts verbally. Consequently, to paraphrase an old expression, it may be that children's actions are more developed than their words. In our conceptual analysis that follows, we argue that by observing children's play, we can infer particular levels of perspective-taking earlier than Selman, who relied entirely on interview data, suggests. Because this book deals specifically with the early years of childhood, our conceptual analysis will focus on the first three of Selman's stages.

At **Stage 0** (3- to 6-years-old), *egocentric role-taking*, children can understand that others may have their own distinctive thoughts and feelings about things; however, they cannot distinguish between their own perspective and that of others in the same social situation. Instead children judge that all others view this shared social experience in an identical fashion.

At **Stage 1** (6- to 8-years-old), *subjective role-taking*, children make the distinction between self- and other-centered viewpoints of the same social situation, but cannot interpret either their own or the other's actions and thoughts from the other's perspective. A major advance made at this stage is the understanding of another's intentions.

In **Stage 2** (8- to 10-years-old), *self-reflective role-taking*, children can think that others think of them in particular ways. Furthermore, children understand that other people's perspectives of them can have implications for behaviors toward them. As Flavell writes,

The fundamental insight of Level 2 may come down to this: I know I could conceivably tune in on your cognitive perspective because we are both subjects or persons rather than objects; I also know that you could do the same to me for the same reason; it follows that you may be doing so at the very moment I am and that your tuning may therefore pick up my tuning. Such an insight, whenever it comes, must represent a giant step in the development of social cognition (1977, p. 133).

Having briefly described the first three of Selman's stages (there are two others), we can now relate them to perspective-taking and play. To make our case we will focus primarily on Selman's Stage 1, subjective role-taking. The work of Garvey (1977) is particularly relevant here. Garvey has suggested that there are, at least, two essential criteria in order for cooperative social pretense to occur. First, the child must be able to discriminate between literal (real) and nonliteral (pretend) meanings. For example, in social fantasy discourse the participants must recognize when their play partners are just pretending (as in the initiation of a Luke Skywalker, rough-and-tumble episode) and when they really mean it (true aggression). The ability to make such distinctions requires that children correctly read the intentions of their playmates, a skill that falls clearly at the Stage 1 level.

The second criteria noted by Garvey concerns rule abstraction. Cooperative dramatic play requires children to comprehend and follow specific rules that apply to particular play episodes. These rules include an understanding of turn-taking norms and a focus on keeping the players on track in their chosen and mutually agreed upon roles. In short, to play successfully in a sociodramatic fashion, children must be able to infer intentions, make distinctions between literal and nonliteral behaviors, and conceptualize role expectations for themselves and their play partners.

These skills, which can be observed in action during the social-pretense play of preschool-aged children are all criterial for Stage 1 perspective-taking. However, according to Selman, Stage 1 role-taking is not fully in children's social-cognitive repertoires until they are from 6- to 8-years-old! Similar evidence for the belief that perspective-taking levels can be inferred at earlier ages from observations of play than from interviews can be found in Rubin and Pepler's (1980) conceptual analysis of children's games.

Implications for educators

In summary, we have demonstrated that pretense play and social perspective-taking are related, both conceptually and empirically. We have argued also that not all forms of pretense reflect normal growth and development for children. For example, children whose dramatic play in social settings is of a nonsocial nature appear to be rated as maladjusted by their teachers, and they may have difficulties in social cognition. It is important for us to note, however, that it is premature to assume that a high frequency of nonsocial-pretense causes later socio-emotional and social-cognitive problems; at this time, it is safer to say that when children deviate significantly from their age-group norms regarding nonsocial pretense, (e.g., the frequency of production is greater than or equal to one standard deviation from their age group and classroom play norms) they may be demonstrating, in their play, a lag in social and social-cognitive development.

This brings up two critical issues. First, for some children, high frequencies of nonsocial pretend play are quite normal. For example, one would not expect a large amount of cooperative fantasy activity in groups of 1½- and 2-year-olds. Consequently, there would be no reason to conclude that very young children who play on their own in a nonliteral fashion are demonstrating developmental lags.

Second, it is critical that the reader not confuse the display of nonsocial pretense in situations where the child is alone versus with others. It is quite normal, and indeed creative, for 3-, 4-, and 5-year-olds to play alone in their rooms with their imaginary companions, dolls, and action figures and props. Our message is that when such solitary pretend activities are brought into classroom or other group (social) settings, there may be a problem. If one observes 4- or 5-year-olds who spend the bulk of their free play time in nonsocial dramatic play, it may be wise to assess, more formally, the child's developmental progress.

In conclusion, we believe that evidence is now beginning to emerge to suggest that sociodramatic play in early childhood is causally related to social-cognitive development in the early elementary school years. These results follow nicely from our conceptualization of social-pretense as a forum for providing children with opportunities to develop, practice, and demonstrate newly emerging perspective-taking skills. The bottom line is that psychologists, educators, and parents who advocate sociodramatic experiences for young children are on the right track. Our only hope is that the world will not be populated by multitudes of He-Men and Teelas in years to come; after all, not everyone can live in Castle Grayskull!

Jean Berlfein

Teachers can either reinforce classic traditional sex-stereotyped choices or increase children's awareness of all the opportunities open to them in a non-sex-typed society the children themselves may someday build.

References

Brainerd, C. J. (1982). Effects of group and individual dramatic play training on cognitive development. In D. J. Pepler & K. H. Rubin, (Eds.), *The play of children: Current theory and research*. Basel, Switzerland: Karger.

Burns, S., & Brainerd, C. J. (1979). Effects of constructive and dramatic play on perspective-taking in very young children. *Developmental Psychology, 15*, 512–521.

Connolly, J. (1980). *The relationship between social pretend play and social competence in preschoolers*. Unpublished doctoral dissertation, Concordia University, Montreal.

Connolly, J., & Doyle, A. B. (1984). Relation of social fantasy play to social competence in preschoolers. *Developmental Psychology, 20*, 797–806.

Fink, R. S. (1976). Role of imaginary play in cognitive development. *Psychological Reports, 39*, 895–906.

Flavell, J. H. (1977). *Cognitive development*. Englewood Cliffs, NJ: Prentice-Hall.

Garvey, C. (1977). Play with language. In B. Tizard & D. Harvey (Eds.), *Biology of play*. Philadelphia: Lippincott.

Golomb, C., Gowing, E., & Friedman, L. (1982). Play and cognition: Studies of pretense play and conservation of quantity. *Journal of Experimental Child Psychology, 33*, 257–279.

Guthrie, K., & Hudson, L. (1979). Training conservation through symbolic play: A second look. *Child Development, 50*, 1269–1271.

Piaget, J. (1926). *The language and thought of the child*. London: Routledge & Kegan Paul.

Rosen, C. (1974). The effects of sociodramatic play on problem-solving behavior among culturally disadvantaged preschool children. *Child Development, 45*, 920–927.

Rubin, K. H. (1980). Fantasy play: Its role in the development of social skills and social cognition. In K. H. Rubin (Ed.), *Children's play*. San Francisco: Jossey-Bass.

Rubin, K. H. (1982). Nonsocial play in preschoolers: Necessarily evil? *Child Development, 53*, 651–657.

Rubin, K. H. (1986). Play, peer interaction, and social development. In A. Gottfried & C. Brown (Eds.), *Play interactions: The contribution of play materials and parental involvement to child development*. Lexington, MA: Heath.

Rubin, K. H., Fein, G. G., & Vandenberg, B. (1983). Play. In E. M. Hetherington (Ed.), *Handbook of child psychology: Vol. 4. Socialization, personality and social development*. New York: Wiley.

Rubin, K. H., & Krasnor, L. R. (1986). Social-cognitive and social behavioral perspectives on problem-solving. In M. Perlmutter (Ed.), *Minnesota symposia on child psychology* (Vol. 18). Hillsdale, NJ: Erlbaum.

Rubin, K. H., & Maioni, T. L. (1975). Play preference and its relationship to egocentrism, popularity, and classification skills in preschoolers. *Merrill-Palmer Quarterly, 21*, 171–179.

Rubin, K. H., & Pepler, D. J. (1980). The relationship of child's play to social-cognitive growth and development. In H. C. Foot, A. J. Chapman, & J. R. Smith (Eds.), *Friendship and social relations in children*. London: Wiley.

Saltz, E., & Johnson, J. (1974). Training for thematic-fantasy play in culturally disadvantaged children: Preliminary results. *Journal of Educational Psychology, 66*, 623–630.

Selman, R. (1980). *The growth of interpersonal understanding.* New York: Academic.

Shantz, C. U. (1983). Social cognition. In J. H. Flavell & E. Markman (Eds.), *Handbook of child psychology: Vol. 3. Cognitive development.* New York: Wiley.

Smilansky, S. (1968). *The effects of sociodramatic play on disadvantaged preschool children.* New York: Wiley.

Smith, P. K. (1977). Social fantasy play in young children. In B. Tizard & D. Harvey (Eds.), *Biology of play.* Philadelphia: Lippincott.

Smith, P. K., & Syddall, S. (1978). Play and non-play tutoring in preschool children: Is it play or tutoring which matters? *British Journal of Educational Psychology, 48*, 315–325.

Spivack, G., Platt, J. J., & Shure, M. B. (1976). *The problem-solving approach to adjustment.* San Francisco: Jossey-Bass.

Mary Ellen Powers

In helping children explore their own abilities and the environment in which they live, teachers influence children's notions of gender identity, their personal goals, and their choices of friends and activities.

CHAPTER 9

The Play of Boys and Girls

MARSHA B. LISS

When an observer enters a preschool classroom, she or he may first think that it is less structured than the primary classroom. However, it actually has many structured or designated activity areas. Among these are areas for pretend play (house), construction activities (blocks), transportation activities (trucks), and shop activities (woodworking). The observer might further notice that some play areas are occupied by boys and others by girls. This chapter will explore some of these play areas that are often sex-differentiated and raise questions about why they develop.

The presence of sex-differentiated activity in children's play has been examined extensively. The results have been more complex than initially supposed. Situational variables, play history (familiarity, familial influences), availability of play materials, and teacher and peer presence affect play behavior regardless of a child's gender. In this chapter, areas of research such as traditional play preferences and toy choices, family variables, teacher influences, studies of intervention in play choices, and dramatic play will be discussed. While there are some consistencies across studies, there are inconsistencies as well. Readers may draw their own conclusions about the implications of this research for children's development. Experiences and feedback from peers and adults in the impressionable early years form the basis for later behaviors and attitudes. Therefore, one implication of differential experiences related to gender is the development of differential outlooks and future goals.

Play preferences and toy choices

Children's preferences for different toys and play activities have been an area of child development research since the 1930s. Benjamin (1932), Parten (1932), and Vance and McCall (1934) pioneered in this

127

field, identifying the earliest age at which sex-segregated preschool areas appeared in the classrooms they observed. Some of their specific findings have been observed in classrooms as recently as the late 1970s and 1980s. However, during the 50-year span, some preferences have changed along with changes in children's toy preferences overall. The number of articles discussing *what do boys and girls tend to play with in free play?* are far too numerous to cite in entirety, but I will highlight a few and summarize the major traditional male and female preferred areas and those in which crossovers are found.

Some activity areas are predominantly occupied by males. In earliest studies (Bridges, 1927; Parten, 1932; Vance & McCall, 1934), boys were found to prefer blocks, tools, and cars and trucks. Over the course of the next decades, the latter became known as *transportation toys*, a category extended to include cars, trucks, and trains, both miniature and child-size. Transportation toys continued to be mentioned in almost all lists of preferred male activities (e.g., Fagot & Patterson, 1969; Serbin, Tonick, & Sternglanz, 1977; Smith, 1980). Another very consistent male-dominated area is the sandbox, although specific types of sandbox play are not usually described (Fagot & Patterson, 1969; Halliday & McNaughton, 1982; Lott, 1983). A third common area of boys' toy preference is blocks and construction toys (such as Legos®), a preference stable through the years (Fagot & Patterson, 1969; Serbin, Tonick, & Sternglanz, 1977; Smith, 1980).

In recent years, the rather large category of outdoor active play has been added to this list. While mentioned by many researchers (Fagot & Littman, 1975; Fagot & Patterson, 1969; Lott, 1983; Smith, 1980), outdoor active play does not always mean the same thing. Sometimes this play refers to running, other times it refers to climbing, and for kindergarten and older children, it may refer to organized boys' sports activities, especially those involving throwing and catching (Halverson, Roberton, & Langendorfer, 1982).

Lastly, a commonly assumed, but much less studied, defined, or observed (regardless of gender) male-dominated activity is rough-and-tumble play, which includes wrestling and for school-age children physical contact sports (DiPietro, 1981; Smith & Connolly, 1972). Boys are more likely to engage in fighting and killing games, and simulated war games, but these are a subset of both indoor and outdoor active play (Tizard, Philps, & Plewis, 1976). Generally, these activities are group activities that require physical movement in a somewhat nonrestricted area.

Girls' activities, on the other hand, tend to include small-group interactions that are confined in space and physical movement. Again, starting with the earliest descriptions by Bridges (1927), Parten (1932), and Vance and McCall (1934), girls preferred scissors and paper, paints, beads, chalkboards, dolls, and house. Girls' preferences for playing house or family games continue to appear with some regularity according to Fagot and Patterson (1969); Serbin, Tonick, and Sternglanz (1977); and Smith (1980).

Highly related to house play, where the players are the involved characters, is doll play where the players act out scenes with miniature toy people. Doll play was a frequent and preferred girls' activity (Fagot & Patterson, 1969) in several earlier studies, but tends to be less favored today. It has not made the five-best list in recent studies (e.g., Halliday & McNaughton, 1982; Liss & Etaugh, 1983).

The scissor, paper, and painting tasks mentioned in the earlier studies are categorized as arts and crafts in recent literature. Arts and crafts (or some subset of activities in this area) are common preferred activities for girls (Fagot & Patterson, 1969; Halliday & McNaughton, 1982; Lott, 1983; Serbin, Tonick, & Sternglanz, 1977; Smith, 1980). The parallel for girls to boys' active outdoor play is quiet indoor play, a predominantly female activity. Fagot and Littman (1975) also found that girls often engaged in conversation play or in other quiet sedentary indoor play behaviors. Carpenter and Huston-Stein (1980) consider this a highly structured activity. They believe that this activity choice might reflect a liking for structure and teacher presence, rather than a preference for the activity itself.

Books, music, and other listening activities have also been cited as female play areas in various investigations (Fagot & Patterson, 1969; Halliday & McNaughton, 1982; Smith, 1980). Lest it seem that girls never engage in large muscle physical activity, one author (DiPietro, 1981) examined young children's physical play and found that while boys engage in many of the rough-and-tumble or contact physical activities, girls prefer jumping and noncontact physical play activities.

These findings may at first glance seem unchallenged and unchanging. However, there are signs of crossovers in preference — male activities preferred by females and vice versa, or activities without strong male-female differences. For instance, Lott (1983) and Halliday and McNaughton (1982) found no differences between boys and girls in the amount of attention to books or other teacher-related activities. This finding disagrees with Smith (1980) and Carpenter and Huston-Stein (1980) who found more females in teacher-related or teacher-present areas of the room. More startlingly, blocks (Lott, 1983) and climbing (Halliday & McNaughton, 1982) may now be equally preferred by both sexes. Furthermore, Fagot and Littman (1975) found that boys and girls both engage in a great deal of listening activities. Earlier, Fagot and Patterson (1969) reported that this was a female activity. In her observations of children, Lott (1983) found that both sexes played indoors with gym equipment (previously believed to be an outdoor active play activity), played house, participated in story group, and did woodworking.

Despite the impressive history of observations of children in free play, only a few areas maintain consistent sex differences, and these are not always the most preferred areas for that sex overall. For instance, Halliday and McNaughton (1982) found that while boys played more with transportation toys than did girls, this was not a significant difference, and boys did not prefer transportation toys over most other activities. This created a low enough frequency to make the sex difference irrelevant in addition to being statistically nonsignificant. Furthermore, while Lott (1983) found that girls are more accepting of novel toys than boys, Carpenter (1983) found the opposite.

It appears that boys and girls in the 1980s sometimes prefer to play with same-sex peers, in sex-segregated classroom areas, especially if teachers or other adults are present. Left to their own accord, children are freer to play with what and with whom they want. The particular choices made by boys and girls under these circumstances rise and fall in popularity and degree of sex-typing. However, evidence of sex-segregated play areas and play styles continues to appear. How do these sex differences arise? In the following sections, I will highlight some of the variables that influence how and why children play the way they do.

Social influences on play

Family influences

Detailed studies of family influences on play are few, but point in the same direction: A major source of children's early sex-typed play is the home. Familial influences work in two ways: direct feedback and modeling. The modeling of sex-typed play is most pronounced when the parent plays with the child or when the child imitates sex-differentiated parental activities such as domestic activity or driving.

The most obvious way in which parents influence children is by presenting them with toys they consider appropriate for the child's sex. Rheingold and Cook (1975) did the most innovative and widely cited study in this area. They examined children's rooms, focusing on the type of room (its areas and furnishings) and type of toys in the room (most of which were given by the parents). They found clear sex differences across age groups. In fact, an innocent observer could easily distinguish the boys' and girls' rooms by the presence or absence of toys such as sports equipment and transportation toys or dolls and kitchen implements. It is easy to see that children become familiar with sex-typed toys at home and carry this familiarity into the classroom.

Recently, Liss and Etaugh (1983) examined parental input in terms of presents given, and chores performed or assigned at home. In that study, children received more sex-typed presents (for holiday gifts) than they had even requested. For example, girls who wanted baseballs and bats and boys who wanted play kitchens did not get them. Instead, these children received highly sex-stereotyped or traditional items. In addition, boys and girls performed different chores at home. Notably, girls washed dishes, baby-sat, and did laundry, while boys did outdoor chores such as yardwork. Expectations of parental behavior are also evident in toy sales: Toy salespeople persuade parents (especially fathers) to buy more sex-typed toys for male than for female children (Ungar, 1982). Among these male sex-typed purchases are occupational-related items in the sciences (Astin, 1975). Thus, other adults may transmit sex-role expectations to children through their parents.

Moreover, a few studies on how children and parents play together have indicated sex-typing especially on the part of fathers (Lamb, 1977; Langlois & Downs, 1980). These sex-typed interactions represent both modeling and feedback for play behavior. In a related manner, Fling and Manosevitz (1972) found that parents believed their children were more sex-typed (and should be — especially males) than the children's actual sex-typed toy preferences and sex-role orientations indicated.

Another way that parents influence children's sex-typed play has been infrequently studied, but may determine the ease with which some activities (such as climbing) can be performed. Kaiser and Phinney (1983) assessed the relationship between clothing and sex-typing in young preschoolers. Given the age of the children, it is likely that the parents rather than the children purchased and selected the children's clothing. The investigators found that young children are quite knowledgeable about clothing and who wears what and under what circumstances. Who selects clothing may be a subtle difference to parents, but important to children whose very actions may be hindered or aided by type of clothing they wear.

Teacher influences

A parallel influence to the family in the life of the young child is the teacher. The teacher represents another powerful adult whom children presume to be all-knowing and caring, and who becomes an admired individual whose words and deeds children accept as truth. There is considerably more information on teacher influences than on family influences. This may be because research with young children is often conducted in preschool programs.

Several studies have examined how teachers often unconsciously or inadvertently influence children's choices of activities and classroom behaviors. The general finding is that boys are more harshly disciplined and chastised for sex-nontraditional or cross-gender play than girls. Fagot has shown in a series of studies (Fagot, 1977; Fagot & Leinbach, 1983) that teachers play an important role in shaping children's play in much the same way as parents do. Teachers, like parents, tend to reinforce traditional sex-role preferences and same-sex choices of activities and playmates.

Teacher-impact studies also show differences in how males and females are treated in the same settings. In a classic study, Fagot and Patterson (1969) found that preschool teachers constructed environments that catered to girls' traditional sex-typed behaviors of quiet attention, but clashed with boys' more active styles. They termed this type of classroom a *feminizing environment.*

In addition, conflict between school-appropriate behavior and traditional sex-typed play (especially for boys) is evident in the teacher-impact studies. In a study of the introduction of new toys into the preschool setting, boys were encouraged in masculine directions more than girls were encouraged in feminine directions (Serbin, Connor, & Iler, 1979). Teachers, especially females, tend to scold boys more (in expectation of wrongdoing), while at the same time praising them more (Etaugh & Harlow, 1975; Meyer & Thompson, 1956). Overall, this tendency results in increased attention to males in the classroom. To examine the effect of teacher feedback on children's sex-typed play, Serbin, Tonick, and Sternglanz (1977) instructed teachers to reinforce cross-gender play in preschoolers. Their results confirmed the trend: Children increased play in cross-gender activities and with cross-gender playmates when they were reinforced for such behaviors.

Peer influences

In addition to adult influences, children are attuned to their peers' thoughts and opinions about their play and adapt their play form to the group setting. Some of the work in these areas falls under the category of play modification (Kobasigawa, 1968; Liss, 1979; Liss & Doyle, 1982). Boys, especially, tend to influence other boys to avoid sex-nontraditional items (Ross, 1971). Most impressive is Serbin, Connor, Burchardt, and Citron's (1979) finding that a peer's presence drastically reduces the amount of play with cross-sex toys compared to solitary play. This finding was most pronounced in the presence of opposite-sex peers.

Intervention or modification studies

The last few sections have alluded to studies in which an adult or a peer had an impact on the child's play behavior, either through direct statements or by their presence. This section will discuss those studies, as well as others that have intentionally used modeling as a means of play behavior modification.

Flerx, Fidler, and Rogers (1976) read children non-sex-typed stories (i.e., no traditional roles) and found that these presentations, although brief, reduced children's stereotypical thinking. Along these lines, DiLeo, Moely, and Sulzer (1979) found that modeling could be used to modify children's tendencies to play with same-sex toys and encourage them to opt for opposite-sex toys — a stronger tendency for girls than for boys. These modeling effects have been found in children as young as 20-months-old (Fein, Johnson, Kosson, Stork, & Wasserman, 1975).

Liss (1979) found that children accept the behavior and play choice of a same-sex peer they have seen in a televised play session. These children choose cross-gender toys more frequently than children who have not seen such models. However, a subsequent study using the same television materials, but varying the play situation, did not confirm this result. In the earlier work, the investigator showed children the model and then allowed them to play alone with the toys. In the later work (Liss & Doyle, 1982), two children viewed the same modeling materials separately and then were brought together to play. The effects of modeling disappeared when the peer was there.

The presence of another individual, especially an opposite-sex peer, can limit a child's interest in cross-gender play. Serbin, Connor, Burchardt, and Citron (1979) found that a peer could serve this limiting role while Hartup, Moore, and Sager (1963), and Rekers (1975) indicate that mere presence of an adult can also serve this function.

Another method of modifying children's play choices is direct intervention by another individual. Serbin and colleagues (Serbin, Connor, Burchardt, & Citron, 1979; Serbin, Connor, & Iler, 1979; Serbin, Tonick, & Sternglanz, 1977) found that cross-sex play could be increased by teacher attention and approval for these activities. Furthermore, the longer the experimental period, the greater the duration of the effect. In an open school setting, with continued emphasis on equal access and approval for boys and girls, children show few sex-typed behaviors and attitudes (Bianchi & Bakeman, 1983). This applied experience indicates the potential durability and utility of teacher intervention.

Cross-gender play activities are related to the acquisition of both social and cognitive skills. The reader is referred to Liss (1983) for a more complete discussion of the correlates of play behavior in both cognitive and social domains. Numerous studies describe the academic, attitudinal, and social effects of play with sex-traditional and sex-nontraditional toys in same-sex and opposite-sex peer groups. The vast majority of studies support the trends summarized in this chapter.

Fantasy and dramatic play

Young children's fantasy or dramatic play is receiving increasing attention from several perspectives. First, some investigators have examined sex and age differences in the amount of this behavior. Second, others have described qualitative differences in boys' and girls' pretend play. And third, some tentative hypotheses have been generated concerning the outcome of these differences for future social structures and cognitive functioning.

The work on quantitative differences between boys and girls in fantasy and dramatic play is equivocal at best. One study (McLoyd, 1980) found dominance by females, others found dominance by males (Sanders & Harper, 1976), but the majority of studies (Pulaski, 1970; Smith, 1980; Tizard et al., 1976) indicate that qualitative differences (styles) outweigh quantitative differences (amounts).

Qualitative differences focus on the types of equipment or props used in play and the types of roles children adopt. Johnson and Roopnarine (1983) found that girls use fewer concrete props (real or imitative objects) in their fantasy play and rely mostly on abstract themes. Several studies which have focused on how boys and girls engage in fantasy play confirm what an innocent observer in a toy store might conclude: Boys engage in adventure tales and take on the roles of heroes (often fashioned after movie and television characters), while girls are more involved in domestic activities and take on the roles of family members. This finding has been reported by Fein (1981), Grief (1976), and Singer (1973).

Connolly, Doyle, and Ceschin (1983) extended this work on fantasy play by examining sex differences in play and its social and cognitive correlates. They found that the type of fantasy play predicted types of social interactions and children's use of materials. These authors concluded that fantasy play is extremely important in developing social

Tom Cheek

Evidence from several sources indicates that play encourages experimenta-tion and flexibility, attributes that contribute to creative thinking.

skills for boys and girls, despite the fact that the stories and types of interactions by the sexes are different. Connolly et al. (1983) additionally question whether encouraging boys and girls to engage in fantasy play normally associated with the opposite sex would change their social skills and if so, how.

Summary and implications for teachers

It seems that as much as we have learned about the play of boys and girls, there is more to ask and more to know. There is a long history of research examining boys' and girls' preferences for different types of toys and a more recent history of research examining how boys and girls play with these same toys or in similar situations. Additionally, we know that differences between boys and girls are not unchangeable; rather, the play of boys and girls is highly susceptible to change from direct feedback, presence of others, modeling by adults or peers, and from casual interactions. We also know that environmental influences from many sources, such as peers, teachers, families, television, and books, impinge on children's choices and play styles. Perhaps the most accurate conclusion is that there are as many similarities as there are differences and we still have much to learn about the combinations of circumstances that expand children's play behaviors.

As educators we must realize the enormous and important responsibility we have to the children in our charge. Young children arrive in school with histories of sex stereotyping collected from the family, media (especially Saturday morning television), and daily life encounters. In helping children explore their own abilities and the environment in which they live, teachers influence children's notions of gender identity, their personal goals, and their choices of friends and activities. Teachers can either reinforce classic traditional sex-stereotyped choices or increase children's awareness of all the opportunities open to them in a non-sex-typed society the children themselves may someday build. These choices are a heavy burden for educators but a welcome challenge for a changing society.

References

Astin, H. S. (1975). Sex differences in mathematical and scientific precocity. *The Journal of Special Education, 9,* 79–91.

Benjamin, H. (1932). Age and sex differences in the toy preferences of young children. *Journal of Genetic Psychology, 41,* 417–429.

Bianchi, B. D., & Bakeman, R. (1983). Patterns of sex-typing in an open school. In M. B. Liss (Ed.), *Social and cognitive skills: Sex roles and children's play* (pp. 219–233). New York: Academic.

Bridges, K. M. B. (1927). Occupational interests of three-year-old children. *The Pedagogical Seminary and Journal of Genetic Psychology, 34*, 415–423.

Carpenter, C. J. (1983). Activity structure and play: Implications for socialization. In M. B. Liss (Ed.), *Social and cognitive skills: Sex roles and children's play* (pp. 117–145). New York: Academic.

Carpenter, C. J., & Huston-Stein, A. (1980). Activity structure and sex-typed behavior in preschool children. *Child Development, 51*, 862–872.

Connolly, J., Doyle, A., & Ceschin, F. (1983). Forms and functions of social fantasy play in preschoolers. In M. B. Liss, (Ed.), *Social and cognitive skills: Sex roles and children's play* (pp. 71–92). New York: Academic.

DiLeo, J. C., Moely, B. E., & Sulzer, J. L. (1979). Frequency and modifiability of children's preferences for sex-typed toys, games, and occupations. *Child Study Journal, 9*, 141–159.

DiPietro, J. A. (1981). Rough and tumble play: A function of gender. *Developmental Psychology, 17*, 50–58.

Etaugh, C., & Harlow, H. (1975). Behaviors of male and female teachers as related to behaviors and attitudes of elementary schoolchildren. *The Journal of Genetic Psychology, 127*, 163–170.

Fagot, B. I. (1977). Consequences of moderate cross-gender behavior in preschool children. *Child Development, 48*, 902–907.

Fagot, B. I., & Leinbach, M. D. (1983). Play styles in early childhood: Social consequences for boys and girls. In M. B. Liss (Ed.), *Social and cognitive skills: Sex roles and children's play* (pp. 93–116). New York: Academic.

Fagot, B. I., & Littman, I. (1975). Stability of sex role and play interests from preschool to elementary school. *Journal of Genetic Psychology, 89*, 285–292.

Fagot, B. I., & Patterson, G. R. (1969). An in-vivo analysis of reinforcing contingencies for sex-role behaviors in the preschool child. *Developmental Psychology, 1*, 563–568.

Fein, G. G. (1981). Pretend play in childhood: An integrative review. *Child Development, 52*, 1095–1118.

Fein, G., Johnson, D., Kosson, N., Stork, L., & Wasserman, L. (1975). Sex stereotypes and preferences in the toy choices of 20-month-old boys and girls. *Developmental Psychology, 11*(4), 527–528.

Flerx, V. C., Fidler, D. S., & Rogers, R. W. (1976). Sex role stereotypes: Developmental aspects and early intervention. *Child Development, 47*, 998–1007.

Fling, S., & Manosevitz, M. (1972). Sex typing in nursery school children's play interests. *Developmental Psychology, 7*, 146–152.

Grief, E. B. (1976). Sex role playing in preschool children. In J. S. Bruner, A. Jolly, & K. Sylva (Eds.), *Play: Its role and development in evolution*. New York: Basic.

Halliday, J., & McNaughton, S. (1982). Sex differences in play at kindergarten. *New Zealand Journal of Educational Studies, 17*, 161–170.

Halverson, L. E., Roberton, M. A., & Langendorfer, S. (1982). Development of the overarm throw: Movement and fall velocity changes by the seventh grade. *Research Quarterly for Exercise and Sport, 53*, 198–205.

Hartup, W. W., Moore, S. G., & Sager, G. (1963). Avoidance of inappropriate sex-typing by young children. *Journal of Consulting Psychology, 27*, 467–473.

Johnson, J. E., & Roopnarine, J. L. (1983). The preschool classroom and sex differences in children's play. In M. B. Liss (Ed.), *Social and cognitive skills: Sex roles and children's play* (pp. 193–218). New York: Academic.

Kaiser, S. B., & Phinney, J. S. (1983). Sex typing of play activities by girls' clothing style: Pants versus skirts. *Child Study Journal, 13,* 115–132.

Kobasigawa, A. (1968). Inhibitory and disinhibitory effects of models on sex-inappropriate behavior in children. *Psychologia, 11,* 86–96.

Lamb, M. E. (1977). The development of parental preferences in the first two years of life. *Sex Roles, 3,* 495–497.

Langlois, J. H., & Downs, A. C. (1980). Mothers, fathers, and peers as socialization agents of sex-typed play behaviors in young children. *Child Development, 51,* 1237–1241.

Liss, M. B. (1979). Variables influencing modeling and sex-typed play. *Psychological Reports, 44,* 1107–1117.

Liss, M. B. (1983). Learning gender-related skills through play. In M. B. Liss (Ed.), *Social and cognitive skills: Sex roles and children's play.* New York: Academic.

Liss, M. B., & Doyle, T. (1982, April). *Sex-typing and play: When modeling doesn't work.* Paper presented at meeting of the Western Psychological Association, Sacramento, CA.

Liss, M. B., & Etaugh, C. (1983, August). *Home, school and playroom: Training grounds for adult sex roles.* Paper presented at meetings of the American Psychological Association, Anaheim, CA.

Lott, B. (1983). Behavioral concordance with sex role ideology related to play areas, creativity, and parental sex typing of children. *Journal of Personality and Social Psychology, 36*(10), 1087–1100.

McLoyd, V. C. (1980). Verbally expressed modes of transformation in the fantasy play of Black preschool children. *Child Development, 51,* 1133–1139.

Meyer, W. J., & Thompson, G. G. (1956). Sex differences in the distribution of teacher approval and disapproval among sixth-grade children. *Journal of Educational Psychology, 47,* 385–397.

Parten, M. B. (1932). Social participation among preschool children. *Journal of Abnormal and Social Psychology, 27,* 243–262.

Pulaski, M. (1970). Play as a function of toy structure and fantasy predisposition. *Child Development, 41,* 531–537.

Rekers, G. A. (1975). Stimulus control over sex-typed play in cross-gender identified boys. *Journal of Experimental Psychology, 20,* 136–148.

Rheingold, H. L., & Cook, K. V. (1975). The contents of boys' and girls' rooms as an index to parental behavior. *Child Development, 46,* 459–463.

Ross, S. A. (1971). A test of generality of the effects of deviant preschool models. *Developmental Psychology, 4,* 262–267.

Sanders, K. M., & Harper, L. V. (1976). Free play fantasy behavior in preschool children: Relations among gender, age, season and location. *Child Development, 47,* 1182–1185.

Serbin, L. A., Connor, J. M., Burchardt, C. J., & Citron, C. D. (1979). Effects of peer pressure on sex-typing of children's play behavior. *Journal of Experimental Child Psychology, 27,* 303–309.

Serbin, L. A., Connor, J. M., & Iler, I. (1979). Sex-stereotyped and nonstereotyped introductions of new toys in the preschool classroom: An observational study of teacher behavior and its effects. *Psychology of Women Quarterly, 4,* 261–265.

Serbin, L. A., Tonick, I. J., & Sternglanz, S. H. (1977). Shaping cooperative cross-sex play. *Child Development, 48,* 924–929.

Singer, L. L. (1973). *The child's world of make-believe: Experimental studies of imaginative play.* New York: Academic.

Smith, A. B. (1980). The family, schools and sex roles. In G. H. Robinson & B. T. O'Rourke (Eds.), *Schools in New Zealand society: A book of readings.* Auckland: Longman Paul.

Smith, P. K., & Connolly, K. (1972). Patterns of play and social-interaction in preschool children. In R. B. Jones (Ed.), *Ethological studies of child behavior.* London: Cambridge University Press.

Tizard, B., Philps, J., & Plewis, I. (1976). Play in preschool centers: Play measures and their relation to age, sex and IQ. *Journal of Child Psychology and Psychiatry, 17,* 251–264.

Ungar, S. B. (1982). The sex-typing of adult and child behavior in toy sales. *Sex Roles, 8,* 251–260.

Vance, T. F., & McCall, L. T. (1934). Children's preferences among play materials as determined by the method of paired comparisons. *Child Development, 5,* 267–277.

Rick Reinhard

An adult can facilitate children's symbolic play by making suggestions, asking questions to clarify, and elaborating on themes and roles.

Part 4:
Benefits of Play

In some preschool and kindergarten programs, academic activities increasingly occupy a substantial part of the curriculum. This trend may reflect the uninformed view that play is an educationally frivolous activity, and not properly a part of school. Certainly, there has been much romanticizing about the benefits of play, and, until recently, little systematic evidence. Two approaches to the beneficial aspects of play are illustrated in Chapters 10 and 11.

Debra Pepler (Chapter 10) examines the link between play and creativity. Evidence from several sources indicates that play encourages experimentation and flexibility, attributes that contribute to creative thinking. While some problems have only one correct answer, there may be several ways to find it. Most of life's problems lend themselves to more than one solution. The research described by Pepler supports the view that opportunities for play may contribute to a balanced school curriculum in which divergent and convergent ways of thinking are equally valued.

Studies of the benefits of play have examined a wide range of cognitive, social, and emotional aspects of development. These studies have used varied procedures to enhance play through some form of adult intervention. Roz and Eli Saltz (Chapter 11) discuss experimental efforts to encourage children's play. These authors conclude that training in fantasy and pretend activities enhances children's spontaneous behavior in these areas. Moreover, this training is associated with improvements on a variety of measures related to children's ability to organize and remember information, consider the perspective of others, and gain control over their own impulses. While some educators have argued that the best way to teach social and intellectual discipline is to regulate children's activity, the findings reviewed by the Saltzes indicate that the self-regulatory and organizing aspects of play may achieve these ends.

Although we use play in various ways in the classroom for our own purposes, we need to remember that the children have purposes of their own, and need to deal with such purposes largely by themselves, making use of this vital and universal kind of communication.

CHAPTER TEN

Play and Creativity

DEBRA PEPLER

There is a widespread belief among developmental psychologists and educators that play is a primary medium through which children develop cognitive skills, particularly those skills related to creativity or divergent thinking (Bruner, 1974; Sutton-Smith, 1967, 1968). The purpose of this chapter is to examine the link between play and creativity and to consider the implications for those working with young children. To this end, I will first examine theoretical perspectives on the relationship between play and creative thinking. Second, I will review the research that demonstrates a relationship between play and creativity and the research that shows play to facilitate creativity.

Theories linking play and creativity

Major theories of play contribute two common themes concerning the ways that play contributes to the development of creativity. One theme stresses experimentation and flexibility in play. Another stresses the transition from concrete to abstract thought facilitated through play.

Experimentation and flexibility in play

Once children have discovered the properties of an object through specific exploration or have mastered a skill, they begin to experiment actively with the object or action. In this experimentation, identified as *diversive exploration,* children seem to ask, "What can I do with this object?" (Hutt, 1982). Diversive exploration is presumed to be a process in play that contributes to creativity. Characterized by a relaxed and varied approach to play objects (Hutt, 1982), it involves trial and error and chance combinations of responses (Piaget, 1962), and is a form of *variation-seeking* with an object or with children's own behaviors (Sutton-Smith, 1975). The benefit of this experimental mechanism in play is that it provides a broad repertoire of skills and responses and

143

perhaps encourages flexible thinking, which, in turn, enhances creativity.

The transition from concrete to abstract thought

Several major theorists have postulated that play facilitates the transition from concrete to abstract thought (Piaget, 1962; Smilansky, 1968; Vygotsky, 1976). According to Piaget, the symbolic representations produced in play (for example, pretending that a stuffed dog is a real dog) form part of the process through which a child develops abstract thought. Vygotsky (1976) clarified the way that the transformation from concrete to abstract thought occurs. He explained that when children pretend that a stick is a horse, for example, the stick "becomes a pivot for severing the meaning of horse from a real horse" (Vygotsky, 1976, p. 546). In play, young children's thought is freed from real-life situational constraints and moved from the concrete to the abstract at an age when children may be otherwise incapable of abstract thought.

Several researchers have demonstrated a developmental sequence from the concrete to the abstract in play. As children's thinking matures, they rely less on the similarity of the object being symbolized in play (Fein, 1975) and move from using the self as agent to using objects as agents (Watson & Fischer, 1977). Presumably, the ability to consider objects in more abstract and less centered terms, which is practiced in play, would facilitate creativity on tasks that require a variety of free associations.

In summary, the significance of the transition from concrete to abstract thought in play lies in the opportunity it provides for children to focus beyond the obvious, to make novel associations, and to engage in imaginative activity during play and subsequent divergent problem solving. Taken together, the theories that examine the influence of play on development suggest that play may contribute to creativity by enabling children to experiment with objects, to generate novel responses, and to practice symbolic thinking. It remains to be shown whether these processes in play correlate with increases in creativity.

Are play and creativity related?

Interest in the link between play and creativity has stemmed primarily from research that demonstrated a correlation between several play behaviors and divergent thinking. Lieberman (1965) was among the first to examine this relationship. She asked kindergarten teachers to rate their children on five aspects of playfulness: physical spontaneity, social spontaneity, cognitive spontaneity, manifest joy, and sense of humor. Lieberman found strong correlations between these playfulness traits and three divergent thinking factors: *ideational fluency* (the ability to generate a large number of responses that meet a certain criterion), *spontaneous flexibility* (the ability and disposition to vary responses), and *originality* (the ability to generate unique responses). In other words, those children who were most playful were also most creative.

Singer and Rummo (1973) also examined the relation between playfulness and creativity as measured by ideational fluency. They found that highly creative boys were more communicative, curious, humorous, playful, and expressive. For girls, none of the playfulness measures was related to creativity alone, but interacted with measures of IQ. These findings suggest a relation between styles of play and creativity, at least for boys.

Hutt and Bhavnani (1976) also found a relation between style of playful interaction and creativity that was unique to boys. They assessed 3- to 5-year-old children in their interactions with a novel toy and categorized them as: (1) *nonexplorers* who looked at a toy, but did not investigate it in any way; (2) *explorers* who actively investigated the toy, but did not go beyond specific exploration; and (3) *inventive explorers* who investigated the new toy and then used it in imaginative ways as in diversive exploration. More girls were categorized as nonexplorers and more boys were categorized as inventive explorers. A test of divergent thinking was given to these children. Inventive play was found to be positively correlated with the measures of divergent thinking, but primarily for boys.

Johnson (1976) examined the relation of fantasy play styles and creativity. He observed 3- to 5-year-old children during free play at nursery school and categorized their fantasy play as social or nonsocial. Johnson found that only social fantasy play related to performance on divergent thinking tasks (multiple uses and story completion). He suggested that the factor common to both divergent thinking and social fantasy play might be the ability to generate a variety of ideas. Perhaps more ideas are generated in group fantasy play than in solitary fantasy play and this facilitates creative thinking.

Sutton-Smith (1968) examined the link between play experience and creativity more generally by presenting kindergarten boys and girls with male and female sex-typed toys and asking them for alternate uses for the toys. The boys and girls were presumed to be equally familiar with the toys, but to have differential play experiences with same-sex and opposite-sex toys. The relationship between play experience and creativity was demonstrated; boys and girls gave more unique responses for the toys identified with their own sex. Sutton-Smith suggested that the novel responses associated with an object during play contributed to the creativity of responses about that object in the task situation. Children may be able to think more creatively about a toy when they have played with it in a variety of ways.

The weakness of these and other correlational studies, as Hutt (1982) cautioned, is that it is impossible to determine whether play experiences *cause* changes in creativity or whether play and creativity are simply related. In other words, children who play more creatively may also think more creatively; hence, it cannot be said that their creativity results from play experience. Therefore, it is important to determine whether play enhances creativity and to identify the features of the play experience that relate to creativity.

Does play enhance creativity?

The initial research efforts to determine the effects of play on creativity typically involved presenting children with objects during play or nonplay sessions and subsequently testing them on divergent thinking tasks. One of the first such studies was conducted by Dansky and Silverman (1973). They assigned 4- to 6-year-old children to one of three conditions: play, imitation, and neutral (coloring). The children were given 10 minutes to play, imitate, or color and tested immediately thereafter on an alternate uses task. Although there were no differences among the groups on standard responses (referring to a use for which the object was designed), the children in the play group were superior to those in the other two groups on the number of nonstandard responses for the object. Dansky and Silverman suggested that the children who had played may have come into the testing situation with a more playful attitude, thereby approaching the divergent task with more flexibility, curiosity, spontaneity, and interest.

In a subsequent study, Dansky and Silverman (1975) tested the generality of the effect of play on creativity. Children were exposed to one set of materials in a play, imitation, or intellectual task condition and were then asked the alternate uses for a different set of materials. The children in the play condition produced significantly more standard and nonstandard uses than children in the other groups. Dansky and Silverman concluded that the results of their two studies "lend strong support to the notion that play creates a set, or attitude, to generate associations to a variety of objects whether or not these objects are encountered during play activity" (1975, p. 104).

A study conducted by Li (1978) followed Dansky and Silverman's research by examining two questions. First, do children in a play condition give more novel associations for an unfamiliar object? Second, is the make-believe aspect of play the link to creative thinking? Children aged 4 and 5 years were randomly assigned to one of four groups: free play, make-believe play (with prompting to think about the objects in a pretend way), imitation, and control. The children were given 10 minutes of individual experience and tested immediately afterward on an alternate uses task. The results indicated that both the free play and make-believe play subjects were superior to the imitation and control subjects in responses to a familiar item. Make-believe subjects gave more nonstandard responses to an unfamiliar item than the free play group.

Dansky (1980a) also examined the role of make-believe or fantasy as a primary factor in play that contributes to creativity. Prior to treatment, preschool subjects were categorized during free play as either *players* (who engaged in make-believe) or *nonplayers*. These children were then assigned to one of three conditions: free play, imitation, or problem solving. After a 10-minute treatment session, the children were asked to name the uses for unfamiliar objects. Dansky found that the beneficial effects of free play on a creativity task were limited to those children who typically engaged in make-believe play in the classroom. Based on this and earlier findings, Dansky postulated that certain cognitive processes involved in make-believe or fantasy play, such as free association and symbolic thinking, are similar to those involved in creative thinking.

An effect of play on creativity was also found in two studies that Pepler (1979) and Pepler and Ross (1981) conducted on play and problem solving. In the first study 3- and 4-year-old children were assigned to one of four conditions: play with convergent materials, play with divergent materials, observation of convergent activity, and observation of divergent activity. The play materials, five sets of nine pieces which fit into five formboards, could be used as puzzles (convergent activity) or play blocks (divergent activity). Children in the convergent play condition played with the pieces and the formboards; children in the divergent play condition played only with the pieces. The control groups observed the experimenter engaging in convergent or divergent activity. All children participated individually in three 10-minute sessions and were given a battery of divergent problem-solving tasks after the third session. Children in the divergent play group gave more unique responses on a divergent thinking task than all other groups.

The second study was similar to the first except that a nonplay control replaced the observation conditions and the divergent thinking tasks were modified. In this study, the divergent group again gave more unique responses than the other groups. These findings indicate that children who had divergent play experiences were more imaginative in their responses to divergent thinking tasks, suggesting that it is not play per se, but play with unstructured materials that contributes to creativity.

In summary, there is considerable support for the effect of play on creativity. Taken together, these studies indicate that children given play experiences perform better on creativity tasks than children with imitation, intellectual, convergent, or neutral experiences.

Several processes by which play may contribute to creativity are suggested by the research.

- First, there may be a generalized transfer of a playful attitude or a flexible response set from the play to problem-solving situations. Hence, children with play experiences may be more flexible, curious, spontaneous, and interested in the task (Dansky & Silverman, 1973, 1975).

- Second, there may be a more specific transfer of novel responses generated by investigation and experimentation in play. Children with play experiences were found to make more use of previous play activities to generate responses on a creativity task (Dansky & Silverman, 1973).

- Third, symbolic activity in play may facilitate creative performance. The results suggest that those children who benefited most from play experience were those whose play was likely to include make-believe elements. It has been postulated that the cognitive skill of shifting one's thinking from concrete to abstract during symbolic play may be similar to the skill required to generate a variety of novel responses on a creativity task (Johnson, 1976; Singer & Rummo, 1973).

These processes, presumed to mediate the link between play and creativity, may also interact with individual and situational factors.

Which children benefit more from play?

Children's play styles appear to illustrate that experimentation and symbolic activity, the two processes postulated by the theories, link play and creativity. The role of experimentation and flexibility is suggested by research indicating that playful, curious, and inventive children were likely to be more creative on a divergent thinking task than those children who did not display these playful characteristics (Hutt & Bhavnani, 1976; Lieberman, 1965; Singer & Rummo, 1973). These children might be less constrained by the situation and more likely to explore their environment in unusual ways than children who were not playful and curious.

The role of symbolic thinking in mediating the link between play and creativity is suggested most clearly by the work of Dansky (1980a). He found that only those children whose spontaneous play included make-believe elements would benefit from free play experience and perform better on a creativity task. Pulaski (1973) also found that children who showed a high predisposition to fantasy in free play were likely to be more imaginative in a task situation. The importance of symbolic thinking may also be suggested by Singer and Rummo's (1973) study, in which they found expressiveness and communicativeness to be related to divergent thinking.

In summary, although play may provide an opportunity for all children to engage in experimentation and symbolic activity, some children are more playful, curious, and imaginative than others and it is for these children that play most clearly enhances creativity. This is not to say that children who lack playful, inventive, and symbolic play styles cannot learn to engage in exploration or fantasy play. Several studies have indicated gains in performance on creativity tasks following training in verbal exploration (e.g., Pellegrini, 1984) or fantasy play (e.g., Dansky, 1980b). The role of a teacher, therefore, should be to encourage active exploration, experimentation, and fantasy play for all children.

Which play situations enhance creativity?

Certain characteristics of the play situation may enhance or inhibit creativity.

Degree of structure of play materials

Pulaski (1973) found that children who had played with minimally structured play materials, compared to those that were highly structured, exhibited greater richness and variety of fantasy in a task situation.

Our research (Pepler, 1979; Pepler & Ross, 1981) also demonstrated this relationship — children who played with the divergent materials performed better on a measure of creativity than children who played with convergent materials. Divergent materials elicited a variety of investigative, constructive, and symbolic activities. In contrast, the formboard in the convergent condition seemed to limit the play to primarily puzzle-solving activities. Therefore, while the convergent play materials provided the opportunity to practice puzzle completion, they did not elicit the processes presumed to be related to creativity, namely experimentation and symbolic play.

Goldman and Chaillé (1981) also reported that children's activities with structured materials were limited rather than flexible and experimental. They suggested, therefore, that play with such structured materials would be unlikely to foster creativity.

Additional support for the contention that highly structured materials limit creativity comes from a study by Dreyer and Rigler (1969). They found that children from Montessori schools, in which the materials are highly structured, were less creative than children from traditional nursery schools. As Montessori (1965) contended, structured materials are designed to elicit attention to certain properties and thereby direct children to self-discovery through play; the discovery that takes place with less structured materials, however, may have more diverse applications.

Social versus solitary play

Some research suggests that social play is more conducive to creativity than solitary play. Johnson (1976) reported high correlations between social fantasy play and divergent thinking measures, but found no such correlations for nonsocial fantasy play.

Griffing (1981) also reported that imagination correlated more highly with sociodramatic play than with nonsociodramatic play. Perhaps the additional requirement to communicate and share pretense in sociodramatic play enhances symbolic thinking, a process in play presumed to contribute to creativity.

Other factors

Other situational factors, such as adult intervention and training, may also influence the development of creativity through play. As I have mentioned, there are several play training studies that demonstrate a link between fantasy play training and creativity (Dansky, 1980b; Feitelson & Ross, 1973). Less intrusive adult interventions may also enhance creativity. For example, there is evidence that parents' provision of an enriched and flexible play environment at home is related to their children's creativity (Bishop & Chace, 1971). A similar relationship might be expected between the preschool play environment and creativity.

Implications for educators

This review of theory and research suggests many aspects of children's play environments that interact to promote creative activity. First, in order to foster young children's creative thinking, certain aspects of the play situation, such as the structure of materials, may be altered to offer a more diversive play experience. Although there is a place for structured materials such as puzzles and formboards, these materials tend to restrict children's play activities. The research indicates that structured play materials, such as coloring books, may provide such strong direction for children's activities that they inhibit the behaviors that might enhance creativity. Less structured items, such as blocks, markers and blank paper, or dramatic play props, tend to foster children's divergent thinking.

Second, young children's creativity may be enhanced by identifying the aspects of their play that demonstrate the rudiments of creativity and by fostering and expanding upon these behaviors. For some children, creative play may be most prevalent with dolls; for others it may be found in active, gross motor play. Some children may exhibit most creativity during play with peers, while other children may be most creative and imaginative on their own. Teachers can build on and diversify each child's interests.

How can adults enhance play? A teacher or parent can foster creativity through play by providing a variety of interesting and unstructured play materials to encourage investigation and experimentation. An adult can facilitate children's symbolic play by making suggestions, asking questions to clarify, and elaborating upon themes and roles. A parent or teacher can also facilitate fantasy play by occasionally joining the play to help initiate the pretense activity. The degree of intrusiveness required of the adult will vary according to characteristics of the children and situation as well as the objectives of the activity.

Although the evidence that play fosters creativity is quite strong, it should be noted that play is not the only means to enhance divergent thinking. Play is, however, the most natural and spontaneous approach and should be encouraged to prepare children to face the complex problems of everyday life.

References

Bishop, D. W., & Chace, C. A. (1971). Parental conceptual systems, home play environment and potential creativity in children. *Journal of Experimental Child Psychology, 12*, 318–338.
Bruner, J. (1974). Child's play. *New Scientist, 62*, 126–128.
Dansky, J. L. (1980a). Make-believe: A mediator of the relationship between play and associative fluency. *Child Development, 51*, 576–579.
Dansky, J. L. (1980b). Cognitive consequences of sociodramatic play and exploration training for economically disadvantaged preschoolers. *Journal of Child Psychology and Psychiatry, 20*, 47–58.
Dansky, J. L., & Silverman, I. W. (1973). Effects of play on associative fluency in preschool-aged children. *Developmental Psychology, 9*, 38–43.
Dansky, J. L., & Silverman, I. W. (1975). Play: A general facilitator of associative fluency. *Developmental Psychology, 11*, 104.
Dreyer, A., & Rigler, D. (1969). Cognitive performance in Montessori and nursery school children. *Journal of Educational Research, 62*, 411–416.
Fein, G. G. (1975). A transformational analysis of pretending. *Developmental Psychology, 11*, 291–296.
Feitelson, W., & Ross, G. S. (1973). The neglected factor—play. *Human Development, 16*, 202–223.
Goldman, J., & Chaillé, C. (1981, April). Object use in the preschool: An underdeveloped resource. Paper presented at the Biennial Meeting of the Society for Research in Child Development, Boston.
Griffing, P. (1981, April). Follow up study of sociodramatic play among Black schoolage children representing two social class groups. Paper presented at the Biennial Meeting of the Society for Research in Child Development, Boston.
Hutt, C. (1982). Towards a taxonomy and conceptual model of play. In S. J. Hutt, D. A. Rogers, & C. Hutt (Eds.), *Developmental processes in early childhood*. London: Routledge & Kegan Paul.
Hutt, C., & Bhavnani, R. (1976). Predictions from play. In J. S. Bruner, A. Jolly, & K. Sylva (Eds.), *Play*. New York: Penguin.
Johnson, J. E. (1976). Relations of divergent thinking and intelligence test scores with social and nonsocial make-believe play of preschool children. *Child Development, 47*, 1200–1203.
Li, A. K. F. (1978). Effects of play on novel responses of preschool children. *Alberta Journal of Educational Research, 24*, 31–36.
Lieberman, J. N. (1965). Playfulness and divergent thinking: An investigation of their relationship at the kindergarten level. *Journal of Genetic Psychology, 107*, 219–224.
Montessori, M. (1965). *The Montessori elementary material*. Cambridge, MA: Robert Bentley.
Pellegrini, A. (1984). The effects of exploration and play on young children's associative fluency: A review and extension of training studies. In T. Yawkey

& A. Pellegrini (Eds.), *Child's play: Developmental and applied*. Hillsdale, NJ: Erlbaum.

Pepler, D. J. (1979). Effects of convergent and divergent play experience on preschoolers' problem solving. Unpublished doctoral dissertation, University of Waterloo, Ontario, Canada.

Pepler, D. J., & Ross, H. S. (1981). The effects of play on convergent and divergent problem solving. *Child Development, 52*, 1202–1210.

Piaget, J. (1962). *Play, dreams and imitation in childhood*. New York: Norton.

Pulaski, M. A. (1973). Toys and imaginative play. In J. L. Singer (Ed.), *The child's world of make-believe*. New York: Academic.

Singer, D. G., & Rummo, J. (1973). Ideational creativity and behavioral style in kindergarten aged children. *Developmental Psychology, 8*, 154–161.

Smilansky, S. (1968). *The effects of sociodramatic play on disadvantaged preschool children*. New York: Wiley.

Sutton-Smith, B. (1968). Novel responses to toys. *Merrill-Palmer Quarterly, 14*, 151–158.

Sutton-Smith, B. (1967). The role of play in cognitive development. *Young Children, 22*, 361–370.

Sutton-Smith, B. (1975). The useless made useful: Play as variability training. *School Review, 83*, 197–214.

Vygotsky, L. S. (1976). Play and its role in the mental development of the child. In J. S. Bruner, A. Jolly, & K. Sylva (Eds.), *Play*. New York: Penguin.

Watson, M. W., & Fischer, K. W. (1977). A developmental sequence of agent use in late infancy. *Child Development, 48*, 828–836.

Sally Gale

Particularly for children whose pretend play skills are just emerging, extending this kind of play by questioning, suggesting new ideas, or taking a role in the play itself, appear to be valuable teaching strategies.

CHAPTER ELEVEN

Pretend Play Training and Its Outcomes

ROSALYN SALTZ AND ELI SALTZ

Jason: "Let's build a boat. A houseboat."

Sam: "Have you ever seen a houseboat? You live in it all day!"

Jason: "Bring those blocks over here, Paul. We need more."

(Twenty minutes later the structure is completed. It consists of big, hollow blocks arranged in several tiers in the shape of a large rectangle. Four long boards, serving as a roof for the boat, have been placed across two long sides of the rectangle. The children are now inside their boat and under the roof.)

Mary (placing small triangular blocks on roof): "We need these for lights."

Sam: " 'Cause when it's nighttime we have to have them."

Jason: "Who wants to start the boat up?"

Sam: "OK. Who's going to steer?"

All together: "Zoom, zoom, zoom!" (Jason and Sam pantomime the use of a steering wheel.)

Sam: "I'll be back in a second. Don't leave no one on!" (Carefully steps out of boat.)

The four children (aged 4½ to 5½ years) involved in the activity described here were engaged in a type of pretend play (also variously termed imaginative, make-believe, dramatic, or fantasy play) which has come to be known as sociodramatic play. This kind of socially interactive pretend play is developmentally quite advanced—it is far from a universal accomplishment, even among older preschool and kindergarten children.

Theorists and researchers in the area of early development have been interested in the possible relationship of such play to positive developmental outcomes. This interest has led to a number of recent studies that have investigated the effects of pretend play on various aspects of children's development. Many of these studies have involved tutoring children in social pretend play skills and then examining the impact of

155

such training on children's cognitive and social development. This research has important implications for developmental psychologists and teachers of young children.

Development of pretend play

Sequence of development

The central characteristic of pretend play is that some aspect of the play must rely on the child's symbolic transformation of immediate reality. This may involve substituting toy objects for real ones (e.g., a doll for a baby, or a block structure for an airplane), representing an imagined action or event by enacting it in play (e.g., "Bang, bang, you're dead" with a finger waved as an imaginary gun), or representing a real or fictional character by role playing (e.g., "I'm the mommy and you're the baby"; or "I'm Batman and I'm saving you.").

Children's pretend play shows a regular developmental sequence that appears to be related to the young child's gradual development and practice of cognitive and social skills. Piaget (1962) holds that the kind of self-directed, interactive dramatic play illustrated would not be expected until a child is at least 3 years of age and has firmly entered what Piaget termed the stage of *collective symbolism.*

Early pretend play focuses on the simple substitution of pretend objects for real ones (e.g., child using a stick as a horsey, feeding a doll baby with a toy bottle). During this period, the pretend play tends to be largely solitary and to need objects that clearly resemble the real ones (e.g., toy stoves, dishes, cars). From 3 to 6 years of age, social pretend play becomes more frequent, and children become increasingly able to dispense with prototypical objects in their pretend play. Gradually, they become able to rely more on their own imaginations and symbolic constructions (as in the sociodramatic play illustrated, when the boat is a block structure and the steering wheel is nonexistent and represented only by the children's gestures and ideations). A relatively advanced level of imaginative capability is also required by a form of sociodramatic play that is often called fantasy play, which relies on fictional characters and fantastic situations (e.g., Peter Pan, Batman and Robin, or fairy tales) rather than real ones.

Functions of pretend play

A number of investigators have found a positive relationship between the frequency with which children engage in spontaneous social pretend play and positive aspects of intellectual and social development (Johnson, 1976; Marshall, 1961; Smilansky, 1968). Others have found that children who engage in such play may be more able than those who do not to achieve the comprehension aspects of early reading. For example, Pellegrini (1980) found that kindergarten children who tended to engage in such symbolic play activities were better able to comprehend words and stories than children who did not.

Do children's pretend play activities directly contribute to their cognitive and social development or do these activities merely reflect the development that has already taken place? Although there is some controversy among psychologists, many see pretend play as facilitative to development in various ways.

Piaget (1962) and Vygotsky (1967) have focused on the relationship of pretend play to cognition. They have suggested that imagination and pretend play are basic to critical aspects of children's cognitive development. Both see pretend play as instrumental to the development of internal systems of representation that gradually free children from their early reliance on the here and now and allow them to think about objects and events that are not immediately present—to think about the past and plan ahead for the future.

For example, Vygotsky found that young children would not even imitate sentences that were not literally supported by their perceptions (e.g., they might refuse to say "It is snowing" unless it really was snowing). He noted that it was in the course of pretend play that children began to use language in nonliteral ways, such as pretending to ride a stick and calling the stick a horse. By permitting the stick to steal the horse's name and become the horse's symbolic representation, Vygotsky felt, children were thereby embarking on the long process of freeing thought from immediate perception. In this way, Vygotsky believed, pretend play made an important contribution to children's gradual development of representational, logical thought.

Theorists have also focused on assumed positive relationships of pretend play to other aspects of development, namely creativity (Singer & Rummo, 1973), learning to appreciate the point of view of others (Garvey, 1977), and social-personality growth in other areas, including the development of the self-concept, impulse control, and cooperative behavior. [See Fein (1981) and Rubin, Fein, & Vandenberg (1983) for comprehensive reviews of these and other theories related to the cognitive and social functions of pretend play.]

As stated earlier, many preschool children do not spontaneously engage to any considerable degree in social pretend play. Smilansky (1968), in her pioneering research, found that socially disadvantaged

Israeli children rarely exhibited such play. She maintained that the reason for this difference was that pretend play was modeled and encouraged in many middle-class homes, but not in the homes of the Israeli children of lower socioeconomic status. Subsequent researchers in several different countries, including Canada, England, Israel, and the United States, have also reported social class differences in the level of social pretend play, with children from low SES families engaging in such play much less frequently than do children from middle-class families (Christie & Johnsen, 1983).

Pretend play training

Can special tutoring in pretend play skills increase the incidence and level of social-pretend play among children? Can it lead to the positive developmental outcomes that have been attributed to children's spontaneous pretend play activities? If so, what kinds of training might prove to be most beneficial? Studies have been conducted which throw considerable light on these questions.

For the most part, play training studies have emphasized interactive role playing in either sociodramatic play, thematic fantasy play (story or fairy tale enactment), or a combination of these. Because so many studies have used or adapted these two play-training models, it may be helpful to describe clearly the basic methods that were used in the Smilansky (1968) and Saltz, Dixon, and Johnson (1977) studies, for paradigms of the sociodramatic and thematic fantasy training procedures.

Sociodramatic play

This term was coined by Smilansky (1968), who also conducted the first large-scale pretend play training study. Its aim was to teach children pretend play skills and to stimulate the kind of interactive social pretend play illustrated by the vignette at the beginning of this chapter. Such play involves reenactment of remembered experiences, role taking, and social interaction among the children. It also involves representational thought because children must react to others in terms of their assumed roles, not the actual characteristics of the children themselves. In addition, of course, such play involves symbolic substitution of pretend for real objects (the boat and roof in the vignette).

During the training, Smilansky and her colleagues took children on outings, for example to fire stations. When the children returned to the preschool, they were encouraged and prompted to reenact their experiences, with teachers taking appropriate roles and giving suggestions, as necessary.

Subsequent researchers revised this model in various ways. The sociodramatic theme, for example, did not necessarily depend on an actual shared field trip, but on a shared experiential background (going to the doctor or the grocery). In some training studies, children used surrogates such as puppets to represent the characters in the sociodrama. In one case, children used dolls made from pipe cleaners as the actors (Freyberg, 1973). Whatever the modification, however, this type of social pretend play training centers on the interactive reenactment of a realistic social situation.

Thematic fantasy play

A type of dramatic play akin to Smilansky's sociodramatic play is the kind of social pretend play that involves fantastic rather than realistic characters and situations (Superman, E.T., Goldilocks). In this type of fantasy play, children are required to imagine and symbolically enact characters and behaviors further removed from their everyday experiences than in sociodramatic play. Such fantasy play, then, may place greater demands on ideation and imagination than does more realistic dramatic play (Saltz et al., 1977; Rubin et al., 1983).

In a series of pretend play training studies, Saltz and his colleagues (1977) introduced the term *thematic fantasy play* to describe a condition in which children reenacted fairy tales *(The Three Billy Goats Gruff, The Three Little Pigs)*. This type of dramatic play training is not only less focused on realistic experiences than is sociodramatic play training, but is also more tightly plotted. A description of the thematic fantasy play training procedures used in the Saltz studies may clarify this method.

After reading the fairy tale to the children, the teacher led a brief discussion of the story theme and motivations of the characters ("Why did the little pig run to the brick house?" "How did the little pig feel when the wolf said, 'I'll huff and I'll puff!'?"). Roles were then chosen or assigned, and the children reenacted the story. Props and costumes were minimal and often chosen or constructed by the children themselves. Children were strongly encouraged to follow the original story line. Reproduction of the original dialogue was not, however, considered important, and rephrasing was accepted. For example, one group of children enacted *The Three Little Pigs* with the following dialogue:

Wolf: "You better let me in!"

Little Pig (crouching behind a wall constructed of blocks): "No way, man!"

Initially, the teacher's role was very directive, perhaps serving as narrator, or frequently prompting, as the children engaged in the actions indicated. If necessary, the teacher might even physically lead a child through an action. At this point the enactment might be mostly pantomime (the wolf blowing the pigs' houses down on cue, the pigs running and screaming). Children exchanged roles from session to session, gradually becoming more adept at role playing and verbal expression and more aware of the story lines. As the children became more experienced, the teacher's active direction was decreased and sometimes even eliminated; the children themselves would often direct each other in the reenactments, as in, "Wolf, you not s'posed to run away now, you s'posed to get stuck in the chimney!"

Other researchers have subsequently conducted studies using story enactments similar to the thematic fantasy play training procedure. Still others have used only sociodramatic play, or have incorporated combinations of sociodramatic, thematic fantasy, or other types of pretend play into their play training strategies. The following section will examine the results of these play training studies.

Results of training studies

We shall see that, in general, training in pretend play activities has been found to improve children's functioning over a wide range of cognitive, social, and emotional behaviors. Furthermore, the data suggest that sociodramatic and fantasy play may not be equivalent: While the two types of play training have similar effects on some types of functioning, they appear to differ in their effects in other realms.

Spontaneous play effects

One of the most consistently found effects of pretend play training is that it leads to an increase in the amount and level of children's spontaneous social pretend play. This was first demonstrated by Smilansky (1968) in a study involving more than 700 children. Similar data have been reported in a number of subsequent experiments (Freyberg, 1973; Smith & Syddall, 1978). Saltz et al. (1977) reported that thematic fantasy training increased spontaneous fantasy play, while sociodramatic play training resulted in a marked increase in children's spontaneous sociodramatic play. Training also appears to affect the quality of spontaneous play: Feitelson and Ross (1973) found that children trained in sociodramatic play later engaged in pretend play activities that were more developmentally advanced than those of children not trained in sociodramatic play.

It is noteworthy that, in these studies, some children did not engage in spontaneous pretend play behaviors *except* after direct play training. Smilansky (1968) found no increase in play for children who participated in the same field trips and had access to the same props as those in the play training group, but who were not involved in the play training sessions. Similarly, Dansky (1980a) reported that simply providing excellent play props was not sufficient to stimulate pretend play. Adult-initiated play training was required in order to facilitate an increase in the frequency and level of the children's socially interactive pretend play.

Cognitive effects

Intelligence test performance. Theoretical considerations suggest that pretend play should enhance representational abilities in young children. Because representational functioning is important in performing well on most intelligence tests, we would anticipate that such enhancement of children's representational abilities should be reflected in increased scores on intelligence tests. At the same time, however, we must bear in mind that beyond the age of 3 or 4 years, intelligence test scores are quite stable. Consequently, casual, short-term experiences are unlikely to have marked effects on such global abilities.

The most extensive training study is the one reported by Saltz et al. (1977). In that study, 145 children received approximately 7 months of training in pretend play activities, 3 days per week, in sessions of approximately 15 minutes per day. The children were preschoolers between 3½ and 5 years of age, mostly from lower SES families. Three types of pretend activities were examined: sociodramatic play, thematic fantasy play, and a condition in which the children listened to and discussed the same stories which were being enacted by the thematic fantasy group. A fourth group engaged in nondramatic activities with the experimenters. It should be noted that this study was conducted within the context of an excellent preschool, so that all the children received a great deal of stimulation in addition to the play training.

By the end of the 7-month training periods, the children in both the sociodramatic and the thematic fantasy training conditions were approximately 10 IQ points superior to both the children who listened to and discussed stories and the children who were in the nondramatic control condition. This effect was statistically significant in each of the 3 years of the study.

A study by Saltz and Johnson (1974) involved a 4-month training interval and only one type of pretend play, thematic fantasy. Here, too, training in pretend play led to significant superiority in IQ scores over a control condition.

One study (Smith & Syddall, 1978) failed to find an effect of play training on intelligence scores. This study compared two training conditions, one involving sociodramatic play training and the other training in various skills, such as clay modeling. Training lasted only 5 weeks, three sessions per week, with only seven children in each condition. The two groups did not differ in intelligence test scores at the end of the 5-week program.

In summary, three studies have evaluated the effects of pretend play training on indexes of intelligence. Two of these studies found that such training had facilitative effects on intellectual performance. The study that did not find such effects was characterized by a very short period of training and very small groups of children. [See Saltz and Brodie (1982) for a more extensive discussion of the Smith and Syddall (1978) research.] This evidence suggests that pretend play training facilitates intellectual functioning, if this training is carried on for a sufficient period of time.

Language and comprehension effects. Common sense suggests that when children interact in a social play situation, they will tend to communicate with each other both verbally and nonverbally. It is reasonable to expect that such practice in communication would enhance children's verbal facility. The surprising finding is not that a relationship was found between pretend play and communicative factors, but that this relationship was generated by relatively small amounts of training in pretend play.

Freyberg (1973) reports that eight training sessions on sociodramatic play conducted during a month's time led children to use longer, more complex sentences compared to a control group.

In a more extensive study, Lovinger (1974) involved 20 lower SES children in daily sociodramatic training sessions for 25 weeks. Sociodramatic training significantly increased sentence length and number of words used in free play by the experimental group compared to the children in the control condition. In addition, the sociodramatic group also scored significantly higher than the control on the Verbal Expression subtest of the Illinois Test of Psycholinguistic Ability. Whether these differences are due to the sociodramatic training per se, or are attributable to the verbal modeling exhibited by the teacher during the training sessions is not easily determined, because the control children did not receive any systematic substitute attention from the experimenter. In either case, sociodramatic training certainly provided the context in which this increase in language skills arose.

Dansky (1980a) reports increased facility with language after only nine sessions of sociodramatic training over a 3-week period. Dansky employed a control condition in which children played with the same equipment as the sociodramatic children, and for equivalent time, but instead of pretend play, these children interacted actively with the experimenter in exploring and discussing the physical characteristics of the objects in the environment. Following training, the sociodramatic children proved to be significantly superior to the control children on a variety of language and comprehension tests: (1) After hearing a story, they were superior at arranging a series of pictures in a manner that corresponded to the story heard. (2) They were superior at repeating a story just heard, keeping the events in the correct sequence. (3) When shown a picture and asked to make up a story about it, the sociodramatic children were superior to children in the other two conditions in number of words used, number of different words used, and number of events described that transcended what was actually shown in the picture. Note that (1) and (2) refer to sequencing of events, and suggest that the story characteristics of pretend play help children to understand that events of their lives may have discernable patterns.

Does pretend play facilitate the detection of patterns, or plots, that relate the individual events that constitute an experience? Results reported by Saltz et al. (1977) are consistent with those of Dansky (1980a) in suggesting that the answer to this question is "Yes."

Saltz et al. (1977) developed a Story Integration Test as a measure of children's ability to relate events depicted in a sequence of pictures. While thematic fantasy and sociodramatic training both facilitated the ability to integrate sequences compared to the control conditions, the children in the thematic fantasy training condition were superior to those in the sociodramatic condition on this task.

These results suggest that the children's ability to detect patterns in a series of events is dependent on more than the quantity of verbal stimulation they encounter. This is indicated by the fact that both the sociodramatic-play and the listen-and-discuss groups experienced roughly the same amount of verbal stimulation as the thematic fantasy group, yet the thematic fantasy children were superior to these others in ability to detect patterns. Nor is experience with sequenced stories critical, since the listen-and-discuss group encountered the same plotted stories that were presented in the thematic fantasy condition. At a verbal level, the listen-and-discuss children were more concerned with analyzing the meaning of sequenced events than were children in any of the other conditions. Apparently the combination of sequencing and *acting* the sequence was the important characteristic of the thematic fantasy condition.

On the other hand, Smith and Syddall (1978) found no differences between their sociodramatic condition and their construction-training control group on a composite score based on vocabulary and comprehension subtests.

In summary, several studies have reported that training in various types of pretend play can facilitate various aspects of language performance in young children, with only Smith and Syddall failing to find an effect. One of the most surprising aspects of these results is the relatively small number of training trials necessary to make a difference.

Creativity and imaginativeness. A number of psychologists have suggested that pretend play should foster children's creativity and imaginativeness (Johnson, 1976; Lieberman, 1977; Singer & Rummo, 1973). Rubin et al. (1983) summarize the intuitive basis for a belief in this relationship in the following manner: "Playfulness and creativity . . . both involve the creation of novelty from the commonplace" (p. 741).

Will training in pretend play stimulate creativity and imaginativeness? Several studies suggest that it may. Feitelson and Ross (1973) found that children trained to engage in sociodramatic play scored significantly higher than the control children on the Torrance Test of Originality. This test measures the number of unusual titles children will invent for pictures. However, no significant differences were found between groups on tests that purported to measure curiosity.

Dansky (1980a) obtained results similar to those of Feitelson and Ross. He found a significant tendency for sociodramatic play training to augment performance on a test of creativity (Guilford's *Alternative Uses* test) and replicated Feitelson and Ross's failure to find a significant effect of sociodramatic play on curiosity. However, sociodramatic training did lead to significantly superior scores on several tests of imaginative thinking, such as imaginative storytelling.

Egocentrism. Young children tend to view the world from their own perspective and often fail to understand that others do not know what they know, see what they see, or feel what they feel. Asked to suggest an appropriate birthday gift for their mother, for example, many young children are likely to indicate some toy they enjoy: "Let's give her a toy car!" Because pretend play involves changing roles so that the children act in the role of someone else, a number of theorists have suggested that pretend play might facilitate the transition from egocentric thought to a mature ability to take the perspective of others (Chandler, 1973; Mead, 1932; Smilansky, 1968).

Perhaps the most careful of the studies relating pretend play to egocentrism is that of Burns and Brainerd (1979). Whereas most of the other studies we shall examine used one or two types of perspective-taking tasks, Burns and Brainerd used a large number of tasks that covered the range from physical perspective-taking ("Do others see what I see?") to social perspective-taking. All the children were from lower SES backgrounds, and from a nonstimulating childcare situation; thus, attention from adults, in general, might improve behavior. For this reason, Burns and Brainerd employed three experimental conditions: a sociodramatic training condition; a construction play training condition, in which small groups of children cooperated in making various things; and a no-treatment control that simply received the pre- and posttests. Each of the training conditions involved 10 training sessions. Results indicated that both types of training were effective in reducing egocentric behavior, compared to the control group. Sociodramatic training was significantly more effective than construction training, but this difference was only moderate.

Smith and Syddall (1978), like Burns and Brainerd (1979), compared a sociodramatic training condition with a construction play training condition. Like Burns and Brainerd, they found that sociodramatic play training was significantly more effective than construction play training in facilitating the development of perspective-taking ability. Iannotti (1978) reports a very interesting study in which he found that sociodramatic play training increased perspective-taking ability in both 5- and 9-year-old children. This suggests that play training may be beneficial long after the preschool years.

Despite the fact that the studies cited (with the notable exception of Burns and Brainerd's) measured performance on few different types of perspective-taking tests (often only one), and that this restricts the generality of their findings, the results of these studies have been consistent in suggesting that sociodramatic play facilitates the reduction of egocentric thought and the development of better perspective-taking abilities.

Conservation of physical and social concepts. Golomb and Cornelius (1977) reported that three training sessions of pretend play resulted in accelerated development of the ability to comprehend that the physical quantity of an object is conserved when the object changes shape (e.g., the child comprehends that a ball of clay does not gain more clay by being rolled into the shape of a sausage, even though it may look bigger). However, other investigators failed to find similar results (Guthrie & Hudson, 1979; Rubin et al., 1983). Thus, training in pretend play does not necessarily facilitate any and all types of cognitive functioning.

Fink (1976), on the other hand, reports that eight sessions of training in pretend play facilitated social-role conservation in the types of tasks used by Sigel, Saltz, and Roskind (1967), ("A father goes to work where he is a doctor; is he still a father?"). Sigel et al. (1967) report that many preschoolers contend that the father is no longer a father when he changes roles and is a doctor. Note, however, that the social role conservation facilitated by play is more similar to the types of activities involved in sociodramatic play than is conservation of physical properties.

Thus, the evidence suggests that pretend play training may have various effects on different aspects of cognitive functioning.

Social and emotional effects

There is evidence to suggest that play training has a beneficial effect on social and emotional development.

Social problem solving. Rosen (1974) found that sociodramatic play training facilitated various types of group problem-solving tasks that required cooperation among the children in a group. Thus, it appears that the play training fostered cooperative interactions, at least among the children who were trained together.

Altruism. Iannotti (1978) examined the effects of sociodramatic training on altruistic behavior. As a test for altruism, each child was given some candy or raisins while the experimenter talked about a low-income boy whose birthday was approaching. The child was then left alone to donate in private. The altruism score was the number of food items shared. For 6-year-olds, almost no altruistic behavior occurred in the control conditions; only the children trained in sociodramatic play shared their candy. This difference was highly significant.

Aggression. There is little evidence that training preschool children in sociodramatic or thematic fantasy has any effect on aggressive tendencies. Iannotti (1978) hypothesized that role changes would foster understanding the feelings of others, and therefore would reduce aggression. Observations of the children indicated no tendency toward differences in frequency of aggressive acts among the various conditions in this experiment.

Impulse control. The behavior of young children is very much under the control of their immediate perceptions. In this sense, these children have little internal control over their behavior, and are impulsive. Vygotsky (1967) has proposed that as children develop more complex internal representations, these representations become a filter between the immediate perceptions and the impulses to respond. Children have impulse control to the extent that they can use internal processes as a basis for refusing to respond to strong external stimuli (resist a desirable toy that mother has declared off limits). Thus, if pretend play fosters the development of internal representations, it should reduce impulsive behavior.

Singer (1961) has presented correlational data that indicate that children who engage in pretend play are more successful at displaying waiting behavior. Experimental evidence in support of Singer's position comes from Saltz et al. (1977) and Saltz and Johnson (1974). Both studies found that training in thematic fantasy play increased waiting time in considering alternatives before making a response.

Sociodramatic play training, on the other hand, had no such effect (Saltz et al., 1977). Several other types of situations that might evoke impulsive behavior were examined in Saltz et al. (1977), such as asking children to guard an attractive toy and not touch it. In these tasks, some children were asked to think of something pleasant to keep their minds off waiting. Under such thinking instructions, children who had been trained in thematic fantasy play were much more successful in waiting than were children in any other condition. Sociodramatic training also facilitated waiting, but not as much as thematic fantasy training.

Effects on emotionally disturbed children. Few studies have examined the effects of sociodramatic play training on emotionally disturbed children. Nahme-Huang, Singer, Singer, and Wheaton (1977) found no effects in such a population. Udwin (1983), on the other hand, found some positive effects in preschoolers, removed from their homes because of abuse or neglect, who were in general found to be emotionally deprived and low in imaginative play. The pretend play training for a child consisted of some sessions of thematic fantasy play and some of sociodramatic play training. Compared to an untrained control group, training resulted in the following significant effects on behavior observed during free play: more positive general affect (mood and emotional tone); increased interaction and cooperation with peers; and a decrease in actual, observed aggressive behavior during play. On test performance, the children trained in pretend play scored significantly higher than the controls on several different measures of creativity and originality.

Conclusions from training studies

We have seen that training in pretend play has positive effects on a number of different cognitive and socioemotional traits and abilities, ranging from general intelligence and creativity scores to altruism and positive peer interactions.

Scientific disagreement appears to be centered on how pretend play produces these effects, rather than on whether the effects exist. We have already summarized some of the proposed explanations from the effectiveness of such play (e.g., Piaget, 1962; Vygotsky, 1967). More recently, Smith and Syddall (1978) have suggested that many of the cognitive effects of training in pretend play may be attributable to the *amount* of verbalization directed by the experimenters toward the children in the play situations. With regard to the egocentrism effects reported above, Rubin (1980) suggests that it is not the pretend play itself that is critical to the increased social understanding of the trained children; it is the related interactions between children that occur in organizing the play that is important. At this time, there is very little well-controlled evidence in support of any of these formulations. Certainly, the question of *how* pretend play training produces effects is an important one that merits further research.

Furthermore, the data suggest that we must be careful not to be too simplistic in trying to discover this *how* of pretend play. There is not a single, unidimensional pretend play; there are at least several types of pretend play, and these do not always function in the same way on different aspects of development. For example, while sociodramatic and thematic fantasy play appear to be very similar in their effects on IQ-type test performance, they may be very different in their effects on impulsivity. Pretend play appears to involve a complex pattern of factors that determine behavior (see Saltz, 1980).

How much pretend play training is necessary to produce changes in cognitive, social, and emotional functioning? The range of training reported in the various studies cited is very wide. For example, in Dansky (1980b) one brief session of imaginative play led those children who were already highly imaginative to perform more creatively than a comparable group who had not had this experience. Saltz and Brodie (1982) suggest that it is unlikely that one brief session greatly enhanced the *ability* of children to be more creative; it is more reasonable to assume that the session primed the children to think in a more original way in that particular situation.

Studies reporting improvement in language skills have involved as few as nine sessions of play training (Dansky, 1980a). While this appears to be a relatively small amount of training to produce improvement in so complex a set of skills, the absolute amount of improvement may also have been modest. In the great majority of studies, it is difficult to evaluate the size of the improvement in any of the skills measured, because standardized tests are seldom used. Of course, because training in pretend play stimulates spontaneous play, the actual experience with pretend play could considerably exceed the nine formal training sessions.

Smith and Syddall (1978) found no difference in IQ between children given 15 sessions of training in pretend play and a control group. On the other hand, Saltz et al. (1977) found a consistent 10-point advantage in IQ for groups trained in pretend play after approximately 75 training sessions. Considering how gradually intellectual skills develop, it would have been suprising to find that a small number of sessions could produce measurable increases in IQ scores. In short, training on pretend play may facilitate cognitive development, but the quality and quantity of pretend play are likely to be important factors in determining its effectiveness.

Certainly, much research remains to be done before the issues raised here can be resolved. However, the cumulative findings of play training studies seem to us to indicate that play training can have a variety of positive developmental outcomes. Other reviewers of the play training research have come to similar conclusions. For example, Rubin et al. (1983) state that there is "now a large body of literature that suggests sociodramatic, dramatic and thematic fantasy play training does have some impact in a wide variety of developmental areas," (p. 753) and Christie and Johnsen (1983) conclude that such play training seems to have "considerable educational value" (p. 112).

Educational implications

In recent years, play of all kinds has been downgraded and in some cases almost eliminated from kindergarten and even some preschool programs. Instead, renewed educational emphasis on teaching the basics has been extended downward to many kindergarten and preschool classrooms. At this level, *basics* is often taken to mean a curriculum devoted to activities and drill which teach shapes, colors, letters, and numbers. Yet, as has been documented in this chapter, researchers in early childhood development have found that pretend play activities appear to further central aspects of children's cognitive, language, and social development. Therefore, encouraging such play may be one of the most important basics in an early childhood curriculum. An acceptance of the educational value of this type of play could lead to more time and resources devoted to play.

Even if, as is the case in many early childhood settings, play is already an integral and valued part of the educational program, not all of the children in these classrooms engage in social pretend play. Others do so only infrequently, fleetingly, and at relatively immature levels. It is encouraging that play training research has found that the pretend play skills of children can be developed and improved by deliberate educational intervention. It will be recalled that providing field trips (Smilansky, 1968; Feitelson & Ross, 1973) or reading and discussing fantasy stories (Saltz et al., 1977) were not sufficient to increase the frequency or improve the level of play for children who did not already engage in a significant amount of such play. In all these cases, active teacher intervention, using play training strategies, was required.

Certainly, it is not being suggested that the results of play training research imply that teachers should always intervene in children's social pretend play. For many children, simply providing stimulation through stories, suggested themes, and props (playing hospital after a group time story and discussion) is often sufficient to encourage them to initiate long periods of independent, self-directed, and highly interactive dramatic play. In these cases, the only encouragement necessary may be for teachers briefly to enter into the pretense if they are invited by the children to do so (doctor to teacher: "Here, I'll fix your arm. You broke it bad!"). Griffing (1983) presents a variety of strategies that teachers of young children can use to encourage such play in their early childhood classrooms.

On the other hand, the play training research does suggest that teachers should not be overly hesitant to interfere in children's play for fear of inhibiting independent play. Particularly for children whose pretend play skills are just emerging, extending this kind of play by questioning, suggesting new ideas, or taking a role in the play itself appear to be valuable teaching strategies.

Similarly, some teachers may be even more reluctant to direct children in dramatic story reenactments (as in the thematic fantasy play studies), because this requires careful structuring, even narration by the teacher, to help the children retain the story line. Yet, it should be remembered that the active and sometimes highly structured play training methods used in these studies did not appear to inhibit children's independent, spontaneous pretend play. On the contrary, after play training, children exhibited more frequent, more sustained, and more elaborate social pretend play during free play periods. It should also be reassuring that the children who participated in the training studies appeared to enjoy the activities involved (e.g., Saltz et al., 1977).

We would certainly caution against the possibility that the concept *training* might be implemented in too grim a spirit. It would be unfortunate indeed if pretend play lost its playful quality by, perhaps, being introduced into some early childhood classrooms as another basic skill that must be instilled into the children by drill and repetition. This is inappropriate and is unlikely to be effective. Recall that play theorists believe that central characteristics of pretend play are that it is enjoyable and that it requires an active and creative symbolic process on the part of the child. It would seem to follow that this kind of process cannot be instilled by rote, but would require the child's willing, active engagement in the play training activities. Experienced teachers of young children will probably agree that, as with all other effective teaching strategies, their own flexibility and sensitivity to individual children's needs and developmental levels will be important to their success as effective play tutors.

Additional implications for early childhood practice may well be forthcoming as a result of future research in the area of pretend play. Much still remains to be learned. Play training research has thus far focused largely on social pretend play. Yet, other forms of pretend play, such as solitary fantasy play, may also have important effects on development (Rubin, this volume). It would seem desirable to explore such possible effects through future play research. Another area that might be important to investigate is whether some form of play training would prove beneficial for developmentally delayed children. In general, it can be concluded that pretend play training research has so far provided much impetus for further study, as well as considerable support for the value of play in early childhood education.

References

Burns, S. M., & Brainerd, C. J. (1979). Effects of constructive and dramatic play on perspective taking in very young children. *Developmental Psychology, 15,* 512–521.

Chandler, M. J. (1973). Egocentrism and antisocial behavior: The assessment and training of social perspective taking skills. *Developmental Psychology, 8,* 326–332.

Christie, J. F., & Johnsen, E. P. (1983). The role of play in social-intellectual development. *Review of Educational Research, 53,* 93–115.

Dansky, J. L. (1980a). Cognitive consequences of sociodramatic play and exploration training for economically disadvantaged preschoolers. *Journal of Child Psychology and Psychiatry, 20,* 47–58.

Dansky, J. L. (1980b). Make-believe: A mediator of the relationship between play and associative fluency. *Child Development, 51,* 576–579.

Fein, G. G. (1981). Pretend play in childhood: An integrative review. *Child Development, 52,* 1095–1118.

Feitelson, D., & Ross, G. S. (1973). The neglected factor—play. *Human Development, 16,* 202–223.

Fink, R. S. (1976). Role of imaginative play in cognitive development. *Psychological Reports, 39,* 895–906.

Freyberg, J. T. (1973). Increasing the imaginative play of urban disadvantaged kindergarten children through systematic training. In J. L. Singer (Ed.), *The child's world of make-believe.* New York: Academic.

Garvey, C. (1977). *Play.* Cambridge, MA: Harvard University Press.

Golomb, C., & Cornelius, C. B. (1977). Symbolic play and its cognitive significance. *Developmental Psychology, 13,* 246–252.

Griffing, P. (1983). Encouraging dramatic play in early childhood. *Young Children, 38*(2), 13–22.

Guthrie, K., & Hudson, L. M. (1979). Training conservation through symbolic play: A second look. *Child Development, 50,* 1269–1271.

Ianotti, R. (1978). Effect of role-taking experiences on role-taking, empathy, altrusism and aggression. *Developmental Psychology, 14,* 119–124.

Johnson, J. A. (1976). Relations of divergent thinking and intelligence test scores with social and non-social make-believe play of preschool children. *Child Development, 47,* 1200–1220.

Lieberman, J. N. (1977). *Playfulness: Its relationship to imagination and creativity.* New York: Academic.

Lovinger, S. L. (1974). Sociodramatic play and language development in preschool disadvantaged children. *Psychology in the Schools, 11,* 313–320.

Marshall, H. R. (1961). Relations between home experiences and children's use of language in play interactions with peers. *Psychological Monographs, 75,* (5, Whole No. 509).

Mead, G. H. (1932). *Mind, self and society.* Chicago: University of Chicago Press.

Nahme-Huang, L., Singer, D. G., Singer, J. L., & Wheaton, A. (1977). Imaginative play and perceptual-motor intervention methods with emotionally disturbed hospitalized children: An evaluation study. *American Journal of Orthopsychiatry, 47,* 238–249.

Pellegrini, A.D. (1980). The relationships between kindergartners' play and achievement in prereading, language, and writing. *Psychology in the Schools, 17,* 530–555.

Piaget, J. (1962). *Play, dreams and imitation in childhood.* New York: Norton.

Rosen, C. E. (1974). The effects of sociodramatic play on problem solving behavior among culturally disadvantaged preschool children. *Child Development, 45,* 920–927.

Rubin, K.H., Fein, G. G., & Vandenberg, B. (1983). In P. H. Mussen (Ed.), *Handbook of child psychology,* 4th Ed., New York: Wiley.

Rubin, K. H. (1980). Fantasy play: Its role in the development of social skills and social cognition. *New Directions in Child Development, 9,* 69–84.

Saltz, E. (1980, September). *Pretend play: A complex of variables influencing development.* Paper presented at the meeting of the American Psychological Association, Montreal.

Saltz, E., & Brodie, J. (1982). Pretend-play training in childhood: A review and critique. In D. J. Pepler & K. H. Rubin (Eds.), *The play of children: Current theory and research.* Basel, Switzerland: Karger.

Saltz, E., Dixon, D., & Johnson, J. (1977). Training disadvantaged preschoolers on various fantasy activities: Effects on cognitive functioning and impulse control. *Child Development, 48,* 367–380.

Saltz, E., & Johnson, J. (1974). Training for thematic-fantasy play in culturally disadvantaged children: Preliminary results. *Journal of Educational Psychology, 66,* 623–630.

Sigel, I. E., Saltz, E., & Roskind, W. (1967). Variables determining concept formation in children. *Journal of Experimental Psychology, 74,* 471–475.

Singer, D. G., & Rummo, J. (1973). Ideational creativity and behavioral style in kindergarten aged children. *Developmental Psychology, 8,* 154–161.

Singer, J. L. (1961). Imagination and waiting ability in young children. *Journal of Personality, 29,* 396–413.

Smilansky, S. (1968). *The effects of sociodramatic play on disadvantaged preschool children.* New York: Wiley.

Smith, P. K., & Syddall, S. (1978). Play and nonplay tutoring in preschool children: Is it play or tutoring which matters? *British Journal of Educational Psychology, 48,* 315–325.

Udwin, O. (1983). Imaginative play training as intervention method with institutionalized preschool children. *British Journal of Educational Psychology, 53,* 32–39.

Vygotsky, L. S. (1967). Play and its role in the mental development of the child. *Soviet Psychology, 12,* 62–76.

Elaine M. Ward

The outdoor environment, developmentally as important as the indoor environment, also requires thoughtful and well-informed adult decisions.

Part 5
Environments for Play

Although the sensitive interactions between children and teachers and parents are vitally important, perhaps the most sustained impact that adults have on child behavior might be found in the way adults design physical features of the early childhood setting. Social harmony, solitary pursuits, and imaginative activity may be encouraged or discouraged by physical aspects of the indoor and outdoor environment. In Chapter 12, Elizabeth Phyfe-Perkins and Joanne Shoemaker discuss the design of indoor play environments — physical space, group size, materials, and appropriately responsive adults. The outdoor environment, developmentally as important as the indoor environment, also requires thoughtful and well-informed adult decisions. Joe Frost (Chapter 13) reviews research on the outdoor play environment. The large number of studies reported by Frost indicate that well-designed playgrounds contribute much to the quality of children's play.

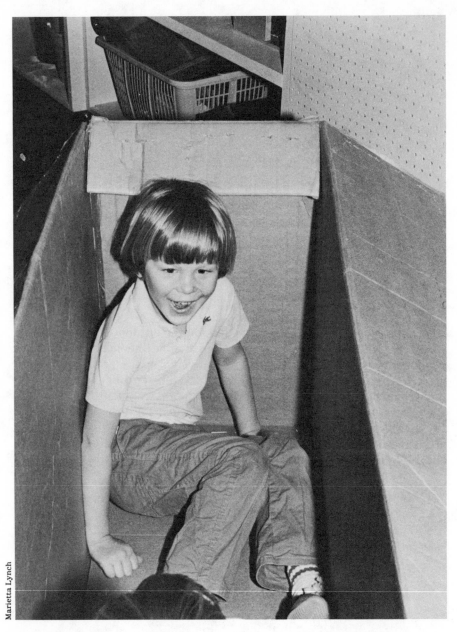

Marietta Lynch

In any environment, children's inventiveness, and the possibility of discovery, are directly proportional to the number and kinds of materials in it.

CHAPTER TWELVE

Indoor Play Environments:
Research and Design Implications

ELIZABETH PHYFE-PERKINS AND
JOANNE SHOEMAKER

Whether they take the position that early interaction with a stimulating environment is crucial for development (Bloom, 1964; Deutsch, 1966; Hunt, 1961) or the more pragmatic approach that environmental design helps manage behavior (Dodge, 1978; Kritchevsky & Prescott, 1969), early childhood educators tend to be interested in the physical aspects of classroom organization. In this chapter we review some of the research concerning the relationship of children's play to the indoor physical environment. We also review the approaches used by several architects and professional designers whose work is consistent with this research and is focused on the creation of indoor play environments for young children. Their work is a result of systematically addressing behavioral and curricular goals defined by educators of young children. Just as we learn by studying various philosophical approaches and early childhood program models, we can also learn by analyzing the physical spaces and equipment created by these designers.

Our goal is to present information that will assist educators in understanding and in implementing environments that support children's play. In order to integrate theory and practice, we present selected research findings first, followed by suggestions and implications for designing and arranging physical space. Specifically we focus on the play environment's capacity to

- control the size of the group in which children interact,
- provide a variety of experiences and spaces planned and designed to enhance young children's play,
- encourage and support children's developing social interaction,
- support adults in their encounters with children, and
- provide a quality setting for each child.

It is Prescott's (1984) belief that

One of the easiest ways to make day care better is to improve the physical environment. Behavior . . . happens in a specific place and time frame composed of a particular configuration of objects and people. If this configuration is changed, cues that elicit behavior and possibilities for responding are altered. Thus an understanding of the physical setting becomes one of the most powerful tools in regulating behavior and in implementing wished-for activities. (p. 44)

We maintain that, intended or not, the design and arrangement of the physical environment reflects the philosophy of the early childhood institution and significantly determines how children will play and live in a space, perhaps for as long as 10 hours a day.

Group size

Research

One of the most important variables in predicting the quality of life of children in child care has been identified by the National Day Care Study (Ruopp, Travers, Glantz, & Coelen, 1979) as the size of the group in which children spend their day. The study defined quality in terms of the developmental benefits to the child and took the premise that children's interactions with peers and adults must be warm, stimulating, and challenging.

In a small group of 12 children, as opposed to a large group of 24, (keeping the adult/child ratio constant) the study found changes in the following child behaviors

- cooperation and compliance (21% more often);
- reflection and innovation, such as considering and offering new ideas (37% more often);
- attention to adults (21% more often). [In contrast,]
- noninvolvement and aimless wandering was **minimized** by 21%, as was attention to groups [e.g., involvement in group activity as opposed to interaction with adults] (31% less often) (pp. 90–97).

Although test scores were not the focus of the National Day Care Study, larger gain scores on the Peabody Picture Vocabulary Test (PPVT) (receptive language) and The Preschool Inventory (general knowledge) were associated with high levels of adult-child interaction in class groupings of 12 or less, participation in small subgroups, and the previously listed child behaviors. The size of the activity subgroup (regardless of overall group size) together with high levels of caregiver-child interaction accounted for one half the difference in gain scores in children's receptive vocabulary (PPVT). Unfortunately, large groups of 24 children tended not to be broken down into small activity subgroups even when sufficient staff were present. Thus, Ruopp et al. (1979) offer a definition of quality child care that includes high levels of developmentally appropriate child behaviors, limiting group size, child involvement in small activity subgroups, and high levels of caregiver-child interaction.

Fitt (1974) found that one preschool classroom arranged with several large areas that contained groups of five to eight children was typified by noisy, large muscle activities, whereas another classroom arranged in small learning areas that contained groups of two to three children was typified by quieter interaction and more task involvement. Pollowy (1974) found a correlation between easily identifiable learning areas and a concomitant increase in the number of child-equipment interactions.

Both large open and small enclosed areas are recommended for differing needs of children in child care. Open areas encourage large motor activity and group glee (Sherman, 1975), but do not allow children to escape stimulation and noise; small spaces allow privacy, introspection, and intimate conversation (Sheehan & Day, 1975). Even though overall room size is often dictated by the program's budget and construction costs, it may be possible to influence the size of activity subgroups and facilitate child-adult interaction by taking into account the design of the physical space. We hypothesize that these changes will increase developmental benefits for children even in large classrooms.

Group size: Physical design implications

Moore, Lane, Hill, Cohen, and McGinty (1979) suggest that classrooms be filled with an array of "resource rich activity pockets" for groups of two to five preschool children, one to three toddlers, or two to five infants. These pockets can contain many types of materials, tapes, books, games, pictures, and toys that relate directly to the activity. In a nature study area, the pockets may include animals, plants, and other materials. In a building area, the pockets may include trucks and cars, buildings, and trains. The block area may also include materials to encourage numbers and counting (section 908, p. 2). These authors also suggest the use of texture, color, and lighting to emphasize the specialness of each area and recommend allowing for storage, surface area, equipment plug-in, and display space in each pocket.

Play spaces can be defined in various ways and to various degrees. The amount of enclosure should be determined by the type of activity and the kinds of behaviors desired. In defining spaces, educators must become sensitive to the physical elements they use, being sure that such features as rugs, platforms, or low shelves clearly convey to children where the area begins and ends.

Changes in floor color, texture, or level; vertical boundaries such as cubbies, book cases, and display units; and changes in lighting level or quality, must be carefully planned to be consistent with the intended boundaries and character of the activity area. A carpet remnant that extends several feet beyond the boundary area confuses children. Remembering that physical objects convey information and messages to children and adults (Proshansky & Wolfe, 1974), educators should convey behavioral information with clear and consistent physical clues.

Variety and complexity of experiences and spaces

Research

In any environment, children's inventiveness, and the possibility of discovery, are directly proportional to the number and kinds of materials in it (Nicholson, 1974). Various naturalistic studies of children in group settings tend to point in one direction—the areas set up in early childhood classrooms, especially the materials provided in them, have a strong influence on children's play. Children in housekeeping corners are frequently observed talking to each other and engaging in dramatic play. A well-equipped block corner seems to offer children opportunities for building and for cooperative play. In the art area, children are often more subdued, less social, and busy with their creations. It seems that if teachers not only select materials that match children's interests and developmental needs, but also plan for diversity, these activity centers can encourage involvement and promote play.

Prescott, Jones, and Kritchevsky (1967), and Kritchevsky and Prescott (1969) have analyzed play equipment based on the level of complexity, variety, and amount of activity per child. The more complex the unit, the more choices there are for children to make in the course of play, and the more potential there is for group play. Complexity sustains attention and fosters dramatic play and social interaction. Simple materials (e.g., swings and tricycles) have one obvious use and do not have subparts. Complex play units (e.g., play house with furniture, water table with equipment) have subparts or involve the juxtaposition of two different types of materials, and allow children to improvise and/or manipulate. Super-complex units involve three or more types of material (e.g., water and measuring equipment added to the sandbox, boxes and boards for use with the jungle gym).

Variety is the measure of the number of different kinds of things there are to do. Variety facilitates free choice in programs where children are expected to play on their own for some length of time each day. The amount to do per child is a calculation of the number of play spaces per child. This figure needs to be larger than one per child if children are expected to choose their own activities at their own speed. Other play spaces must be available to children when they have finished an activity; otherwise adult direction is necessary to move children to and from the few available play spaces.

Kritchevsky and Prescott (1969) suggest scheduling smaller groups of children, or adding complex and super units, as a means of increasing the number of play spaces per child. The authors maintain that the variables of complexity, variety, and amount to do per child, as applied to an analysis of materials in early childhood settings, are related to children's behaviors such as attention span, group participation, dramatic play, nondisruptive free choice of activities, and goal-directed behavior.

Bridges (1927) found that colorful materials that presented self-evident problems and allowed for variation were chosen frequently and sustained the interest of 4-year-olds in a Montessori classroom. However, Bott (1928) observing a traditional nursery, found that raw materials (clay, sand, blocks) and locomotor toys were played with the most. The choice of materials teachers provide to children is important to encourage task involvement and facilitate social interaction (Van Alstyne, 1932). For example, a sufficient number of tricycles and wagons appeared to encourage cooperative play (Murphy, 1937).

Moyer and Gilmer (1955) concluded that toys must satisfy the developmental needs of the child at a particular age and, if this requirement is met, attention spans of 26 to 34 minutes can be expected for 2-year-olds with an increase in attention span according to age for some toys. For children who were required to follow a rigid schedule of activities, an abundance of materials facilitated positive play behavior (Doke & Risley, 1972).

In a series of experimental manipulations, Smith (1974) varied both the types and numbers of toys available to preschool children as well as the amount of space. Variation in the type of play resources produced some interesting findings. When children were provided with only apparatuses (e.g., tables, chairs, baby carriages, climbing frame), they significantly increased their verbal and physical interaction and the incidence of cooperative play. Smith was intrigued by increases in unusual uses of equipment such as positioning tables end-to-end as a platform for walking baby carriages, and the lining up of chairs to form a pretend train.

Most of the studies reviewed by Phyfe-Perkins (1980) reinforce the notion that children interact with different materials in qualitatively and quantitatively different ways. Children find some materials more attractive than others, and they seem to stay with certain activities for longer periods of time. Kounin and Sherman (1979) speculated about the characteristics of preschool activity settings that influence the length of time children remained involved. Settings with high holding power (art, role play, blocks, and sand) seem either to offer a variety of play behaviors or to result in a clear sense of progress or an actual product. Kounin and Doyle (1975) found that when independent art and construction activities are organized so that the steps are self-reinforcing and sufficient materials are available, task involvement is fostered.

Rubin (1977) found differences in levels of play (functional, constructive, dramatic, sociodramatic) according to the engagement of the child in various activities. Children using dough clay, sand, or water were coded in a functional mode of play 75 to 90% of the time; those using paints, crayons, and puzzles were primarily involved in constructive play. Three quarters of the interaction in the role play area was dramatic or sociodramatic. Rubin and Seibel (1979) studied changes in children's activity preferences during a 3-month period. Changes in play categories included the emergence of more constructive play than both functional and dramatic play in the block area. While dramatic play with blocks was primarily cooperative, constructive block play was characterized by solitary and parallel play. The authors concluded:

It would appear as if the degree of "freedom" [in free play] is somewhat determined by the materials available to the children. . . . For example, it was discovered that group-dramatic play was inhibited by the presence of sand and water, puzzles and art activities. This form of play [group dramatic] has recently been suggested, by some, to contribute significantly to the development of social competence and perspective taking skills. (Rubin & Seibel, 1979, pp. 7–8)

The teacher's provision of varied and progressively more complex activity settings, the availability of materials, and the sequencing of activities, can become major influences on children's play. For example, Krantz and Risley (1972) found that the involvement level of children was higher during group story time and that transition into story time was shorter when the story had been preceded by naptime rather than outdoor play. Thus, by being aware of the effects of materials, space, and scheduling, teachers can intervene to prevent problems, increase developmentally appropriate play, and otherwise arrange the environment to support program goals (Prescott, 1984).

Variety of experiences and play spaces: Physical design implications

Olds (1979) states that "the motivation to interact with the environment exists in all children as an intrinsic property of life, but the quality of the interactions is dependent upon the possibilities for engagement that the environment provides" (p. 91). She recommends planning for a minimum of six categories of play experiences for preschool classrooms and classrooms with special needs children (Table 12.1).

After determining the types of experiences to be offered, play spaces for these activities should be designed to support and enhance, both functionally and aesthetically, children's play in each area. Just as a variety of experiences enhances play and learning, a variety of spaces offers children the experience of playing in environments that vary texturally, visually, auditorily, spatially, and kinesthetically. Rho and Drury (1978) suggest that

the complete preschool room ought to include a wide range of textures in large enough quantities so that the children can experience them while moving as well as at stationary tasks. To review a room's textures, think of pairs of characteristics: Hard/soft, rough/smooth, dry/wet, cold/warm, glossy/matte, etc. Then for example, if everything large in the room seems hard, add areas of softness—carpet, pillows, matting, etc. If everything seems flat, add roundness. (p. 76)

Table 12.1   Categories of play experiences (Olds, 1979, p. 102)

Activity	Examples
Quiet, calm activities	Listening, viewing, meeting, reading
Structured materials/activities	Puzzles, construction toys, blocks, manipulatives, group games, instruction
Craft and discovery activities	Paint, clay, collage, pens, crayons, chalkboards, woodworking, science, plants, animals
Dramatic play activities	Puppets, store, fantasy, masks, dress-up, kitchen and doll play, miniatures
Large motor activities	Climbing, sliding, crawling, hanging, tumbling, swinging, rocking, balls, Velcro and magnetic darts, ring toss, Nerf basketball, large blocks, punching bags, Bo-Bo punching clowns
Therapeutic and therapeutically educational activities	Inflatable and foam equipment—water bed and air mattress, for example—with therapeutic value for sensorily and physically disabled children. Casts, braces, X-rays, and models of organs to educate special needs and normally developing children about disabilities and development

To allow children to experiment and explore freely, there must be a match between the character of the space, the curriculum goals of the program, and the behavioral expectations for children engaged in each activity. A home-based child care playroom may have a cozy, richly colored and textured rug for comfort, but the rug's character is not functional for young children engaged in expressive activities such as finger paint or dough clay. Often by specifically listing the curriculum goals of each area, and the behavior expected of young children engaged in the activity, the design of the physical environment can be carefully matched to the experiences and activities offered. In this way a variety of play experiences and play spaces can be provided to support children's play.

Increasing social interaction

Research

Moore (1983) studied children's behavior in preschool settings. In programs where children made choices and worked at their own pace in a variety of well-defined activity settings, children exhibited high levels of social interaction, child-initiated behavior, and child involvement in activities.

Well defined behavior settings have been defined . . . as areas limited to one activity, with clear boundaries from circulation space and from other behavior settings, and with at least partial acoustic and visual separation. Typically they are sized to accomodate 2 to 5 children plus one teacher, and include storage, surface area, equipment plug-ins. . . . They are contrasted with poorly defined activity areas, i.e., areas where the spatial definition is low, where the area is too large or too small for the group size, or where the resource and work surfaces are not readily available for the particular activity. (p. 26)

Prescott (1984) warns that without adult planning, open-structure settings can easily become disorganized and may eventually lack challenge for children. However, in these settings she sees potential for the child for initiative, child-child interactions, mobility, and manipulation of the environment. "Open settings must have well-developed space and adults who know how to problem solve and keep track of children" (p. 60).

Rubin (1977) found differences in levels of social participation according to child involvement in various activities. Children using dough clay engaged in solitary or parallel play 65% of the time. Puzzles, sand or water play, and painting and coloring had similar social play profiles of 80% solitary or parallel play. Cooperative social interaction was scored 50 to 55% of the time for children engaged in house play and in play with cars or vehicles.

Furniture arrangement may be another effective means to influence children's social interaction. One implication of the research may be relevant to the practice of arranging an entire class of children in a large circle for group discussion time. Sommer (1969) found that although adults preferred to sit opposite rather than next to one another for conversational purposes, they avoided sitting opposite one another with more than 5 feet between them. Thus, a large circle of children may not support the developmental goal of language development usually attributed to circle time.

Norum, Russo, and Sommer (1967) investigated the seating preferences of pairs of preschool children when they were given variously cooperative, parallel, and competitive tasks to complete at a table. Pairs completing the cooperative task tended to sit side by side. During the competitive task children sat at 90° angles to each other around the corner of the table, and in the parallel coactive task children sat at opposite corners. Very few children sat directly across from one another, but girls tended to sit side by side, the most intimate arrangement, significantly more often than boys did. The authors concluded that the task-induced relationship between the children affected the proximity of their chosen seating patterns.

Physical design implications

If we are going to promote complex social interactions among children, the studies mentioned suggest providing young children with

- well-defined areas for groups of two to five children,
- protection from disruptions and intrusions,
- a sufficient number of small areas, and
- options for different seating patterns depending on the chosen task.

In addition, equipment and furniture scaled for two or three children should be considered. Mueller and Bergstrom (1982) suggest using large play equipment to foster peer interaction and propose that "perhaps slides, tunnels, and rocking boats are ideal 'spacing' devices" (p. 204) that permit very young children to interact with limited physical contact. Wheeled toys designed to be used by two or three children; wall mirrors large enough to reflect more than one child; group easels; benches and slides large enough for two or three children; and tents, playhouses, and empty closets with a curtain at the entrance (instead of a door) invite children to play together.

Simple alterations in the physical environment, such as positioning a water table so that children can be on either side of it, encourage children to establish visual contact with each other. Aquariums or animal cages, likewise placed at right angles to the wall, allow children to interact around an interest area, yet maintain some physical separation.

Adult encounters with children

Implications of adult behaviors

We need to examine what adult behaviors enhance the play and social interaction of children in preschool settings. Ruopp et al. (1979) found certain adult behaviors were associated with higher levels of child behaviors such as reflection, innovation, cooperation, and on-task attention. Adults who promoted these child behaviors spent:

- more time in social interaction with the children: praising, responding, comforting, questioning, and instructing;
- more time interacting with small activity subgroups; and
- less time observing children (passive monitoring as opposed to analytic study of behavior).

Stallings (1975) found that verbally responsive, nondidactic teachers who asked open-ended questions and interact frequently with one or two children (as opposed to addressing the entire group) were associated with increased task persistence, independence, verbalizations, cooperation, and self-esteem on the part of the children.

Phyfe-Perkins (1981) in a review of 67 studies on the effects of teacher behavior on preschool children's behavior found consensus around optimal adult teaching styles. Some of the crucial aspects of the immediate behavior of successful teachers include their ability to be encouraging, warm and friendly, involved with individuals and small groups, and attentive to two issues simultaneously. Adults need to keep the momentum going, effect smooth transitions, use positively worded instructions, minimize direct leadership of large groups, and maximize a child-centered approach in which children, rather than adults, make most of the decisions. Children taught by adults who possess these traits are high on measures of task involvement, language comprehension, social participation, constructive use of materials, spontaneity, creativity, sympathy, and independence, and low on measures of dominative and hostile behavior.

A smaller, more recent group of studies has explored the contribution of the scheduling, organization, and placement of equipment and activity segments. Adults' arrangement of the environment, as well as their attention to children, is clearly important. Pollowy (1974) found that the supervisory involvement of adults increased wherever equipment distribution restricted the child's activity or access. However, according to Hart and Risley (1975), limited access to some materials can be used to increase the instances of incidental teaching and thus achieve cognitive goals in an informal child-centered manner.

Physical design implications

In designing a play environment for young children, the quality of the environment for the adults in this setting must also be considered. Ferguson (1979) speaks most directly to the relationship between the environment and adult behavior. She describes her design of infant play yards as "soft and comfortable and nurturing for adults; which enable adults to be soft and comfortable and nurturing for the children" (p. 20). Her design thus matches the physical setting with behavioral expectations for adults as well as children. Comfortable seating is located in areas where the adult's presence and interaction will enhance children's play. Less comfortable seating is provided in areas where less adult-child interaction will encourage more independent play.

Programs espousing one-to-one adult-child interactions as a goal need to examine whether the play environment offers physical supports to encourage and support this interaction. A large hammock, an adult-sized rocking chair, and areas scaled and comfortable for one adult and one child, will increase the incidence of these interactions by addressing the needs and comfort of both children and adults with appropriate spaces and equipment.

Another crucial aspect is the adults' need for total room awareness while interacting with a small group or one child. Using low dividers of 3 to 3½ feet in height may allow adults to participate on the children's eye level yet see the room in a brief glance.

The quality of the child's experience

Research

Child care spaces are places for living 8 to 10 hours a day. According to Prescott (1984) this is a more radical view than the characterization of child care as a school. Thus, we need to examine how the physical environment can provide for these quality of life variables frequently absent from traditional schools. In thinking about providing a physical space that supports play and social interaction, it appears that privacy and softness are essential.

Canter and Kenny (1975), suggest that privacy is the ability to regulate the input and output of information to and from oneself. They see this need to regulate information as the basis of all human behavior in relation to spatial features of the environment. Gramza (1970) has explored children's preference for privacy by manipulating the degree of enclosure of play boxes from two sides to six sides. Children preferred complete enclosure in varying sizes of boxes. In examining the attributes of closed space with one side open that might attract children, Gramza constructed 32-inch cubes of either opaque, translucent, or clear Plexiglas. Children consistently preferred the opaque and translucent boxes, lending support to the idea that the attraction of enclosed space includes a visual limitation as well as a physical boundary.

Prescott (1978), in a comparison of home child care and two types of center-based child care, noted that the child may more easily find private space in the home than in the classroom. She associated the provision of private space with the presence of softness. Indicators of softness include:

- child/adult cozy furniture [such as] rockers [and] large pillows
- large rug or full carpeting
- grass on which children can play
- sand for children to play in
- dirt for digging
- animals to hold and fondle
- single-sling swings
- dough [clay]
- water play opportunities
- very messy materials such as mud, finger paint, clay, shaving cream
- laps, adults holding children (p. 16)

In Prescott's study, homes had high softness ratings. Closed-structure child care centers (in which teachers made most of the decisions) contained three or fewer of these elements. These centers also ranked lowest in provisions for privacy. Although the observed child behaviors cannot be linked solely to the presence or absence of privacy and softness, closed-structure settings registered much lower frequencies of children being physically active, giving orders, selecting and choosing, asking for help, giving opinions, and engaging in playful intrusions than did either open-structure settings or home settings. Home care settings had the highest frequencies of these behaviors just mentioned, as well as the highest softness and privacy ratings. It seems self-evident that young children may need a chance to rest and control or limit their interaction with the world when they feel the need—not just at naptime.

Physical design implications

Bednar and Haviland (1972) observed that privacy has many aspects: visual, acoustical, physical, and psychological. Osmon (1971) broadened the design implications of privacy by recommending four different configurations for "places to pause for awhile" (p. 43). He suggested small enclosed spaces; in-between spaces that are well defined but allow children to see out; places located to overlook activity; and places of interest with frequently changed or changing objects such as a fish tank surrounded by pillows.

The concept of softness is often expressed through color and texture. Educators might also consider including soft lines and soft forms (curves rather than straight lines) in the structure of setting and in the choice of furnishings and play equipment.

A major characteristic of soft architecture is defined by Sommer (1974) as "personalization, the ability to put one's individual imprint on one's surroundings" (p. 19). To design soft environments for children, we need to examine what there is in the setting that reflects the presence of children.

In a description of a school for young children in Reggio Emilia, Italy, Gandini (1984) described a transparent collage made of items such as shells, traditional decorations, and items brought in from home or from excursions outside the center. "Children are encouraged to bring in tokens of their home experience connected with daily or special events" (p. 18). Each child's treasure is placed in a transparent plastic bag that teachers assemble into a collage hung in front of a window. Children may congregate and engage in counting games, attribute guessing games, or conversations about the events that made these objects special.

Other elements that contributed to the responsiveness of the environment include chairs and pillows that conform to the body; hammocks, water beds, and rocking chairs that react to a child's movements; and large pieces of lightweight play equipment such as foam blocks, inflatable balls, hollow blocks, and plastic milk crates. These elements allow children to influence and control their environments, even to create their own spaces within the larger, more stable play environment.

Implications for educators

Spontaneous interactions with materials, adults, and other children are the basis for a play curriculum, as children test, explore, and learn from the observed consequences of their own actions. In order for the child to "have power to introduce her own innovations" (Bronfenbrenner, 1979, p. 205), it is imperative that the environment be responsive. We propose that if early childhood educators believe in the importance of the child's interaction with the world of people and objects as the major means of growth and development (Franklin & Biber, 1977; Hunt, 1961; Piaget, 1951), then the design of the indoor space becomes critical in planning for the experience and learning of young children. As part of an ongoing evaluation of their program, teachers might look at the following elements:

- the group size in which children commonly interact,
- the variety of play experiences and play spaces available and how they are used,
- the provision for one-to-one and small group interaction, and
- the degree of personalization and physical comfort afforded adults and children.

Of special importance in understanding the influence of the physical environment on behavior is the need to analyze space to see if it supports a full range of play behavior. Observing the behavior of individual children provides teachers with a complementary analysis of the quality of the play environments. The following questions are suggested:

- Quantitatively, how much play does the child engage in?
- Qualitatively, how much is social? On what cognitive levels?
- Does the physical space provide the child with opportunities to demonstrate competence yet continue to offer challenges?
- Is the environment soft and responsive? Can the child find privacy and places to pause throughout the day?
- Does the environment, as well as the people in it, respond to the child's actions predictably?
- What choices and responsibilities does the child encounter?
- Does the child engage in a variety of interactions with objects, peers, and adults?

Perhaps the art and skill of designing the early childhood environment to support the maximum involvement of each child, with materials and with each other, is one that ought to be developed. Certainly, a first step can be carefully observing young children at play, together with an analysis of the physical design aspects of the indoor space.

References

Bednar, M. J., & Haviland, D. S. (1972). *Role of the physical environment in the education of children with learning disabilities.* New York: Education Facilities Laboratories.

Bloom, B. (1964). *Stability and change in human characteristics.* New York: Wiley.

Bott, H. (1928). Observations of play activities in the nursery school. *Genetic Psychology Monographs, 4,* 44–88.

Bridges, K. M. B. (1927). Occupational interests in three-year-old children. *Pedagogical Seminary and Journal of Genetic Psychology, 34,* 415–423.

Bronfenbrenner, U. (1979). *The ecology of human development.* Cambridge, MA: Harvard University Press.

Canter, D., & Kenny, C. (1975). The spatial environment. In D. Carter (Ed.), *Environmental interaction.* London: Surrey University Press.

Deutsch, M. (1966). Early social environment: Its influence on school adaptation. In F. Hechinger (Ed.), *Preschool education today.* Garden City, NY: Doubleday.

Dodge, D. T. (1978). *Room arrangement as a teaching strategy.* Washington, DC: Dodge.

Doke, L. A., & Risley, T. R. (1972). The organization of day care environments: Required versus optional activities. *Journal of Applied Behavioral Analysis, 5,* 405–420.

Ferguson, J. (1979). Creating growth-producing environments for infants and toddlers. In E. Jones (Ed.), *Supporting growth of infants, toddlers and parents.* Pasadena, CA: Pacific Oaks College.

Fitt, S. (1974, August). The individual and his environment. *School Review.* 617–620.

Franklin, M. B., & Biber, B. (1977). Psychological perspectives and early childhood education: Some relationships between theory and practice. In L. G. Katz (Ed.) *Current topics in early childhood education* (Vol. 1). Norwood, NJ: Ablex.

Gandini, L. (1984). Not just anywhere: Making child care centers into "particular" places. *Beginnings, 1*(2), 17–20.

Gramza, A. F. (1970). Children's preferences for enterable play boxes. *Perceptual Motor Skills, 31,* 177–178.

Hart, B., & Risley, T. B. (1975). Incidental teaching of language in the preschool. *Journal of Applied Behavioral Analysis, 4,* 411–420.

Hunt, J. McV. (1961). *Intelligence and experience.* New York: Ronald.

Kounin, J. S., & Doyle, P. H. (1975). Degree of continuity of a lesson's signal system and the task of involvement of children. *Journal of Educational Psychology, 67,* 159–164.

Kounin, J. S., & Sherman, L. W. (1979). *School environments as behavior settings.* Manuscript submitted for publication.

Krantz, P., & Risley, T. (1972). *The organization of group care environments: Behavioral ecology in the classroom.* Lawrence: University of Kansas. (ERIC Document Reproduction Service No. ED 078 915)

Kritchevsky, S., & Prescott, E. (1969). *Planning environments for young children: Physical space.* Washington, DC: NAEYC.

Moore, G., Lane, C., Hill, A., Cohen, U., & McGinty, T. (1979). *Recommendations for child care centers.* (Report R79-2). Milwaukee: University of Wisconsin, School of Architecture and Urban Planning.

Moore, G. T. (1983). *The role of the socio-physical environment in cognitive development* (WP 83-5). Milwaukee: University of Wisconsin, Center for Architecture Urban Planning Research.

Moyer, K. E., & Gilmer, B. (1955). Attention spans of children for experimentally designed toys. *Journal of Genetic Psychology, 87,* 187–201.

Mueller, E., & Bergstrom, J. (1982). Fostering peer relations in young normal and handicapped children. In K. Brown (Ed.), *The social life of children in a changing society.* Hillsdale, NJ: Erlbaum.

Murphy, L. B. (1937). *Social behavior and child personality.* New York: Columbia University Press.

Nicholson, S. (1974). The theory of loose parts. In G. Coates (Ed.), *Alternative learning environments.* Stroudsburg, PA: Dowden, Hutchinson, & Ross.

Norum, G., Russo, N., & Sommer, R. (1967). Seating patterns and group tasks. *Psychology in the Schools, 4,* 276–280.

Olds, A. (1979). Designing developmentally optimal classrooms for children with special needs. In S. Meisels (Ed.), *Special education and development: Perspectives on young children with special needs.* Baltimore: University Park Press.

Osmon, F. L. (1971). *Patterns for designing children's centers.* New York: Educational Facilities Laboratories.

Phyfe-Perkins, E. (1980). Children's behavior in preschool settings: A review of research concerning the effects of the physical environment. In L. G. Katz (Ed.), *Topics in early childhood education* (Vol. 3). Norwood, NJ: Ablex.

Phyfe-Perkins, E. (1981). *Effects of teacher behavior on preschool children: A review of research* (EECE Cat. #194). Champaign: University of Illinois, College of Education.

Piaget, J. (1951). *Play, dreams and imitation in childhood.* New York: Norton.

Pollowy, A. M. (1974). The child in the physical environment: A design problem. In G. Coates (Ed.), *Alternative learning environments.* Stroudsburg, PA: Dowden, Hutchinson, & Ross.

Prescott, E. (1978). Is day care as good as a good home? *Young Children, 33*(2) 13–19.

Prescott, E. (1984). The physical setting in day care. In J. T. Greenmen & R. W. Fuqua (Ed.), *Making day care better.* New York: Teachers College Press, Columbia University.

Prescott, E., Jones, E., & Kritchevsky, S. (1967). *Group day care as a child rearing environment: An observational study of day care programs.* Pasadena, CA: Pacific Oaks College. (ERIC Document Reproduction Service No. ED 024 453)

Proshansky, E., & Wolfe, M. (1974). The physical setting and open education. In T. G. David & B. D. Wright (Eds.), *Learning environments* (pp. 30–48). Chicago: University of Chicago Press.

Rho, L., & Drury, F. (1978). *Space and time in early learning.* Cheshire, CT: Cheshire Board of Education.

Rubin, K. H. (1977). Play behaviors of young children. *Young Children 32,* 16–24.

Rubin, K. H., & Seibel, C. G. (1979, March). The effects of ecological setting on the cognitive and social play behaviors of preschoolers. Paper presented at the annual meeting of American Educational Research Association, San Francisco.

Ruopp, R., Travers, J., Glantz, F., & Coelen, C. (1979). *Children at the center: Final report of the National Day Care Study.* New York: Abt Associates.

Sheehan, R., & Day, D. (1975, December). Is open space just empty space? *Day Care and Early Education, 47,* 3, 10–13.

Sherman, L. W. (1975). An ecological study of glee in small groups of preschool children. *Child Development, 46,* 53–61.

Smith, P. K. (1974). Aspects of the playgroup environment. *Psychology and the Built Environment.* England: Architectural Press.

Sommer, R. (1974). *Tight spaces, hard architecture and how to humanize it.* Englewood Cliffs, NJ: Prentice-Hall.

Sommer, R. (1969). *Personal space: The behavioral basis of design.* Englewood Cliffs, NJ: Prentice-Hall.

Stallings, J. (1975). Implementation and child effects of teaching practices in Follow Through classrooms. *Monographs of the Society for Research in Child Development, 40,* (7–8, Serial No. 163).

Van Alstyne, D. (1932). *Play behavior and choice of play materials of preschool children.* Chicago: University of Chicago Press.

Joe L. Frost

Contemporary super-structures, properly designed and installed, promote a wide range of play activities within a limited space.

CHAPTER THIRTEEN

Children's Playgrounds: Research and Practice

JOE L. FROST

History of the playground movement

The playground movement began in Europe and the United States in the late 1800s. Just as with similar social movements of the period, programs and facilities rapidly expanded in an attempt to plan life and recreational activities for children and youth (Rainwater, 1921). A political leader, von Schenckendorff, developed the first play areas in Berlin during the 1880s (Sapora & Mitchell, 1948). These open play areas were covered with sand and contained play apparatus for children 2 to 8 years of age. Between 1918 and 1933 widespread attention was given in Germany to the development of indoor and outdoor play facilities unsurpassed anywhere in the world. It is noteworthy that in 1826 the German schoolmaster Frederich Froebel was the first to take a strong position for the educational merits of play and his ideas resulted in the first kindergarten.

The playground movement in the United States had a feeble start in the late 19th century. Before 1900, only 10 cities had established playgrounds. The first was Boston in 1886, followed by Chicago, Philadelphia, Pittsburgh, Baltimore, Hartford, New Haven, New York, San Francisco, and Albany. The original Boston playground was initiated by Dr. Marie Azkrewska (Sapora & Mitchell, 1948). Impressed by children playing in Berlin sand heaps, she wrote to Ellen Tower, Chairman of the Committee of the Massachusetts Emergency and Hygiene Association. Women of the organization placed three piles of sand in the yards of the Children's Mission on Parmenter Street and America's first formal playground was created! Through inquiries from other cities and lectures by Ellen Tower on the success of sandgardens, the idea spread. The reasons given for the sandgardens reflected the social problems of the period: the dangers of playing in the streets; the provision of wholesome environments to counter juvenile delinquency; and the increasing congestion of cities and the resulting need for safe, supervised play areas.

In 1889, Boston opened the Charles Bank Outdoor Gymnasium for adolescent boys and men, equipped with apparatus, track, and space for games. A section was added for girls and women 2 years later. This forerunner of park playgrounds led in 1903 to the development of the South Park playgrounds in Chicago, and a Chicago tax bill of $10 million for park playgrounds. These recreation facilities provided for both indoor and outdoor activities. The famous Hull House Playground opened in 1894 under the leadership of Jane Addams. It was termed a *model playground* and set the standard for later school playgrounds. Public support for the movement was also marked by the opening of several school playgrounds in New York in 1899.

Most early school and public park playgrounds resulted from the efforts of private citizens who wanted their children to have larger and safer places to play than city streets and backyards. The conflicts about control and related issues stimulated the development in 1906 of the Playground and Recreation Association of America (later the National Recreation Association) to coordinate the establishment of playgrounds. An initial task of this group was to draft an Outline for Playground Law (Curtis, 1917/1977). The final document recommended: (1) size of the play area at schools, (2) time limits devoted to play, (3) provisions for employing play supervisors, (4) types of play apparatus and equipment, (5) formulas for state funds for maintenance of school playgrounds, and (6) the establishment of a department for play and physical training within state boards of education.

Three years later, the Association (1909) identified the social ends to be attained through play. They were cleanliness, politeness, formation of friendships, obedience to law, loyalty, justice, honesty, truthfulness, and determination. Two points relevant to this early period should be noted. First, the early proponents of playgrounds were not merely romantics or idealists. Luella A. Palmer, assistant director of kindergartens in New York City, wrote that play develops bodily organs, develops keen and quick thought, widens mental horizons, and promotes social development (Palmer, 1916). Second, playground pioneers created playgrounds to compensate for the loss of country resources resulting from crowded city living. "The apparatus furnished what might be given by the natural resources of the country and the play things which the country child can make for himself" (Palmer, 1916, pp. 251–252).

In 1928, the National Recreation Association developed innovative guidelines for selecting playground apparatus. These guidelines recommended that a preschool playground contain six chair swings, a sand box, a small slide, and a simple low climber. Elementary school playgrounds were recommended to contain six swings on a frame 12 feet high, a horizontal ladder, a slide 8 feet high with a chute 16 feet long, a giant-stride, a balance beam, a horizontal bar, and optional equipment such as traveling rings, seesaws, and low climbing devices. The guidelines also specified the design of equipment. For example, swings should be galvanized pipe with hardboard seats; slides should only be wide enough for one child to encourage taking turns, with an 8-inch platform at the top; climbing structures should be various combinations of galvanized pipe. Design, materials, and construction should ensure economical maintenance, safety, simplicity of supervision, and developmental and recreational values (Butler, 1958). These guidelines established precedents in design that continue to be profoundly influential today. **Unfortunately, these guidelines are hopelessly inadequate in the light of contemporary theory and research on play and playgrounds.**

Recent developments

Throughout the Western countries, playground development has roughly paralleled the industrialization process, accompanied by urbanization, growing affluence, increased education, greater awareness of health needs, and interest in physical fitness. Major social factors influencing the movement in the United States were awareness that one third of World War I military recruits were unfit physically; availability of federal funds for recreation and park facilities during the Great Depression; and economic prosperity following World War II.

Despite this accelerated interest in playgrounds, virtually no progress in design was seen in the first half of this century. Professionals continued to suggest playground equipment remarkably similar to that prescribed in the early 1900s. One of the popular texts on play and recreation (Sapora & Mitchell, 1948) recommended that the fully equipped playground include swings, teeter totters, stride, horizontal bar, horizontal ladder, seesaws, slides, parallel bars, traveling rings, swinging rings, merry-go-round, balancing board, sliding pole, vaulting horses, jungle gym, and balance beam. It is to their credit that these authorities recommended shaded areas and resilient play surfaces: "loose gravel makes an unsure footing . . . concrete is not only too hot in the summer but the jar from playing on it is tiring" (p. 379).

Inventiveness during the first half of this century tended to be restricted to unrealistic alternatives bent to the whims of adults rather than children. The late Lady Allen of Hurtwood (1968) described six periods of playground development:

(1) the prison period with level asphalt and concrete — "An administrator's heaven and a child's hell,"
(2) the ironmongery period with its "proliferation of prison bars,"
(3) the concrete pipe period reflecting "paucity of invention,"
(4) the novelty period with painted steam rollers and fire engines — "the pride of the town clerk,"
(5) the maze period, "over-elaborate, over-clever, too slick — the pride of the architects," and, finally,
(6) the do-it-yourself period with playgrounds where children can "test themselves against new challenges in complete freedom" (pp. 18 – 19).

This final period signaled the first profound change in playground development. The first waste material or adventure playground was established in Emdrup, Denmark in 1945 by a landscape architect, C. T. Sorensen and his associates (Hurtwood, 1968). Wanting children in crowded cities to receive the same opportunities for creative play as those in the country, he set up a large area with old cars, boxes, timbers, boards, and tools. This initial effort inspired hundreds of adventure playgrounds in Scandinavian countries and, later, in industrial countries around the world. The most comprehensive ones, in Denmark and Sweden, contain extensive areas for building, cooking, gardening, climbing, playing games, and caring for animals. The Danish intent is to provide recreation facilities for both children and adults in close proximity to their homes. Trained play leaders work with children in a cooperative manner. The dozens of adventure playgrounds scattered about London also were influenced by Lady Allen. Her London adventure playgrounds for handicapped children are still in operation.

The adventure playground movement has been slow to gain a footing in the United States. The American Adventure Playground Association was formed in 1976, but its influence on playgrounds has been minimal. Resistence to so-called junk playgrounds is firmly entrenched in American beliefs that adults know best, concern that playgrounds be sanitary and neat, and prevailing practice rooted in early 1900s guidelines stressing ease of maintenance, physical fitness, and outmoded theories of play (e.g., play as relaxation, expenditure of surplus energy, or preparation for adulthood).

Playgrounds today

Playground types

Adult-made playgrounds can be classified into four types: traditional, designer or contemporary, adventure, and creative (Frost, 1978).

The *traditional* playground is typically a flat, barren area equipped with steel structures such as swings, slide, seesaws, climbers, and merry-go-round, fixed in concrete and arranged in a row. The equipment is designed for exercise play exclusively. The *designer* or *contemporary* playground is typically designed by a professional architect or designer using manufactured equipment, usually wood, and expensive stone and timber terracing. It is intended to have high aesthetic appeal for adults. The *adventure* playground is a highly informal playground within a fenced area stocked with scrap building material, tools, and provision for animals and cooking. One or more play leaders are available to assist children as needed. The *creative* playground is a semiformal environment combining features of the other types to meet the needs of a specific community or school. It often represents a compromise between highly formal playgrounds and the junk or adventure playground. A wide range of manufactured and handmade equipment and loose materials is provided, depending on their availability and the play needs of children.

Traditional playgrounds remain the most prevalent type, but contemporary playgrounds are gaining ground, particularly in public parks. Unfortunately, adventure playgrounds are generally unacceptable to most American adults. Creative playgrounds are growing in popularity, especially in preschools. But what about the quality of America's playgrounds?

Playground quality

A Play Group of the American Alliance for Health, Physical Education, Recreation and Dance completed a national survey of playgrounds in 1986. Results are being analyzed. The most extensive previous surveys were conducted by Vernon (1976) and Monroe (1983).

Vernon surveyed a randomly selected sample of 269 Texas public elementary schools. She found playground equipment designed for exercise play (traditional playgrounds) with little or no provision for dramatic or construction play. Playgrounds were not established by careful design, and very little attention was given to outdoor play when schools were planned. Parent-teacher associations were a common source of funds for playgrounds because school districts frequently had no budget for building playgrounds. Fewer still provided a maintenance and development budget, and more than 60% had no plans to improve their playgrounds in the future. The equipment was standardized — monkey bars, slides, swings, seesaws, and merry-go-round — surrounded by hard-packed earth and asphalt, all consistent with the guidelines of the early 1900s. Teacher aides supervised outdoor play more often than teachers and both teachers and principals preferred to assign play periods to aides or physical education teachers.

In a more recent survey, Monroe used the comprehensive Modified Playground Rating System adapted from the Playground Rating System (Frost & Klein, 1979, 1984). She surveyed playgrounds at 56 of 443 Title XX child care centers (commercial and nonprofit) in Texas, selected by random, stratified sample. The most common equipment was of the traditional steel, fixed variety, and the most common surfaces were grass, concrete, and asphalt with many playgrounds having concrete or asphalt even in fall zones under equipment. In contrast to public school playgrounds, the preschools had a range of portable equipment including tricycles (74% of the playgrounds surveyed) and tires (63%). Fewer than 35% of the playgrounds contained blocks, boxes, barrels, rocking boats, saw horses, ropes, spools, or boards. Trained observers rated the playgrounds on 20 content, 10 safety, and 10 functional characteristics. The mean score for all playgrounds on content (equipment, materials) was 39.9 (100 possible). The mean score on safety was 65 and the mean score on functional characteristics (e.g., encourages play, complements cognitive play) was 59.4. With a composite mean of 55 out of a possible 100, the playgrounds were rated as follows: excellent — none, good — 5, fair — 25, poor — 22, and nonfunctional — 2.

Although the same instrument was not used in these two studies, the surveys suggest that preschool playgrounds are of higher quality than public elementary school playgrounds. No extensive survey of public park playgrounds is available. Meanwhile, national attention has focused on playground safety, which is one of the important features assessed in these studies.

Playground safety

There are two fundamental problems with most playgrounds: They are inappropriate to the developmental needs of children and they are hazardous (Frost & Klein, 1979/1984). Risk taking is essential in outdoor play, but most playgrounds contain hazards that could be removed without reducing challenge. These hazards are caused primarily by inappropriate equipment design, improper installation, inadequate maintenance, and hard surfaces under and around equipment. The best estimates on playground injuries and fatalities come from the National

Electronic Injury Surveillance System (Rutherford, 1979), which reported that in 1977, an estimated 150,773 children were treated in emergency rooms following injuries on playgrounds. Seventy-one percent of all injuries on playgrounds resulted from falls onto hard surfaces, either ground cover (asphalt, concrete, hard-packed earth) or sections of equipment.

In addition, an unacceptably high number of injuries and deaths result from poorly designed equipment (pinch and shear points, protruding elements, excessive heights, entrapment areas), improper installation, and poor maintenance. Despite the available cause-effect documentation on playground injuries, no mandatory guidelines or standards are imposed on equipment manufacturers.

A problem of potentially grave consequences was brought to public attention by Freedberg (1983) and Youth News in a publication aptly titled *America's Poisoned Playgrounds*. A survey conducted in New York, Philadelphia, Chicago, and San Francisco revealed a number of playground problems related to the use and disposal of toxic materials. In an unknown number of communities across the nation, abandoned landfills and warehouses containing toxic wastes are being used as play areas by children. Playgrounds are often placed in the most undesirable locations, including areas near freeways and other places with extensive auto emissions. Pesticides used in parks and playgrounds pose another hazard because children may play in newly sprayed areas. Finally, toxic materials such as arsenic-copper combinations and pentachloraphenol are widely used by play equipment manufacturers. The use of such materials is virtually unregulated. There are no mandatory regulations for the use of chemicals in playground equipment at the local, state, or national levels.

Standards for play equipment and playgrounds

For more than a decade, sporadic efforts have been made to establish standards for play equipment and playgrounds (Henniger, Strickland, & Frost, 1982). The American Academy of Pediatrics (1969) developed a draft of standards for home playground equipment that were abandoned in 1971. In 1972 the United States Bureau of Product Safety issued a report on the dismal picture of playground hazards in the United States and Canada. In the same year, the University of Iowa (McConnell, Parks, & Knapp, 1973) was commissioned by the Consumer Product Safety Commission (CPSC) to study safety on public playground equipment. About this same time, the Playground Equipment Manufacturer's Association and the National Recreation and Park Association were developing proposed voluntary equipment standards to be published by the CPSC (1973).

Failure of these efforts to result in acceptable standards led to petitions by Butwinick (1974) and Sweeney (1974) to the CPSC to initiate the development of standards. A draft of proposed standards was developed by the National Recreation and Park Association (1976), but this draft was subjected to intense criticism by the equipment industry, playground designers, and the CPSC itself. Subsequently, the CPSC commissioned the National Bureau of Standards (NBS) (1978a, 1978b) to revise the proposed standards and conduct impact tests on playground surfaces. Two reports issued by this agency were not accepted as standards but were revised and made available to the public as handbooks by the CPSC (1981a, 1981b).

An analysis of the original NBS reports was conducted by Frost (1980) and of the CPSC handbooks by Henniger, Strickland, and Frost (1982). There are still no mandatory standards for the manufacture of play equipment; consumers must exercise special precautions when selecting, installing, and using play equipment. The CPSC handbooks contain examples and illustrations of outmoded equipment and are, in most respects, useful guidelines to help ensure a reasonably *safe* play environment. The handbooks, however, do not address the equally important factors of *how* children use play environments or the developmental implications of their use.

How children use play environments

Perhaps the most extensive series of studies on children's play behaviors and equipment choices in outdoor play environments has been conducted at the University of Texas at Austin during the past decade. Abbreviated versions of many of these studies are available in Frost and Sunderlin (1985). These studies were initiated by the Texas State Survey of Public School Playgrounds (Vernon, 1976), conducted in 1974 and 1975 and reported earlier in this chapter. Several of the studies used the four playground categories described — traditional, designer/contemporary, adventure, and creative.

Frost and Campbell (1977) and Campbell and Frost (1985) compared the play behaviors of second grade children in two types of play environments — traditional and creative — using adaptations of the Piaget-Smilansky cognitive play categories and the Parten social play categories (Table 13.1).

The two play environments differed in the frequency of cognitive play. Functional or exercise play was significantly higher on the traditional playground, consuming more than three fourths (77.9%) of the play there versus less than half (43.7%) of the play on the creative playground. More dramatic play was observed on the creative (39%) than on the traditional (2%) playground. More constructive play took place on the creative playground, while more games with rules occurred on the traditional playground.

Among the social play categories, cooperative play was the most frequently occurring category on both playgrounds (traditional 45.6% and creative 50.2%). More solitary play (11% versus 3.4%) and associative play (12% versus 8.5%) occurred on the creative playground than on the traditional playground.

Table 13.1 Play Categories

Type of play	*Child's behavior*
Cognitive	
Functional	Repetition of actions for the fun of it
Constructive	Manipulation of objects to construct or create something
Dramatic or symbolic	Substitution of an imaginary situation or object in pretend play situations
Games with rules	Acceptance of prearranged rules and adjustment to them in organized play
Social	
Solitary	Child plays alone and independently
Parallel	Child plays *beside* rather than *with* other children
Associative	Child plays with other children but each child plays as she or he chooses
Cooperative	Child plays as a member of a self-organized play group striving to attain some common goal

Significantly more parallel play took place on the traditional (29.5%) than on the creative (12.6%) playground.

The presence of different materials and equipment on the two playgrounds had a marked effect on all play categories. Results of this study support the contention that environment has a significant effect on behavior (Gump, 1975) and that settings in which events and behavior occur have inherent regulatory features (Prescott, Jones, & Kritchevsky, 1972).

The wider selection of equipment on the creative playground appeared to stimulate more solitary play, leading children to play apart from others or on separate equipment. However, in this solitary play, children exhibited a range of cognitive activity, an observation that lends support to the position of Moore, Everston, and Brophy (1974), who resist the assumption that solitary play should be categorized lower in hierarchical order than other cognitive forms of play.

The diversity of dramatic and constructive play materials and equipment on the creative playground clearly stimulated these forms of play, whereas their absence on the traditional playground resulted in more functional, parallel play, and games with rules, a finding similar to that of Frost and Campbell (1985).

These findings for second grade children support Strickland's (1979) study of third grade children. He also found that, in comparing a traditional to a creative playground, the latter was more often chosen for dramatic play by both boys and girls. He added the intriguing observation that on the creative playground children *were* the characters in dramatic play and actually acted and talked out roles, while on a traditional playground they merely talked them out. Key materials in these dramatic play sequences were the loose or transportable items (spools, tires, boards, sand, wheeled vehicles), available on the creative playground but absent on the traditional playground.

Availability of equipment and materials also affects form, intensity, and nature of play. Frost and Campbell (1977) and Campbell and Frost (1985) found that second grade children prefer action-oriented to static equipment. On a conventional playground children selected action-oriented swings, merry-go-rounds, and seesaws over fixed apparatus and slides. On a creative playground, play houses (supplied with movable props for dramatic play) were the most popular equipment, followed by movable materials and a boat that could be rocked by the children to stimulate sea travel. On a creative playground the play was spread over a wide range of equipment. Conversely, the equipment on a traditional playground was primarily fixed and limited in variety. On a creative playground, equipment designed for functional play (slides, climbers, swings) was selected for play less than one fourth of the time while equipment or materials designed for dramatic play (sand, loose materials, boat, and car) were selected for more than half of the play.

Expansion of the above studies to include a broader age group, 5- to 8-year-olds, resulted in even more startling findings (Frost & Strickland, 1978). When given free choice of three playgrounds constructed adjacent to one another, children selected a creative playground 64% of the time, a traditional playground 23% of the time, and a special manufactured, fixed, multipurpose structure advertised as a complete playground 13% of the time. An interesting sidelight is that the costs of the playgrounds, respectively, were $500, $2,500, and $7,000. The results of this study strongly suggest that it is faulty to assume that a single structure or combination of structures designed primarily for one form of play (exercise or functional) is sufficiently varied to accommodate the free play choices or developmental play needs of young children.

Similarly, obstacle course equipment arranged in a circular pattern and designed for movement through a series of gross-motor challenges may not function as intended in free play situations (Frost & Vernon, 1976). When 200 six- to eight-year-old children were observed daily for 8 weeks during free play with access to an adjacent creative playground and obstacle course of 10 different structures, only two 6-year-olds and four 7-year-olds used the obstacle course in the manner for which it was designed: to complete the circle while attempting each challenge in turn. It appears that obstacle courses are unsuitable for free play, but may have value for directed activity such as physical education classes.

In contrast to traditional equipment and obstacle courses, contemporary super-structures feature a wide range of motor functions and play possibilities combined into one interlinking structure, thus increasing complexity and challenge. A single unified super-structure provides most of the play opportunities of a traditional playground and does so in one relatively small area. In addition, play and safety are enhanced by the addition of sand underneath and around the structure (Frost & Klein, 1979, 1984), variety in play behaviors is stimulated (Bowers, 1976), and time at play and peer interaction are increased (Bruya, 1985).

Super-structure value is further enhanced by the provision of loose parts or transportable materials that can be used under and around the super-structure for dramatic and constructive play (Frost & Klein, 1979, 1984; Strickland, 1979). Indeed, an abundance of loose or transportable materials seems to be the nucleus of a good playground because these items offer flexibility, diversity, novelty, and challenge and are readily adaptable to use in conjunction with fluid materials, such as sand and water as well as with fixed structures (Frost & Klein, 1979, 1984; Frost & Strickland, 1978; Strickland, 1979; Noren-Bjorn, 1982).

A creative outdoor playground, featuring a variety of fixed and movable equipment, influences play differently than does a typical nursery school indoor environment (Henniger, 1977). The outdoor environment stimulates social play as frequently as the indoor environment. Results from Henniger's study, as well as others in the University of Texas project, show that with the right equipment and careful teacher planning and encouragement, any desired type of play can be stimulated in the outdoor environment and that the outdoor environment has advantages over the indoors for certain types of play and for certain children.

In particular, the indoor environment fostered more dramatic play for girls and younger children, while the outdoor environment stimulated nearly all of the functional play of both boys and girls. Older boys performed most of their dramatic play outdoors, a finding that supports Sanders and Harper (1976). Culture and environment appear to influence differences in the behavior of boys and girls (Lee & Voivodas, 1977). These factors appear to have been involved in these studies, which revealed sex differences for all groups studied, ages 4 through 8. In the Campbell and Frost (1985) study, boys engaged in dramatic play on the creative playground about twice as frequently (45% of total play) as did girls (28% of total play). Bell and Walker's (1985) study of 3-, 4-, and 5-year-olds revealed that boys dominated play on the super-structure, boat, and play house, while girls controlled a separate portion of the playground containing an open air log cabin and swings.

In contrast to 4- through 8-year-old children, toddlers engage in less complex forms of social and cognitive play (Winter, 1983). More than 60% of the social play of toddlers (25 to 34 months) in Winter's study was proximal (playing near others but in their own way), followed by 19% relational (playing in own way but communicating with others), 17% independent (playing alone), and 3% interactive (playing with peers in a common activity). In cognitive play, the combination category (performing two or more movements in an identifiable pattern or placing two or more objects into spatial relationships) accounted for more than half of all play. Repetitive play accounted for 36% and dramatic play about 10%. These findings are consistent with Piaget's theories concerning the age of emergence of various forms of play and imply that the materials and equipment for play should be age/stage specific.

With respect to equipment choices, Winter found that toddlers prefer loose or transportable materials to stationary equipment. The versatility of these items seemed to account for their popularity, a reasonable explanation if one considers the infinite ways to play with sand, the most popular play material for toddlers. It is noteworthy that toddlers also differ in equipment choices and play behavior by gender. For example, boys preferred items inviting active gross motor participation (tricycle, wagon, balance beams) but girls preferred fine motor manipulation and sedentary activity (sand, tea set, cooking pots).

Steele and Nauman (1985) examined the play of infants and toddlers (10 to 35 months) on a play environment containing large and small sandboxes, complex and simple slides, open and closed cubes, and cardboard boxes taped shut. The younger children chose, in descending frequency, the open cube, large sandbox, simple slide, slide with tunnel, small sandbox, and closed cube. Small sand areas elicited a high degree of play by the older toddlers, as did closed cubes and complex slides. Clearly, greater complexity and variety should be added to playgrounds as children develop. The equipment in this study was designed for infants and toddlers and the high frequency of use by the children suggests that designers should scale equipment to children's size/age/developmental levels.

Comparison of types of playgrounds

The research on playgrounds shows that traditional, fixed playgrounds are poor places for children's play from both safety and developmental perspectives (Hole, 1966). Holme and Massie (1971) note that traditional playgrounds suffer from low use rates compared to alternative play places, such as roads and lots, not designed as playgrounds. Traditional playgrounds have low attendance rates compared to contemporary or adventure playgrounds (Hayward, Rothenberg, & Beasley, 1974) and creative playgrounds (Frost & Campbell, 1977; Frost & Strickland, 1978). Adventure playgrounds are popular in certain European countries but not widely accepted in the United States. Yet Vance (1977) reported data from 14 agencies in five states showing that adventure playgrounds were superior to conventional playgrounds: They were less expensive to maintain; community participation was greater; and the number of injuries was about the same or lower.

In sum, the growing body of evidence points to a play environment for young children that contains a variety of both fixed, complex equipment and simple, transportable materials. Large, fixed structures cannot be readily manipulated or modified by children so complexity must be built in by design. On the other hand, movable materials or loose parts can be manipulated and arranged by children in almost unlimited fashion. Because preschool children are able to create characters and situations through mental imagery, props or materials need not be theme specific or suggestive — raw materials such as sand, water, tires, lumber, and spools serve quite well.

Creative and adventure playgrounds, with provisions for various forms of social and cognitive play, clearly surpass conventional and contemporary playgrounds in play value. With attention to safety guidelines (Consumer Product Safety Commission, 1981a, 1981b; Frost & Henniger, 1979; Henniger, Strickland, & Frost, 1982), adventure playgrounds can be reasonably safe while ensuring challenge and variety. Such playgrounds also accommodate extra features that greatly enhance play and learning — animals, nature areas, digging and construction areas, cooking, and organized games — a far cry from the fixed, single function, exercise-oriented equipment of the early playgrounds and their present day copies.

Process for playground improvement

The teacher plays an important role in planning, developing, and using playgrounds. Few administrators, school designers, or teachers are trained in playground design or in play theory and practice. A selected list of readings for those designing or modifying playgrounds appears in Table 13.2.

In general terms, teachers who assume responsibility for playground design should begin by familiarizing themselves with the literature, visit a few high quality playgrounds (Appendix B in Frost & Klein, 1984, is a checklist to evaluate playgrounds), and consult with reputable specialists with a child development background before finalizing site plans or purchasing equipment. High quality playgrounds are complex and require the integration of space, boundaries, service utilities, play equipment, portable materials, storage facilities, wheeled vehicle tracks, landscaping, and classrooms. Age and numbers of children, their developmental needs, and the curriculum of the program are additional important factors to consider.

Table 13.2 Readings for adults involved in designing or modifying playgrounds

Consumer Product Safety Commission. (1981). *A handbook for public playground safety. Volume I: General guidelines for new and existing playgrounds.* Washington, DC: U.S. Government Printing Office.

Frost, J. L., & Henniger, M. (1979). Making playgrounds safe for children and children safe for playgrounds. *Young Children, 34*(5), 23–30.

Frost, J. L., & Klein, B. L. (1984). *Children's play and playgrounds.* Playgrounds International, P.O. Box 33363, Austin, TX 78764.

Frost, J. L., & Sunderlin, S. (Eds.). (1985). *When children play.* Wheaton, MD: Association for Childhood Education International.

Garvey, C. (1977). *Play.* Cambridge, MA: Harvard University Press.

Hogan, P. (1982). *The nuts and bolts of playground construction.* West Point, NY: Leisure Press.

Rouard, M., & Simon, J. (1977). *Children's play spaces: From sandbox to adventure playground.* Woodstock, NY: The Overlook Press.

Although the design and development of good playgrounds is essentially a professional task, children, parents, and school administrators should be involved at all stages. Ideally, orientation sessions about the nature and value of play and the qualities of good playgrounds will be conducted for all parties involved in playground design, beginning with the initiation of playground planning and continuing into the implementation or use period. Teachers with extensive training in child development are usually better equipped to provide leadership than adults with more limited training. Studious, cooperative teams of adults and children can and do develop better play spaces for children.

References

American Academy of Pediatrics. (1969). *Proposed voluntary standard for children's home playground equipment.* Evanston, IL: Author.

Bell, M. J., & Walker, P. (1985). Interactive patterns in children's play groups. In J. L. Frost & S. Sunderlin (Eds.), *When children play.* Wheaton, MD: Association for Childhood Education International.

Bowers, L. (1976). *Play learning centers for pre-school handicapped children.* Tampa, FL: University of South Florida.

Butler, G. D. (1958). *Recreation areas: Their design and equipment* (2nd ed.). New York: Ronald Press.

Butwinick, E. (1974). Petition requesting the issuance of a Consumer Product Safety standard for public playground slides, swinging apparatus and climbing equipment. Washington, DC: Consumer Product Safety Commission.

Bruya, L. D. (1985). The effect of play structure format differences on the play behavior of preschool children. In J. L. Frost & S. Sunderlin (Eds.), *When children play.* Wheaton, MD: Association for Childhood Education International.

Campbell, S., & Frost, J. L. (1985). The effects of playground type on the cognitive and social play behavior of grade two children. In J. L. Frost & S. Sunderlin (Eds.), *When children play.* Wheaton, MD: Association for Childhood Education International.

Consumer Product Safety Commission. (1981a). *A handbook for public playground safety: Volume 1. General guidelines for new and existing playgrounds.* Washington, DC: U.S. Government Printing Office.

Consumer Product Safety Commission. (1981b). *A handbook for public playground safety: Volume 2. General guidelines for new and existing playgrounds.* Washington, DC: U.S. Government Printing Office.

Consumer Product Safety Commission. (1973). Proposed technical requirements for heavy duty playground equipment regulations. Washington, DC: Author.

Curtis, H. S. (1977). *The play movement and its significance.* Washington, DC: McGrath Publishing Company and National Recreation and Park Association. (Original work published 1917)

Freedberg, L. (1983). *America's poisoned playgrounds.* Conference on Alternative State and Local Policies, 2000 Florida Ave., N.W., Washington, DC.

Frost, J. L. (1978). The American playground movement. *Childhood Education,* *54*(4), 176–182.

Frost, J. L. (1980, January). *Commentary: Public playground equipment.* Submitted to the U.S. Consumer Product Safety Commission.

Frost, J. L., & Campbell, S. (1977). *Play and play equipment choices of young children on two types of playgrounds.* Unpublished manuscript, The University of Texas at Austin.

Frost, J. L., & Campbell, S. D. (1985). Equipment choices of primary age children on conventional and creative playgrounds. In J. L. Frost & S. Sunderlin (Eds.), *When children play.* Wheaton, MD: Association for Childhood Education International.

Frost, J. L., & Henniger, M. (1979). Making playgrounds safe for children and children safe for playgrounds. *Young Children, 34*(5), 23–30.

Frost, J. L., & Klein, B. L. (1979). *Children's play and playgrounds.* Boston: Allyn & Bacon. (1984). Playgrounds International, P.O. Box 33363, Austin, TX 78764.

Frost, J. L., & Strickland, E. (1978). Equipment choices of young children during free play. *Lutheran Education, 114*(1), 34–46.

Frost, J. L., & Sunderlin, S. (Eds.). (1985). *When children play.* Wheaton, MD: Association for Childhood Education International.

Frost, J. L., & Vernon, L. (1976). *Movement patterns of first and second grade children on an obstacle course.* Unpublished manuscript, The University of Texas at Austin.

Gump, P. V. (1975). Ecological psychology and children. In E. M. Hetherington (Ed.), *Review of child development* (Vol. 5). Chicago: University of Chicago Press.

Hayward, D. G., Rothenburg, M., & Beasley, R. R. (1974). Children's play and urban playground environments. *Environment and Behavior, 6*(2), 131–168.

Henniger, M. (1977). *Free play behavior of nursery school children in an indoor and outdoor environment.* Unpublished doctoral dissertation, The University of Texas at Austin.

Henniger, M., Strickland, E., & Frost, J. L. (1982). X-rated playgrounds: Issues and developments. *Journal of Physical Education, Recreation and Dance, 53*(6), 72–77.

Hole, V. (1966). *Children's play on housing estates.* London: HMSO.

Holme, A., & Massie, D. (1971). *Children's play: A study of needs and opportunities.* London: Michael Joseph.

Hurtwood, L. A. (1968). *Planning for play.* Cambridge, MA: MIT Press.

Lee, P. C., & Voivodas, G. K. (1977). Sex role and pupil role in early childhood education. In L. G. Katz (Ed.), *Current topics in early childhood education.* Norwood, NJ: Ablex.

McConnell, W. H., Parks, J. T., & Knapp, L. W., Jr. (1973, October). *Public playgrounds equipment.* University of Iowa College of Medicine, Iowa City.

Monroe, M. L. (1983). *Evaluation of day care playgrounds in Texas.* Unpublished doctoral dissertation, The University of Texas at Austin.

Moore, N. V., Evertson, C. M., & Brophy, J. E. (1974). Solitary play: Some functional considerations. *Developmental Psychology, 10,* 830–834.

National Bureau of Standards. (1978a). Suggested safety requirements and supporting rationale for swing assemblies and straight slides. Washington, DC: Consumer Product Safety Commission.

National Bureau of Standards. (1978b). Suggested safety requirements and supporting rationale for public playground equipment. Washington, DC: Consumer Product Safety Commission.

National Recreation and Park Association. (1976). Proposed safety standard for public playground equipment. Washington, DC: Consumer Product Safety Commission.

Noren-Bjorn, E. (1982). *The impossible playground*. West Point: Leisure Press.

Palmer, L. A. (1916). *Play life in the first eight years*. Boston: Ginn.

Playground and Recreation Association of America. (1909). *Proceedings of the Third Annual Congress of the Playground Association, 3*(3).

Prescott, E., Jones, E., & Kritchevsky, S. (1972). *Day care as a child-rearing environment*. Washington, DC: NAEYC.

Rainwater, C. E. (1921). *The play movement in the United States*. Chicago: University of Chicago Press.

Rutherford, G. W. (1979). *HIA hazard analysis report*. Washington, DC: Consumer Product Safety Commission.

Sanders, K. M., & Harper, L. V. (1976). Free play fantasy behavior in preschool children: Relations among gender, age, season and location. *Child Development, 47*, 1182–1185.

Sapora, A. V., & Mitchell, E. D. (1948). *The theory of play and recreation*. New York: Ronald Press.

Steele, C., & Nauman, M. (1985). Infants' play on outdoor play equipment. In J. L. Frost & S. Sunderlin (Eds.), *When children play*. Wheaton, MD: Association for Childhood Education International.

Strickland, E. V. (1979). Free play behaviors and equipment choices of third grade children in contrasting play environments. Unpublished doctoral dissertation, The University of Texas at Austin.

Sweeney, T. (1974, May). Petition to the Consumer Product Safety Commission. Cleveland Heights, OH: Coventry School PTA.

United States Bureau of Product Safety. (1972, September 17). *Public playground equipment*. Washington, DC: Food and Drug Administration.

Vance, B. (1977). The president's message. *American Adventure Play Association News, 1*(4), 1.

Vernon, E. (1976). *A survey of preprimary and primary outdoor learning centers/playgrounds in Texas public schools*. Unpublished doctoral dissertation, The University of Texas at Austin.

Winter, S. (1983). *Toddler play in an outdoor play environment*. Unpublished doctoral dissertation, The University of Texas at Austin.

Joe L. Frost

Diversity of materials and equipment clearly stimulates dramatic and constructive play.

The Teacher's Place in Children's Play

MARY S. RIVKIN

"A teacher," observed Henry Adams, "affects eternity; he can never tell where his influence stops" (1931, p. 300). The tremendous responsibility undertaken in teaching, alternately exhilarating and terrifying to the thoughtful person, requires that knowledge of teaching and children be enterprising. Readers of this volume will have encountered such knowledge and will surely seek to translate it into practical applications for their situations. In its entirety, this book supports the longstanding belief of early childhood educators that play is intrinsic and indispensable to a young child's life.

Beyond corroborating this basic belief, this book provides information about sustaining and encouraging play in three broad areas. First, in presenting evidence of developmental play sequences, the chapters shape the reader's thinking about individual manifestations of play and their relationship to total development. In describing the social interactions of play, the book suggests arenas of teacher influence. Finally, by describing the complex and significant influence of environments on play, these chapters illuminate ways—many highly accessible—to stimulate and enrich children's play.

Vandenberg's introductory chapter demonstrates how thoughts about play have changed and developed during this century, providing us with the current perspective that play, like other aspects of human behavior, follows a developmental sequence involving increasing complexity and capability. For instance, we place young infants side by side and watch them play, usually only occasionally aware of each other; we see 3-year-olds sit side by side at the clay table and scarcely speak even though they have chosen where to sit; we see 5-year-olds engrossed in a drama with action figures, so involved with each other they are oblivious of us! Knowing how play develops, and can sometimes go awry as Rubin and Howe point out, gives a framework within which the educator can stimulate peer interactions and create environments that are developmentally appropriate.

In considering their interactions with children during play, teachers have to be simultaneously aware not only of developmental stages, but also of their own attitudes and values. In this regard, Sutton-Smith's reminders about the dark side of play are appropriate: Not all play is pleasant and sweet, and the way we deal with it reveals as much about ourselves as about the child concerned. For example, in the following description, Shane's behavior presents an observant teacher with a familiar set of choices.

In the 4-year-old classroom, Shane and several other children were inside an Indian tepee — a climber covered with a sheet. Soon, Shane emerged, announcing firmly, "I'm not." He proceeded to a nearby table where small plastic blocks were spread out. He fingered some blocks, held one up, studied it, ran over to the tepee and used it to shoot inside. Rob emerged, shooting back with an imaginary bow and arrow. Undeterred, Shane walked to the other end of the tepee and again shot inside. Making sure, he also lifted the side of the sheet and shot some more. Finished with his massacre, he expended a few more bullets on unconcerned children in the vicinity. He returned to sit briefly at the block table, got up, shoved the gun in his pocket, and walked to the easel where he chatted with Carrie and began to draw a big, brown bus.

How should teachers respond, if at all, to Shane? Should we remind him of the traditional prohibition against guns in nursery school? Should we praise him for taking a symbolic instead of a physical route out of interpersonal difficulties? Should the incident be overlooked, because classroom life is proceeding without actual calamity? Or should Shane be understood as a boy representative of a male-dominated, violence-prone culture, and ought the teacher intervene for cultural change? Liss notes the powerful forces that create gender difference and reminds us that teachers are counted among those forces for good and ill.

Teacher interactions with children are significant in other areas as well. McCune writes how the development of sensitive adults help an infant explore play. Furthermore, Pepler's discussion of creativity indicates how interaction with attentive adults can support pretend play. Finally, the Saltzes show how adults can train children to pretend play, encouraging in them the skills for successful peer interaction. As the following incident demonstrates, children sometimes need help in making the social connections they seek.

Carrie and Laura bustled about the play kitchen in the 4-year-old class. Shane rushed in shouting, "It's our house!" and sat down expectantly. Carrie coldly looked through him and over the partition to Rob who was playing with blocks. "Time for dinner, Rob. Time for dinner, Rob."
Rob, intent on his building, answered, "NO."
Carrie sighed, "I want him to come for dinner." She and Laura left the area.
Shane stood up and left too. He drifted for a while, eventually lying down on the rug with a book.

Here is a situation of three children very much wanting sociodramatic play but not achieving it in a sustained way. Bids and rejections dominated. A sensitive teacher might have intervened, perhaps by suggesting a play theme, by adopting a brief play role in which modeling and prompting might occur, or even by introducing an evocative prop or two. As Fein and Schwartz write, peer interactions are of interest to children from babyhood; teachers need to encourage the skills that make them successful.

Interacting with children's play requires that teachers be able to take the perspective of the child, which, as King reminds us, is often quite different from our own. Transcending our own egocentrism requires observation, imagination, and sensitivity. As an illustration, the reader may contrast the two beginning teachers observed in our 4-year-old classroom in October.

Charlie and Rob were in the housekeeping area, under the table, which was a ghost house. Charlie squeaked and yowled softly. Miss Baker approached. She watched the table as she returned the chalkboard that normally formed a wall of the house area to its usual place. The boys stuck out their heads and asked her why. "We just want it closed off," she said.

"We just want to play haunted house," rejoined Charlie.

"Okay, you can."

"I'd like to be a ghost and hide under the table," Charlie said.

Miss Baker asked, "All ghosts do is hide under the table? Not anything else?"

"Yeah, people walk in here. They get frightened!" said Charlie.

Miss Baker left, and Charlie resumed his squeaky sounds from under the table.

Miss Lewis then approached the area and bent over to look under the table. "Charlie, why don't you come out and sit in a chair?"

Charlie said, "We're playing haunted house."

Miss Lewis countered, "We play that *outside*."

Charlie said, "We want to *here*."

Miss Lewis persisted, "I don't think it's a good idea to play on the floor." She retreated as Charlie emerged. Rob followed, and together they sat at the table. They pretended to eat the plastic fruit there, quite cheerfully.

In this vignette, the first teacher interacted with the players in a non-interfering, supportive way. She learned what they were doing, ascertained its limits, found them acceptable for the classroom, and went on.

By contrast, the second teacher immediately judged the play unacceptable, seemingly because it defined the table in an unconventional way. Challenged by the players, she denied their validity by additional reasons: Such play must occur outside only, and the floor is not a place to play (although blocks were being used on the floor where she stood!). Perhaps too in her reaction was a feeling about the play's content; themes of scariness and ghostliness carry a threat to the deliberate sunniness of a well-run middle-class nursery school. The dark side of play emerged again, this time to alarm an adult. Hence she insisted the children redirect their play from a creative, albeit seasonal, theme to a more stereotypical form.

Time to observe, trust in children's innate sense of meaning, and courage were exhibited in support of children's play by the first teacher and not by the second. Another quality that helps teachers support children's play is memory of one's own childhood: How did you respond to cupboards, closets, and under-tables when you were about a yard-stick high? Such spaces exhibit different potential to young children than to adults.

As we interact with children, we encourage, stimulate, and sometimes repress children's play. However, much of children's play does not depend upon our personal interaction but rather on the environment we provide for it. Pellegrini shows how different types of play centers support different types of play and the valuable language skills that are practiced there. Phyfe-Perkins and Shoemaker outline the numerous variables of play settings and some of their consequences; the subject is intricate. As each setting is different, each teacher needs to study carefully and continuously how the classroom environment affects play.

Indoor environments have great flexibility for innovation and alter-ation; hence teacher responsibility is great there. Frost would prefer that outdoor environments have the same flexibility of materials and arrangement that indoor environments have because of the greater creativity afforded children. However, as outdoor environments tend to be fixed for longer periods of time (some playground equipment has served three generations!), teachers need to supplement the givens of an environment with movables and changeables, and, again, careful obser-vation as to what play occurs where and with what, in order to create maximum opportunity for children's play.

In thinking about children's play — how it develops and how teachers enable and contribute to it — we should perhaps think also of ourselves and our own playfulness. Although, as Paulo Freire (1985) has written, society tries to eradicate our individual playfulness, it is just this quality that enables us to appreciate and enjoy children's play, and to experiment with — play with — the physical and psychological envi-ronments and actions that sustain and enrich such play. Furthermore, by keeping in touch with our childhood and youth, we are more com-plete adults: To be "truly adult," Erik Erikson (1972) has written, we must be "playful at the center" (p. 158).

References

Adams, H. (1931). *The education of Henry Adams*. New York: Modern Library.
Erikson, E. (1976). Play and actuality. In M. W. Piers (Ed.), *Play and development*. New York: Norton.
Freire, P. (1985). *The politics of education*. (D. Macedo, Trans.). South Hadley, MA: Bergin & Garvey.

Information about NAEYC

NAEYC is . . .

. . . a membership supported organization of people committed to fostering the growth and development of children from birth through age 8. Membership is open to all who share a desire to serve and act on behalf of the needs and rights of young children.

NAEYC provides . . .

. . . educational services and resources to adults who work with and for children, including

- *Young Children, the* Journal for early childhood educators
- **Books, posters, brochures, and videos** to expand your knowledge and commitment to young children, with topics including infants, curriculum, research, discipline, teacher education, and parent involvement
- An **Annual Conference** that brings people from all over the country to share their expertise and advocate on behalf of children and families
- **Week of the Young Child** celebrations sponsored by NAEYC Affiliate Groups across the country to call public attention to the needs and rights of children and families
- **Insurance plans** for individuals and programs
- **Public policy information** for informed advocacy efforts at all levels of government
- The **National Academy of Early Childhood Programs,** a voluntary accreditation system for high quality programs for children
- **The Child Care Information Service,** a computer-based, centralized source of information sharing, distribution, and collaboration.

For free information about membership, publications, or other NAEYC services . . .

. . . call NAEYC at 202-232-8777 or 800-424-2460 or write to NAEYC, 1834 Connecticut Avenue, N.W., Washington, DC 20009-5786.

Index of Names

219

Index of Subjects

A

Academic performance, differences in 11, 119

Achievement
    academic 141, 157
    in "good play" 7
    in sociodramatic play maturity 95–109

Adult
    behavior 177–209
    comforting 186
    implications for 40–41, 57–59, 73–75, 80, 86–89, 108–109, 122, 136, 151–152, 169–171, 186–187, 189–191, 208–209, 213–216
    influences on play choices 131–132
    instructing 186
    interacting with small groups 186
    interventions in play 20–21, 46, 56, 57, 108, 116–118, 133–134, 141, 150, 151, 155–171
    modeling 52, 56, 100, 130, 133, 136, 162, 215
    play leaders 198, 199
    play tutoring skills 155–171, 214
    praising 186
    preparing play environment 131–132, 157, 175–209
    presence, effect on play 46, 127, 130, 133, 166
    questioning 186
    responding 186

Affect viii, 106–108, 114, 115, 141, 165, 167, 168
    anger 107, 108
    anxiety 108
    enslaving 3
    fear 107, 108, 215
    freedom 3, 11, 182
    intense importance 13
    panic 3
    positive 114, 167, 186
    self-esteem 186
    spontaneity 3, 5, 146
    tension 3

Aggression vii, 10, 12, 37, 38, 121, 128, 165, 167, 214
    controlling monsters 105, 107

Altruism vii, 165, 168

Animals, play of 12, 23

Anthropology vii, viii, 1, 7, 29, 30, 79

Attachment vii

Attention span 181, 186

Atypical children 43, 46, 55, 56, 122
    abused/neglected 167
    autistic 56
    developmentally delayed 55–56, 171
    emotionally disturbed 167
    physically handicapped 198

B

Behavior, children's
    goals 177, 184
    management 177
    purposeful 181

Benefits of play viii, 18, 39, 57, 108, 109, 114, 141–171, 178, 179, 196

C

Child's viewpoint 1, 29–41

Childish 9

Classification 48, 55, 86

Classrooms/schoolrooms See Environment

Cognitive development (See also Classification, Memory) viii, 7, 10, 18, 20–23, 45, 55, 63, 108, 114, 118, 121, 122, 134, 141, 143, 148, 156, 157, 161, 168, 169, 190, 200, 202, 203, 206
    concrete operational 20
    conflict 115
    decentration 115–116
    physical conservation 166–167
    preoperational 20
    presymbolic 43–89
    reversibility 115, 116
    sensorimotor 20, 46–48, 54, 98
        banging 47, 48
        manipulating 47, 48, 54
        mouthing 46, 47
        visual scanning 46, 47
    skills 166–167
    social role conservation 166–167

Cognitive structuring. See Thinking

Communication vii, viii, 12, 13, 21, 35, 36, 79–89, 95, 109, 113, 114, 116, 145, 149, 162
    metacommunication 10, 21, 22, 35, 101–103
    nonverbal 36, 101, 102, 162
    symbolic 69
    verbal 35, 36, 102, 120, 160, 162

Competence (See also Altruism, Independence, Social—development, Social—skill)
    coping skills 107, 109